WICKED WOMEN
OF
YORE

WERE THEY REALLY WICKED?

D.LAWRENCE-YOUNG

CRANTHORPE
MILLNER

First published by Cranthorpe Millner Publishers (2022)

ISBN 978-1-80378-096-2 (Paperback)

www.cranthorpemillner.com

Cranthorpe Millner Publishers

Historical & Other Novels by D. Lawrence-Young

Fawkes and the Gunpowder Plot
Tolpuddle: A Novel of Heroism
Marlowe: Soul'd to the Devil
Will Shakespeare: Where was He?*
The Man Who Would be Shakespeare
Will the Real William Shakespeare Please Step Forward**
I, Master Shakespeare
Of Guns and Mules
Of Guns, Revenge and Hope
Arrows Over Agincourt
Away, Away from Botany Bay
Anne of Cleves: Unbeloved
Catherine Howard: Henry's Fifth Failure
Six Million Accusers: Catching Adolf Eichmann
Mary Norton: Soldier Girl
Two Bullets in Sarajevo
King John: Two-Time Loser
Go Spy Out the Land
Entrenched
Emma Hamilton: Mistress of Land and Sea
My Jerusalem Book (Editor)
Kill the King ***
Villains of Yore ***
Colonel Blood, Soldier, Robber, Trickster***
Doctor Lopez: Trapped in the Royal Web
Daggers in Men's Smiles

*Reissued as: Welcome to London, Mr Shakespeare
**Reissued as: Who Really Wrote Shakespeare?
***Also published by Cranthorpe Millner

As David L. Young

Communicating in English (Textbook)
The Jewish Emigrant from Britain: 1700-2000 (contrib. chapter)
Out of Zion (contrib. chapter)

Website: www.dly-books.weebly.com

'Wicked: sinful iniquitous, vicious, given to or involving immorality, spiteful, ill-tempered, intending or intended to give pain.'

Oxford English Dictionary

'What is more wicked than a woman once was?'

Riddles Wisely Expounded – Medieval riddle

Contents

Chapter One
Wicked Women in the Bible..................................1

Chapter Two
Messalina (c.17-48 CE) Nymphomaniac & Serial Killer...29

Chapter Three
Alice Kyteler (1263-1325?) The Irish Witch...41

Chapter Four
Queen Isabella of England (1295-1358) The 'She-Wolf' of France...55

Chapter Five
Jeanne de Clisson (1300-1359) The Avenging Pirate..77

Chapter Six
Elizabeth Báthory (1560-1614) The Aristocratic Hungarian Serial Killer...............................89

Chapter Seven
Guilia Tofana (c.1620-c.1651?) The Italian Mass Poisoner..101

Chapter Eight
Mary Read (1685-1721) and Anne Bonny (1697-1721?) & Other Female Pirates.......................111

Chapter Nine
Jeanne de Valois-Saint Remy (1756-1791) The French Con Artist..125

Chapter Ten

Zheng Yi Sao (1775-1844) The Chinese Pirate Chief...144

Chapter Eleven

The 'Mad' Queen Ranavalona of Madagascar (c.1788-1861)..152

Chapter Twelve

Mary Willcocks alias Princess Caraboo (1792-1864)..168

Chapter Thirteen

Sarah Rachel Russell (1814-80) Victorian Cosmetician, Blackmailer & Con artist...189

Chapter Fourteen

Mary Ann Cotton (1832-1873) Serial Killer...210

Chapter Fifteen

Minnie Dean (1844-1895) New Zealand's Baby Killer..225

Chapter Sixteen

Belle Starr (1848-1889) Wild West Outlaw..242

Chapter Seventeen

Bertha Heyman (1851-1901) The Prussian-USA Con Artist..256

Chapter Eighteen

Thérèse Humbert (1856-1918) French Con Artist Par Excellence..273

Chapter Nineteen

Kate Leigh (1881-1964) & Tilly Devine (1900-1970) Rival Australian Organised Crime Bosses...286

Chapter Twenty

Marguerite Alibert (1890-1971) Courtesan to Prince Edward (VIII) & Other High-flyers………………..306

Chapter Twenty-One

Ilse Koch (1906-1967) Nazi Concentration Camp Overseer at Buchenwald &Majdanek……………….319

Chapter Twenty-Two

Bonnie Parker (1910-1934)……..……………………326

Chapter Twenty-Three

Phoolan Devi (1963-2001) The Indian Bandit Leader turned MP & Lawmaker…………………………...344

To my wife, Beverley, who helped me with various computer problems during the writing of this book, and who definitely is not a wicked woman.

Also many thanks to Gary Dalkin, my long-suffering editor, who can spot a missing comma or a wicked woman at fifty paces.

Chapter One

Wicked Women in the Bible

Women who have been considered as 'wicked' are not new. They have been around for thousands of years. They appear at the very beginning of history, as in the Judeo-Christian period, and include the first woman in the Old Testament, in the Book of Genesis. At the same time, we read in the New Testament of over a dozen specific commandments to keep away from such women. Men are warned that if they do not do so, then they will surely suffer.

Several of the Old Testament commands concentrate on the dangers that can come from a woman's mouth and not from the rest of her potentially alluring body. In the Book of Proverbs (5:3-4) it says that although a woman's lips are like 'honeycomb' and 'her mouth is smoother than oil, her end is bitter as wormwood, sharp as a two-edged sword'. The Book of Proverbs 22:14 later reinforces this and says, 'The mouth of strange women is a deep pit; he that is abhorred of the Lord shall fall straight in'.

The Book of Proverbs 6: 24-26 teaches us that in addition to being aware of 'the flattery of the tongue of a strange woman', we must not 'lust after her beauty' nor 'let her take thee with her eyelids'. If you do not follow this

1

*command, then you will be 'brought to a piece of bread',
that is, worth nothing. Perhaps all of the above may be
summarised in the Book of Proverbs 23:27-28, which
informs us that 'A whore is a deep ditch; and a strange
woman (harlot) is a narrow pit. She also lieth in wait for
a prey and increaseth the transgressors among men'.*

*It should also be noted that perhaps the New Testament
is even stricter and more specific than the Old Testament
regarding women who may lead men astray. 1 Corinthians
(14:34) instructs us by saying, 'Let your women keep silent
in the churches... but they are commanded to be under
obedience as also saith the law'. 1 Timothy (2:9-10)
preaches that women must 'dress modestly, with decency
and propriety', while later in the same book (5:13), it says
that women must not even gossip because they will
'become idlers, but also busybodies who talk nonsense,
saying things they ought not'.*

*All of the above proves that from the very beginning of
Biblical history, men were always to be on their guard
regarding women and that in their turn, women had to
conduct themselves modestly and passively. The New
Testament has more about men staying in control and
keeping hold of their power than women actually being
wicked. It is this question of a woman's passive behaviour
vis-à-vis men where the first wicked woman makes her
appearance in the world. However, there is a problem, for
depending on how strong your belief is in the Judeo-
Christian faiths, the first wicked woman was either Eve or
Lilith.*

The first wicked woman that most people hear about is Eve, who appears in the opening chapters of the Old Testament. However, at the same time she was wandering around in the Garden of Eden, Adam was aware of another allegedly wicked woman, Lilith, who does not appear at all in the Book of Genesis. In fact, when she does appear, it is much later in the Bible, in the Book of Isaiah.

Eve, whose name comes from the Hebrew word *chavâh*, meaning 'the living' or 'life', is seen in the Bible as the 'mother of all living' (Genesis 3:20). Eve, as the first woman, wife and mother was the mother of Cain and Abel and 'other sons and daughters'. Her so-called wickedness stems from the fact that she persuaded Adam 'to eat the fruit of the Tree of Knowledge of Good and Evil', an act which had been strictly forbidden by God. Some commentaries claim that it was not her fault, as she had been told to do so by Satan, who spoke to her disguised as a serpent. As a result, humanity was to suffer in three major ways, causing her to be seen as such a wicked woman. She brought death to the human race; women were, after her, to suffer pain in giving birth, and future relationships between men and women were to become a battle of the sexes, an ongoing power struggle full of strife.

Lilith

By John Collier, 1887

In contrast, Lilith, appears only once in the Old Testament in Isaiah (34:14): 'Wild cats shall meet with desert beasts, satyrs shall call to one another; there shall Lilith repose, and find for herself a place to rest'.

Who was Lilith, who some see as a demon figure and Adam's first wife, before Eve? She is mentioned in several ancient books, such as the Babylonian *Talmud* and also in

Zohar Leviticus (19a) as a 'hot fiery female' who first cohabited with man. It is also possible that she appeared in some ancient Mesopotamian religious writings and also in some antiquated Sumerian and Assyrian cuneiform texts.

But whenever and wherever she first appeared, her roots in Jewish folklore may be first seen in the satirical *Alphabet of Sirach* (c.700-1000 CE), an anonymous text of forty-three chapters which was inspired by the ancient Greeks. In this work Lilith abandoned Adam after she refused to become subservient to him, and for this she had to leave the Garden of Eden. At this point God saw that Adam did not like to be alone, and therefore according to Genesis (2:21-22), when Adam was in a deep sleep, He took one of Adam's ribs and formed a woman, Eve, from it.

Meanwhile, Lilith had sexual relations with Samael, the archangel, and became a dangerous demon of the night. In revenge for being thrown out of the Garden of Eden, it was claimed that Lilith became a sexual wanton who, according to various commentators and interpreters, would also steal babies in the night. In the Hebrew version of the Bible, Lilith's name is translated as 'night creature', 'screech owl', or 'night hag', her name being closely connected to the Hebrew word *leilah*, meaning night. In all, Lilith represents a female figure who did not bow down to God and man's rule and it is her rebellious attitude that has made her an inspiration for the modern feminist movement.

Lot's wife

Salt rocks today known as Lot's wife at the Dead Sea, Israel

Seventeen chapters later in the Book of Genesis (19), Abraham's nephew, Lot, was living in the wicked city of Sodom by the Dead Sea (now the site of a huge potash and salt factory). Two angels told him and his family to flee the city as God was going to rain fire and brimstone on the cities of Sodom and Gomorrah as a punishment for their collective wickedness. The angel also told Lot that when he fled he and his family were not to look back. According to the usually accepted account, Lot's wife ignored the warning and was turned into a pillar of salt (Genesis 19:26). Other accounts say that she abandoned her fleeing family, returned to Sodom and died in its destruction.

Like Lilith and Eve, Lot's wife is not named in Genesis. However, according to some traditions and in the *Midrash*, a Jewish interpretation of the Bible, she was called Ado or

Edith. We are told that she disobeyed God and her husband and, as a rebellious wife, she had to pay the price. Incidentally, in the *Quran*, Lot was told to leave but not to take his wife. She stayed behind and was killed when Sodom was destroyed.

Lot and his daughters

Lot and his daughters (c.1635-1638) by Artemesia Gentileschi

But that is not the end of the wicked rebellious women in Lot's family. At the end of the same chapter (Genesis 19:31-38), Lot's two remaining daughters believe that they are the last two women left in the world. As a result, 'they made their father drink wine', had sexual relations with him over the next two nights and bore him two sons as a result. They justified these incestuous acts by saying, 'that we may preserve the seed of our father'. The *Quran* does not mention this incestuous act of rape.

7

Potiphar's wife

Potiphar's wife seducing Jacob by Antonio Maria Esquivel, 1854

Another wife who is deemed wicked in the Bible is Potiphar's wife. This woman was a high-ranking Egyptian, the wife of the captain of Pharaoh's guard. Although she was not given a name in the Book of Genesis (39:5-20), Jewish and Islamic commentators have identified her as Zuleikha.

The story of Potiphar's wife is quite straightforward. For whatever reason, the Bible does not say why she called on Joseph, her Hebrew slave, 'a goodly person, and well favoured' (Gen. 39:7) for a sexual encounter – 'lie with me' – (perhaps she was bored and looking for excitement?) but he refused. She was insulted by this and when he made a speedy exit, she grabbed his garment which the Bible does not specify. She showed it to her husband as evidence that Joseph had attempted to rape her, and as a result he was arrested and thrown into prison. But all was not lost for the young man who was, according to some authorities, a mere seventeen years old. His good qualities were appreciated in prison and several years, and two important dreams, later, he was released to become the Pharaoh's chief minister. The Bible does not mention Potiphar's wife again after her attempted seduction.

So how wicked was this woman? Christian, Jewish and Moslem sources all basically agree that Potiphar's wife was a sinner and/or that Joseph was a model of piety. However, there is more to this than just a story of good versus bad. Some ancient interpretations of this story say that Joseph was punished because he chose to be loyal to a slave-master rather than pleasing a beautiful woman.

But however you look at this story, she has become the prototype for a literary motif – the older 'establishment' woman, a 'cougar' in modern parlance – seducing a younger man. This story has been retold over many centuries in the main European and Arabic languages.

Seeing that she is not named in Genesis, she was later called *la Dame* in the French 15th century mystery plays, *Mistère du vieil testament* and *Les Mystères de la Procession de Lille, la Donna* in the Italian *Rappresentatione di Giuseppe figiuolo de Giacobbe* and *Potiphars Weib* in the German *Fastnachtspiel* (1608). The 17th century Mexican poet, Sor Juana Inés de la Cruz, calls her simply *la Mujer* – the woman.

Potiphar's wife did however acquire a literary name. Sometimes she was called *Sephora* (from the Hebrew

Biblical name, *Zipporah*) and she was also known as *Aegla* in Greek. In 1523, Pandolfo Collenuccio called her *Berencia*, and in the 16th century she was merely referred to as *Misraia* – Hebrew and Arabic for 'the Egyptian woman' by Aegidius Hunnius, the Lutheran theologian.

Delilah

Delilah by Gustave Moreau, 1896

Despite her later variety of names, Potiphar's wife never achieved the 'fame' that Delilah of 'Samson and Delilah' did. Interestingly, Delilah's name, like that of Lilith is a wordplay on the Hebrew word, *leilah* – night – while Samson is another play on words, based on the Hebrew word, *shemesh* – sun. Therefore it would seem that not only does the woman beat the man in this case, but that the night overcomes the all-powerful sun. Her story, of a woman actively disobeying her man (they were never married), as well as being connected with harlotry, are reasons why she has been portrayed as a wicked woman by Judeo-Christian commentators.

The Bible never defines Delilah as a harlot or defines the role that she played in society. However, she is often understood to be a harlot because she is mentioned only one sentence away in the text from when Samson spent the night with another harlot in Gaza, (Judges 16:1-3). It is also often assumed that she was a Philistine woman, because we read that Samson was attracted to that nation's women. In addition, later in the story we learn that Delilah had dealings with important Philistine leaders who, because of the ongoing war between the Israelites and the Philistines, would not have betrayed Samson's secret to her own people.

After Samson met Delilah, he fell in love with her. This was a potentially dangerous situation as she came from the Valley of Sorek, a border area between the warring nations. It was at this point that three of the 'lords of the Philistines' (Judges 16:5) decided to exploit this situation and ask her to find out what made this leader of the Israelites so strong. The situation may have been played out like this.

*

The sun was slowly sinking over the Valley of Sorek, the border area between the warring territories of the Israelites and the Philistines. Neither country could get the upper hand in this long drawn-out struggle and each country was prepared to use any method it could to defeat its enemy.

However, despite the hostile situation, Samson, the Nazirite and Israelite strongman and leader, together with Delilah, a Philistine beauty of a somewhat dubious background, were sitting on a border area hillside, arms around each other. They were casually watching the last rays of the sun dissolving behind the low hills as they heard the sheep-bells quietly tinkling in the distance.

"What a shame our two countries have to keep fighting each other," Samson said as he pulled Delilah even closer to him. "I would love it if only you could come and live with me and so I could hold you like this every night."

"Yes, I hate having to sneak away all the time to meet you," Delilah whispered as she stroked Samson's warm chest.

"And then I would be able to buy you anything you want: dresses, clothes of all sorts made of the finest material, jewellery. Anything."

For an answer, Delilah squeezed his arm and kissed him fully on his mouth in the way she knew he loved. She could feel him wrapping his arms around her so tightly that in any other situation she would have cried out. Just then she heard a shout from over the distant hills and knew that she would have to return to her village.

"Be here tomorrow at sunset in this same place," she whispered, "and I'll have a surprise for you." And before he could say anything, she slipped out of his arms, ran down the hill and disappeared into the evening mist.

That night three Philistine lords came to visit her with details of an important mission for the young Philistine woman.

"Delilah," the oldest lord began, "we know that you are seeing Samson the Nazirite almost every night and we want you to do us and your people a favour. We want you to find out how he gets his great strength. Is it from –?"

"How do you know this? How do you know what I do at night?" a frightened Delilah demanded.

The second lord just tapped the size of his long beak-like nose. "Don't ask. Just know that we know."

The third lord nodded his shaggy head in support. "We know everything about you and that man. Where you meet, how often, and what you do."

"So will you help us?" the first and second lords asked together, leaning towards the nervous Delilah.

"I don't know, my lords. You see, I –"

"We will make it worth your while," the first lord said, placing a full jingling pouch of coins on the table. "If you succeed, we will give you eleven hundred pieces of silver."

"Yes, each one of us," the second lord added, jingling yet another pouch of coins in front of her eyes.

"Do you mean that if I find out the secret of his strength, the three of you will give me thirty-three hundred pieces of silver?"

The men nodded.

Delilah took an apple out of a bowl on the table and took a bite out of it. She was not hungry, but she needed to buy a few minutes to think. It is true that she liked her strong boyfriend very much, but did she love him? And thirty-three hundred pieces of silver! What couldn't she do with that? It was more money than she had ever seen in her whole life. She could buy more clothes and jewellery with it, eat better food and perhaps have a bigger house. It was all so tempting. At last she nodded. She saw that she had no choice.

The following night, before setting off for Samson's house, she bathed herself in rosewater and made sure that her make-up was perfect. She put a vial of her favourite perfume into a small bag to put on just before she arrived. Later, after they had kissed and embraced, Delilah gave Samson a fine white linen shirt she had sewn and embroidered herself. After he had tried it on he took it off so he would not crush it, and she slid closely over to him on the sofa, loosened the top three ties of her chemise and saying, "Tell me, my love, how is it you are so strong? Does your strength come from the food you eat? And how strong are you anyway? Are all the stories I hear about you true?"

"I must not tell you the secret of my strength," he replied, "but just bind me up with seven of those green withes, those tough green branches over there in the corner, and see if I can break free."

She followed his instructions and tied the withes as tightly as she could. Within a minute he smiled at her and snapped them as if they were merely threads of cotton.

"Try again with something stronger," he said. "What about those new ropes lying there on the balcony?"

This time she bound his arms to his chest and wound the ropes several times around him before she tied the tightest and most complicated knot she could. Then she slid back along the sofa to watch him struggle to free himself.

"Ha! Let's see you get out of that," she smiled proudly.

But as pride comes before a fall, within a minute, pieces of torn rope were lying scattered on the floor. He rubbed his hands together and smiled back at her.

"I don't believe it," she cried. "It's a trick."

"No, my love," Samson replied. "It's no trick. It's just that I am very strong. That's all."

"But how?"

"Ah, that I cannot tell you, but perhaps you should try a third time."

"How? With what?"

Samson clicked his fingers. "I have an idea. Tie me up and bind seven of the locks on my head to that loom by the window. Let's see if that works."

Filled with determination, Delilah bound his long hair to the loom and did her best to tie them tightly into place. No-one could get out of that she thought and then wondered if perhaps she had tightened them too much, even for Samson.

"Does it hurt?" she asked.

"No," he replied releasing himself from the loom. "It didn't hurt at all."

"I don't believe it," was all she could say. "It's just not possible."

He smiled at her, pushed his hair back into his hairband and hugged her tightly.

"Oh, you must please tell me," she pleaded. "If you don't, I won't believe that you truly love me. It's like you don't trust me. I'm beginning to think that all you want from me is my body."

"That's not true," he protested, kissing her upturned face. "I love you, I love you, I love you."

"Then if you do, prove it. Tell me what makes you so strong. Please, please, please."

Samson nodded. "Alright then, but you must promise not to tell anyone, ever. Do you promise?"

Delilah nodded.

"Delilah, say I promise and swear by the God of Israel that I will not tell anyone in the whole wide world."

"But I don't believe in your God of Israel."

"But swear anyway."

Delilah did so, and Samson told her that he was "a Nazirite unto God from my mother's womb" and the secret of his enormous strength came from not having his hair cut at all. "If I be shaven," he added, "then my strength will go from me." (Gen.16:17)

As soon as Delilah learned his secret, she informed the Philistine lords, who paid her, and then she made Samson 'sleep upon her knees'. Contrary to popular belief, Delilah did not cut off Samson's locks herself, she left that to 'a man' (a servant or soldier?) who promptly shaved off seven locks of the Israelite strong man's hair. She then called on the waiting Philistines to tie him up while he was now lying defenceless. They bound him 'with fetters of brass' and took him to Gaza. There the Philistines gouged out his eyes and set him to work in prison grinding grain for them.

But here the Philistines' plan came undone. Samson's hair began to grow again and, at the same time, his strength returned to him. The Philistines, who were unaware of this, took him to the temple of Dagon to show off their captive to the rest of their people, where they mocked him. Then the blind Samson asked a young boy to lead him to the pillars of the crowded temple, which was 'full of men and women: and all the lords of the Philistines'. After praying to God, Samson pushed against the temple's pillars, and crying, "Let me die with the Philistines," he brought down the whole building onto the three thousand celebrants, killing himself and all of those within.

*

Even though the Book of Judges does not say, according to some commentaries, Delilah was one of those celebrants. However, the Bible does mention later that Samson's 'brethren and all the house of his father' pulled his body out of the ruins and gave this twenty-year Judge of Israel a decent burial at Manoah, where his father was buried. (Judges 16:31)

This story has been open to many interpretations. Some Jewish texts, such as the *Talmud*, the central text of Rabbinic Judaism, state that Delilah used sex to entice Samson and the Midrash uses this story as a warning to Jewish men about the dangers of straying after non-Jewish women. Christian theology condemns Delilah, and St. Ambrose defines her as a Philistine prostitute. Some Christian commentators also compare Samson's betrayal with that of Jesus, who was betrayed by Judas Iscariot.

But however we understand this story, it has supplied

literature, music and film with a powerful motif. Two of the best-known examples are *Samson Agonistes* by John Milton (c.1671), and Handel's opera, *Samson* (1742). Another loose reworking of the story and musical interpretation is Andrew Lloyd Webber's *The Phantom of the Opera* (1986) while Tom Jones' pop-song *Delilah* became a very successful hit in 1968. A similar success based on the story was Cecil B. De Mille's film, *Samson and Delilah* (1949), which starred Hedy Lamarr as Delilah and Victor Mature as Samson. In this version however, there is some free interpretation of the original text. Delilah really does love Samson and feels remorse that she tricked him. As a result, she 'stands by her man' at the very end and is killed with him when he destroys the Philistine temple.

Jezebel

Jezebel by John L.B. Shaw, 19th century

One woman who probably never felt any remorse for her wicked ways was Jezebel. Like Delilah, her name has become synonymous with wickedness. This Phoenician princess, like Delilah, was a non-Jewess who married a strong Jewish leader, in this case, King Ahab of Israel. Her name is the Anglicised version of *Izebel*, which has been translated as 'Where is the person or place on high?'

At first, the Bible credits Jezebel's husband, Ahab, with being a strong ruler who maintained a stable government, but then he 'took to wife Jezebel' (1 Kings 16:31), and being influenced by her, he started worshiping false gods. She, as a supporter of over eight hundred prophets of Baal, caused him to sin (1 Kings 21:25) and suppress the worship of the true God of Israel.

One of the most blatant examples of her wickedness occurred when she noted that her husband was feeling dejected because he could not buy Naboth the Jezreelite's vineyard. She caused the latter to be stoned to death by the local villagers after he was falsely accused of committing blasphemy. (1Kings 21:14) This then allowed Jezebel to tell her husband that he could now take possession of the vineyard. However, when he went to do so, he met the prophet, Elijah, who pronounced God's punishment for him for stealing the dead man's property. All of the males in Ahab's family would perish, his dynasty would end and he and Jezebel would have the blood of their corpses licked by dogs. (1 Kings 21:21-24).

Some of this prophecy came to pass, but as Ahab expressed deep remorse at what he had done he was spared an immediate death. He died three years later in battle.

However, when his men were preparing his body for burial and cleaning his chariot, dogs did indeed lick the blood lying there, and so Elijah's words came true.

Jezebel, the wicked woman who both encouraged forsaking the worship of the true God and who incited her husband to steal Naboth's vineyard, among other crimes, met the similar humiliating death as predicted.

Jehu, the future King of Israel and an army commander who fought against the worship of Baal, came to the palace to confront Jezebel. Instead of acting modestly during a change of regime, she 'painted her face' and appeared to mock him from an upper window. Jehu ordered two or three eunuchs to throw her out of the window. (2 Kings 9:33) This they did and when Jehu's men came to bury her as a king's daughter, all that they found was her 'skull, her feet and the palms of her hands'. The rest of her body had been eaten by dogs. Elijah's prophecy had again come true.

Like Delilah, Jezebel's name became forever linked with female wickedness. She instituted the rule of Baal instead of the worship of God, while putting herself above the law when she exploited her royal power to steal Naboth's vineyard. Her name has been forever associated with immorality and harlotry, although the Bible never specifically calls her a harlot. Like several of the iniquitous women already referred to in this chapter, perhaps her greatest crime was that the above examples of her wickedness stemmed from the fact that she was anything but a passive and obedient wife and that she was an idol-worshipper. This, the Jewish and Christian religions were not prepared to accept. It was against everything that their patriarchal societies stood for.

Athaliah

Athaliah by Guillaume Rouillé, 1553

Even though Jezebel met a disgusting fate, this was not the end of her family. She and Ahab had three children, their sons Ahaziah and Jehoram and (possibly, the Bible is not clear here) Athaliah their daughter. Ahaziah was wicked in the sense that he allowed his mother to strengthen the worship of Baal even after being reproved by Elijah for doing so. He died soon afterwards from injuries he sustained when he 'fell down through a lattice in his upper chamber'. (2 Kings 1:2).

Ahaziah was succeeded by his younger brother, Jehoram, who worshipped the true God instead of Baal. He was unable to put down a rebellion led by King Mesha of Moab, and in the end, he was shot through the heart by an arrow by Jehu, (2 Kings 9:23-24), the commander who had previously ordered Jehoram's mother, Jezebel, to be thrown out of a window. This was seen as a punishment for his parents having stolen Naboth's land, something made clear when Jehoram's body was disrespectfully cast out into that vineyard.

As soon as Athaliah heard of Ahaziah's death, she usurped the throne and further encouraged the worship of Baal. In addition, 'she arose and destroyed all of the seed royal of the house of Judah' (2 Chron. 22:10) in order to strengthen her own position. For six years she reigned as the only Queen of Judah, and was surprised when she heard that Jehoash, her grandson who had survived the family massacre, was alive and leading a rebellion against her. When she heard the sounds of the trumpets and of the rejoicing crowds, she 'rent her clothes, and cried, Treason, Treason' (2 Kings 11:14) and rushed to the temple to put down the rebellion. She failed and was captured and since the rebels did not want to pollute the temple with her death, she was killed in the 'king's house' instead. Thus the usurper was usurped.

Both the Second Book of Kings and the First Book of Chronicles condemn her for being wicked, especially as she was a worshipper of Baal. In addition, she ruled as a queen in her own right, and not as the obedient consort of her royal husband.

So far, all of the wicked women mentioned here in the Bible have appeared in the Old Testament. The New Testament features fewer examples. Does this mean that there were indeed fewer wicked women, or is it that if there were, then their heinous deeds were not recorded? Or could it be that Jesus had a much more tolerant view of what women did as opposed to the writers of the Old Testament?

Herodias and Salome

Herodias by Paul Delaroche, 1797-1856, and Salome by Titian, 1488-1576

Two of those whose deeds were recorded in the New Testament were the mother and daughter pair, Herodias and Salome. Herodias, the granddaughter of Herod the Great, married two of her uncles, Herod Philip I and Herod Antipas. She hated John the Baptist, who had strongly castigated Herod Antipas for marrying her after he had divorced his first wife, Phasaelis, a Nabatean princess. Therefore, when her daughter, Salome, captivated Herod

Antipas at a feast with her dancing, he promised that he would give her anything she asked for. She asked for John the Baptist's head to be served on a platter. As a result, the man who had baptised Jesus Christ was executed and Salome received her bloody reward. (Mark 6:22-28). Salome then handed the platter to her mother, and this whole incident has caused Biblical scholars to ask if it was about Herodias having revenge on John the Baptist by exploiting her seductive daughter. If this is true, then Herodias was equally wicked on two counts – she planned the fatal plot, and she also exploited her daughter's sexuality to corrupt her husband and also bring about the death of John the Baptist.

As for Salome, she did not outlive John the Baptist for very long. After talking to the head and kissing it passionately, Herod ordered that she too should be executed. As for Herodias, following a later change of regime, she and her husband were banished and never heard of again.

As with Jezebel and Delilah, Salome has been forever associated with seduction, treachery and deceit. The 'Dance of the Seven Veils' is not mentioned in the Bible, it first appeared in Richard Strauss' opera, Salome (1905). Salome also appeared in literature, such as Oscar Wilde's one-act play *Salomé* (1891), and in well-known paintings by Aubrey Beardsley and Gustave Moreau. In addition, many films in different languages have been made about her since 1923. In 1953 Rita Hayworth starred in the film, *Salome,* which was panned in the USA but well-received in France. Sixty years later, in 2013, Al Pacino wrote, directed and starred in a remake of *Salome* in which he played King Herod.

Mary Magdalene

Mary Magdalene by Titian (1565)

Another wicked woman in the New Testament is Mary Magdalene. However, here there is a problem. Until 591 CE., Mary Magdalene was seen as an apostle, a good and virtuous woman who was mentioned positively in the gospels of Matthew, Mark, Luke and John. She was called Magdalene probably because she came from Magdal, a fishing village by the Sea of Galilee. She accompanied Jesus on his journeys around the Holy Land and witnessed the crucifixion and the resurrection. Because she was so involved in the life of Jesus, in 2016, Pope Francis determined she should be called the 'Apostle to the Apostles'. However, the best-selling novel and film *The Da Vinci Code*, by Dan Brown (2003), did much to spread

25

several untruths about this much maligned woman.

If the above view of her is true, why did Pope Gregory I in 591 CE declare her to be a prostitute? It seems that he blended three women: Mary Magdalene (Luke 8:2), Mary of Bethany (Luke 10:39) and an anonymous 'sinful woman' (Luke 7:36-50) into one figure. As a result, from that date on, Mary Magdalene was tainted with the brush of wickedness and prostitution. This was the situation until 1969 when Pope Paul VI declared that Mary of Bethany, the 'sinful woman' and Mary Magdalene were not the same person, and he removed the last-named woman from the *General Roman Calendar*. Since Mary Magdalene came from the Galilee in the north of the Holy Land and Mary of Bethany came from Bethany, over one hundred miles away to the south near Jerusalem, they cannot have been the same person.

Although Mary Magdalene is today counted as one of the saints by the Catholic, Anglican, Lutheran and Eastern Orthodox Churches, she is still considered to be a prostitute or fallen woman in popular culture. This image of her was reinforced from 591-1969 by such poems as *The Wand'ring Whore*, published in 1660. It was sub-titled, *A Dialogue between Magdalena, a Crafty Bawd, Julietta, an Exquisite Whore, Francion, a lascivious gallant and Gusman, a pimping hector.* In addition there were the Magdalene asylums and laundries which were established as homes and workplaces for 'fallen women' (often the hapless victims of sexual abuse) which operated internationally from 1758 until late in the 20th century.

The Whore of Babylon from Martin Luther's translation of the Bible, 1534

The last wicked woman from the New Testament who appears in this chapter is probably the most problematic. She is the 'Whore of Babylon'. She is problematic because she never existed as a woman, but rather is an abstract religious idea. This 'Whore' is an allegorical and apocalyptic figure of evil who is found in the New Testament as one of several embodiments of evil that plague the world. She is often depicted as a beautiful seductive woman in a red dress who was also made to look more seductive by wearing much ostentatious jewellery.

The Whore of Babylon appears in the Book of Revelations, Chapters 17 (verses 1-18) and 18 (verses 1-10) as well as in 1 Peter. In this last book, 'She who is in Babylon, elect together with *you*; greet you...' (1 Peter 5:13). Incidentally, Babylon has been understood by some not to refer to the actual city of Babylon, which was by then more or less non-existent, but to Rome, which was persecuting the new Christian religion. Rome was also seen as the paradigm of greed, debauchery, brutality and paganism.

In Chapter 17 of the Book of Revelations, the most damning reference to the Whore of Babylon appears in the fifth verse: 'Mystery, Babylon the Great, Mother of Harlots and abominations of the earth'. Four verses later, the seven-headed monster which is associated with her is understood to refer to the seven mountains, a possible reference to the hilly city of Jerusalem. This ties up with Rome since the Romans conquered Jerusalem in 70 CE and destroyed the Second Temple.

Later, Christianity saw the Whore of Babylon as an allegory of evil which combined the peace of Jerusalem with the iniquity of Babylon. This interpretation changed with the Reformation in the 16th century. Major writers of the Reformation, including Martin Luther and John Knox, wrote that the Whore of Babylon referred to the Roman Catholic Church, which was rich and powerful and misused its power, especially through its use of the Inquisition. This view is also held today by the Seven-day Adventists. Another religion, the Jehovah Witnesses, view this 'Whore' as an international empire of fake religions and do not limit this just to Christianity. They also refer to the 'Whore' as 'the Great Harlot'. The Mormon Church also equates this 'Whore' with a great and abominable Church.

Chapter Two

Messalina (c.17-48 CE)
Nymphomaniac & Serial Killer

How many generations of pupils have hated studying Latin? How many have claimed that it was a waste of time and effort in studying a 'dead' language that no-one (apart from a few scholars, priests and cardinals in the Vatican) actually speak. Even the greatest writer in English literature, William Shakespeare, had, according to his fellow dramatist, Ben Jonson, 'small Latin, and less Greek'.

Perhaps, if our Latin teachers had taught us more about the ancient Romans themselves, especially the aristocratic women, instead of concentrating on the eight volumes of Caesar's Gallic Wars, *then thousands if not millions of pupils over the past five hundred years would have enjoyed their Latin studies as much as they enjoyed their school's sporting activities.*

Which pupil would not have been interested in the life of the ambitious, violent and ruthless mother of Nero, Julia Agrippina the Younger? Would not our pupils have loved to have learned about Lucretia, who killed many of her rivals and raped Crixus to make herself pregnant? And what about the manipulative Lyvia who killed and poisoned many of the Roman aristocracy in her quest for power?

Then there is Messalina, perhaps the most wicked of all these ancient Roman matriarchs. Her record included starting a reign of terror, killing many of Rome's senators, marrying Gaius Silius when she was already married to the Emperor Claudius and then plotting to assassinate her first husband. Is not this the sort of material to cause generations of British pupils to happily put their sports equipment aside in order to instead concentrate on their Latin homework?

*

Messalina, or to give her full name, Valeria Messalina, was born on 25th January, sometime between 17 and 20 CE in Rome. Her father was Marcus Valerius Messalla Barbatus, a senator and administrative officer in the Roman army, and her mother, Domitia Lepida, was a beautiful thrice married and influential aristocratic landowner. In other words, Messalina had it all. In addition to being born into such an important family, her uncle, Gnaeus Domitius Ahenobarbus, was related to the Empress Agrippina the Younger and her maternal grandmother was related to Mark Antony, the military and political leader.

We know very little about her until she was about eighteen years old, when she married her first cousin once removed, the Emperor Tiberius Claudius. Her husband was at least thirty years her senior. However, such a marriage to a close family member was typical among the aristocracy of ancient Rome. While it kept wealth and lands within the family, it also meant that the gene pool was reduced, which later caused mental and physical health problems. The couple had two children, Claudia Octavia and a son, Britannicus, who was murdered when he was fourteen by Nero, who saw him as a potential rival to the throne.

It is only after Messalina married Claudius that her name began to circulate in the annals of ancient Rome. However, what we know about her was recorded mainly by two Roman historians, Suetonius and Tacitus, both of whom wrote about her fifty years after her death. Suetonius (69-122 CE) whose history he recorded in his twelve-volume *De Vita Caesarium* is not considered reliable by modern academics. The same may be said for Tacitus (56-120 CE), a famous public orator whose works were based on dubious sources. Both of these men relied too much on non-critical hearsay, yet it is mainly from their unreliable histories that Messalina's unsavoury reputation has been handed down to us. This means that parts of the following should be taken with a grain of salt.

Pliny the Elder (23/24-79 CE), another Roman man of words, compared Messalina to Scylla, a famous prostitute. He recorded that in a competition to see who could have sex with the most men in one night, Messalina won. She had twenty-five partners.

Another Roman writer, the first century poet Juvenal, called her Lycisca (a 'She-Wolf') and noted that she used to work secretly all night in a brothel. He referred to her as the *meretrix augusta* – the great imperial whore – and compared her to Cleopatra, the *meretrix regina*, 'harlot queen', 'who preferred a coarse mattress to the royal bed'. Juvenal added that in order to hide her identity, Messalina would wear a blonde wig and so conceal her black hair.

It seems that as soon as Messalina moved up to the highest levels of Roman society she set out to rid herself of any potential rival members of the imperial family. Within one year she had her husband's niece, Julia Livilla, exiled on charges of adultery with Seneca the Younger, the statesman, philosopher and dramatist. This must have been extremely hard on the accused woman as she had only recently returned to Rome after having been banished upon the death of her brother, Caligula, Rome's third emperor. Soon after this, Claudius (perhaps with Messalina encouraging him) had Julia Livilla executed. Seneca was later allowed to return home after Messalina had died.

Then, some four years after their marriage, Claudius

ordered another niece, Julia Livia, to be executed (perhaps, again, after being encouraged by Messalina?) on charges of incest and immorality. The real reasons for this judicial murder may have been that Messalina thought that Julia's son, Rubellius Plautus, would be a future rival to the imperial throne.

If these murders were not enough, towards the end of her life, Messalina decided to remove Claudius' remaining niece, Agrippina the Younger, and her son, Nero. However, nothing came of these plans, but the atmosphere in the imperial high society must have been rife with fear and suspicion during this period.

It was also soon after she was married that Messalina was behind the deaths of two very important senators, Decimus Valerius Asiaticus, and Appius Silanus. Asiaticus was very wealthy and was responsible for developing some of Rome's most luxurious private villas.

*

"Senator Valerius Asiaticus, you are hereby charged with committing adultery with Poppaea Sabina the Elder. How do you plead?"

"Not guilty."

"You are also charged with the failure to maintain discipline among the soldiers under your command. How do you plead?"

"Not guilty."

"And there is also a third charge brought against you: that you have engaged in disgusting homosexual practices.

How do you plead to this?"

"Not guilty."

"The Senate has recorded your pleas and they will be passed on to the Emperor Claudius for his final judgement. Take him away."

*

Asiaticus was removed while Claudius spent some time thinking what to do. He knew that this whole situation was part of a complicated plot that his wife, Messalina, had initiated so that once the wealthy senator had been executed she could seize his beautiful gardens.

After being forcefully encouraged by Messalina and advised by Claudius' fellow consul, Lucius Vitellius, that it would be politically sound, he ordered the senator to be put to death.

However, instead of being killed, Asiaticus in true Roman fashion committed suicide by cutting his veins open. This whole affair was condemned by the Senate, which blamed Claudius and Messalina for this travesty of justice – especially as Asiaticus had never been given a real trial. Apparently this did not concern Messalina who then hounded Poppaea Sabina so much that, in the end, the poor woman was either forced to commit suicide or died from being beaten by Nero.

As for Senator Appius Silanus, who was also Messalina's uncle, Messalina is reported to have wanted him for her own sexual pleasure. Some two years after her marriage, she, together with Narcissus, a freed slave, concocted a convoluted trick designed for her to gain Silanus for herself.

*

"Narcissus, I wish to exploit your fertile and devious brain."

"Why, my empress, what do you want of me this time?"

"I want you to help me get rid of the Senator Silanus."

"Yes, my Empress, but may I ask why?"

"Because he refuses to come to my bed. The foolish and stubborn man insists on staying loyal to that fat bitch of his wife."

"Yes, I remember now. You mentioned that last week when you returned from the Forum. So how can I help you?"

"This is my idea. You and I will each tell Claudius…"

"Your husband, the emperor?"

"Yes, that we both had the same dream about the Senator Silanus plotting to murder him and –"

"Excuse me, my Empress, but that sounds very coincidental, that the pair of us both have the same dream."

Messalina shrugged. "No matter, Claudius is getting very old and he doesn't always think clearly. Don't worry. If both you and I tell him convincingly enough, I'm sure he'll believe us. I've told him all sorts of strange tales and he's believed me every time. I only have to tell him some impossible story and then expose my body to him and he will believe anything, even that the moon is made of green cheese."

35

"If you are sure, then I agree."

"Good. Then we will invite Silanus here to the palace tomorrow morning after we have each spoken to Claudius we'll see what happens."

*

Messalina's devious plan worked. Silanus was invited over to her villa after Messalina and Narcissus had dripped their poisonous words into Claudius' unsuspecting ear. He was confronted by the emperor and, to Messalina's joy, he was executed soon after.

It was for the same reason, that is, that he refused to sleep with her, that Messalina had Marcus Vinicus poisoned to death. It did not help him that he was the grandson-in-law of the former Emperor Tiberius, a consul and a past proconsular governor of Asia. If the nymphomaniac Messalina lusted after you and wanted you for her bed, then if you valued your life, you did not argue.

One important Roman who did not have to be dragged unwillingly to Messalina's rooms was Gaius Silius (13-48 CE), a senator who was about five years older than her. He had become infatuated with the empress, and she in turn was very keen to requite his feelings. In 48 CE, using her status in the Roman hierarchy, she made him divorce his wife so that he could marry her. However, instead of waiting for her husband, Claudius, to die, they committed bigamy. And this was no secret wedding either. They did so before witnesses, and this was the beginning of the end for Messalina.

While his wife was enjoying having her way through this dubious chain of events, Emperor Claudius was at Ostia, the port city of Rome, some twenty-five miles west of the capital. He had gone there to inspect the new harbour that he was constructing. As Messalina was busy celebrating her latest conquest at a wedding feast, Narcissus, the freedman who had helped her bring about the death of Silanus, changed sides and sneaked away to inform Claudius of his wife's most recent 'acquisition'.

When Claudius heard, he ordered that Messalina be brought into his presence and explain herself. It seems that at this point, she realised that she had gone too far. According to Suetonius:

Terror now operating upon her mind, in conjunction with remorse, she could not summon the resolution to support such an interview, but retired into the gardens of Lucullus, there to indulge at last the compunction which she felt for her crimes, and to meditate the entreaties by which she should endeavour to soothe the resentment of her husband.

In the extremity of her distress, she attempted to lay violent hands upon herself, but her courage was not equal to the emergency. Her mother, Lepida, who had not spoken with her for some years before, was present upon the occasion, and urged her to the act which alone could put a period to her infamy and wretchedness. Again she (Messalina) *made an effort, but again her resolution abandoned her; when a tribune* (army officer) *burst into the gardens, and plunging his sword into her body, she instantly expired.*

Suetonius concluded his description of these dramatic events by recording that when the news of his wife's untimely demise reached Claudius, he simply asked for another chalice of wine.

Juvenal, who described the history of Rome in his five books of *Satires*, referred to 'the lewd glance of Messalina's eyes', and when later describing the Empress' bigamist marriage to Gaius Silius and its aftermath, wrote:

And what shall Silius do? Refuse to wed?
A moment sees him numbered with the dead.
Consent, and gratify the eager dame?
He gains a respite, till the tale of shame,
Through town and country, reach the Emperor's
ear,
Still sure the last – his own disgrace to hear.
Then let him, if a day's precarious life
Be worthy his study, make the fair his wife;
For wed or not, poor youth, 'tis still the same,
And still the axe must mangle the frame!

Was Messalina really a wicked woman?

Perhaps the most important question today concerning Messalina and her murderous plotting, to say nothing of her uncontrolled sexual desires, is, did Messalina truly deserve the reputation that she has? Was she really a serial killer and did she truly allow her sexual instincts to rule her head?

After her death (aged about thirty), the Roman Senate ordered that all statues of her be removed and the name of Messalina be erased from all public and private places – an action known as *damnatio memoriae* which was aimed to remove any remembrance of her from public life. This was not fully carried out however, and several statues and images still survive until this day.

In contrast to this physical removal of evidence of the infamous empress, as we have seen, her name was preserved through history and poetry. As it has been noted, this began decades after her death when none of her contemporaries were still alive to defend her possible good name. In other words, it is important to understand the historiography concerning Messalina when it comes to following her story (as it is with all historical figures) and therefore to question if she was as wicked and as manipulative as she has been painted.

However, it must be remembered that Messalina was living in a time and culture which could be described as 'dog eat dog'. If you wished to survive and ensure that your son or brother or any other family member could later rule or inherit your wealth, then it seems that you had no choice but to remove any possible rival, such as by banishing them or by having them assassinated or commit suicide. Therefore, for example, Messalina saw that she had no alternative but to have the young Britannicus done away with in favour of Claudius' natural son, Nero.

However we may justify her actions, it still does not

seem clear why she insisted on marrying Silius. Her husband was thirty years older than herself and was likely to die (or be killed) in the near future, so why was she in such a hurry to get rid of him? Is it because Narcissus, the freed slave who had helped her permanently remove Silanus, now saw that he had gone too far? By plotting to have Messalina killed, he might have been able to restore his own reputation in the eyes of Emperor Claudius. We will never know.

In contrast to this massive besmirching of her name, the earliest and not completely negative description of Messalina is attributed to Seneca, the contemporary (4 BCE–65 CE) Roman stoic, statesman and satirist. When he wrote about Messalina's daughter, Octavia, he noted that her mother was *incesta genetrix* – an unchaste mother-in-law – but that she was more passive in her marriage with Silius than it had been understood in the past.

Finally, there is another theory that attempts to show that Messalina was not as devious as she had been painted. This argues that the wedding she undertook with Silius was not a genuine wedding, but that it was just part of a ceremony in connection with Bacchus, the god of wine and ecstasy.

Chapter Three

Alice Kyteler (1263-1325?)
The Irish Witch

Modern sculpture of Alice Kyteler by Ani Mollereau,
Kilkenny, Ireland

The iconic image of a witch is that of a gnarled, ugly old woman with a long knobbly nose flying through the air on a broomstick. She wears a black pointed hat and cloak and is often accompanied by a black cat. Nothing could be further from the truth. Often, witches in the past were innocent women who had a special knowledge of herbal medicine and who succeeded in curing diseases when the local herbalist or apothecary had failed. Because these so-

called witches sometimes lived alone and were defenceless, they were often attacked by the Church because they were seen to be beyond the Church's influence. In times of famine and drought they were also attacked by the local villagers in rural areas, especially if their animals died or their crops failed. When the so-called witches were caught, they often had to undergo a cruel 'trial by water'. This meant that the unfortunate woman was tied up and thrown into the local pond or river. On the rare occasion that they did not drown, they would be declared innocent. A variation of this trial by water consisted of plunging the witch's hand into boiling water. If their hand remained unblistered, they too were pronounced innocent.

Despite the good that some of these women did, witches were invariably seen in a negative way and their actions were often linked with Satanism. Witches (invariably women) were often blamed for casting spells with their potions, amulets, special dolls called poppets, as well as using incantations, herbs and mirrors. When they were not allegedly carrying out any of the aforementioned wicked deeds, witches were also accused of necromancy – the conjuring up of dead spirits for divine purposes or prophecy. One of the oldest examples of this may be found in the Old Testament (1 Samuel 28:3-25). Here the Witch of Endor, after being consulted by King Saul, raises the spirit of the prophet Samuel who tells the king about the outcome of an imminent battle against the Philistines.

Witchcraft has continued from then until today and is still practiced in several countries. In Saudi Arabia it is still punishable by death. A recent example of witchcraft in England occurred in 2000 when eight-year-old Victoria Climbié from the Ivory Coast was slowly murdered through witchcraft-based ritual abuse by her great-aunt, Marie-Thérèse Kouao and her boyfriend, Carl Manning. This included starving, torturing, degrading and mutilating the poor girl. She was rescued but unfortunately she died soon after in St. Mary's Hospital, London.

From the Bible, Exodus (22:17) declares that, 'Thou shalt not suffer a witch to live' and Deuteronomy (18:12) states 'All these things [wizards, witchcraft and necromancy] are an abomination unto the Lord' – witchcraft has continued to feature in cultures throughout the ages. Perhaps the best-known witches in literature are those who appear in the opening lines of Shakespeare's play, The Tragedy of Macbeth:

When shall we three meet again?
In thunder, lightning, or in rain?
When the hurlyburly's done,
When the battle's lost and won.
(Act I, sc.1, 1-4)

Later, while practicing their traditional necromancy, they predict Macbeth's future to him after proclaiming:

Double, double toil and trouble:
Fire, burn; and, cauldron, bubble.*(Act IV, sc.1, 1-2)*

Even though these witches were from Scotland, witchcraft is an historical and international concept. Catherine Monvoisin – 'La Voisin' – (1640-1680) came from France, Malin Matsdotter (1613-1676) was Swedish, and both Moll Dyer (17th century) and Tituba (who featured in Arthur Miller's play, The Crucible *(1953) were American. Mother Shipton (c.1488-1561) came from England, Merga Bien (c.1560-1603) was German and Isobel Gowdie (17th century) was from Scotland.*

And if you had crossed the Irish Sea from Scotland to Ireland between c.1263-c.1325 you may have met, or at least heard of Dame Alice Kyteler. This woman was the first person to be condemned for witchcraft in Ireland. However, she escaped being burned at the stake by fleeing the country. Like Mary Ann Cotton, the serial killer who appears later in this book, Alice Kyteler was accused of murdering her four husbands, in addition to being a witch.

*

Alice Kyteler was born in Kilkenny in the south-east of Ireland to a family of successful Flemish merchants. When her father died in 1298, Alice inherited his properties and his business. Soon after, the approximately twenty-year-old Alice married her first husband, William Outlawe, a wealthy local merchant and moneylender. He was twenty years older than Alice and she bore him a son also called William. In later life, as with other rich families who wanted to keep their wealth within the family circle, her son became her chief business partner.

At one point early in her story, the older William Outlawe disappeared and Alice and her second husband, Adam Le Blund from Callan, were accused of killing him. She had married him in 1302 and by now she must have been a very wealthy woman. It was perhaps this wealth that allowed her to ride out the storm of disapproval. The locals may have resented her anyway since she was so rich, having made even more money through Le Blund, who was also a banker and moneylender. An indication of her wealth may come from the fact that her son, William Outlawe, declared that he was looking after £3000 of his parents' money, a sum worth about £710,000 today.

It seems that Le Blund died of a drinking spree, and in doing so left all his wealth to Alice. This meant that she could also marry again. This she did by 1309, when she wed Richard de Valle, a landowner from Tipperary in south-central Ireland who owned many properties in the area. His health having deteriorated, he died in c.1316 one evening after a lavish banquet, his death allowing her to marry yet again. Within a year of de Valle's death, Alice had married her fourth husband, Sir John Le Poer. As with de Valle, despite his former good health, soon after the wedding, Le Poer also began to suffer from various illnesses. He became weak and his fingernails fell out and so too did some of his hair. This had turned silver and started falling out in patches, which was an indication of arsenic poisoning.

Of course, having four husbands die on her was certainly not beneficial for Alice's reputation, especially when she clearly gained financially from each of their deaths. In addition, another reason why she was so resented is that it seems that she kept her vast wealth and connections within the Irish Flemish community (for evidence of which, see the names of her husbands). There were many accusations against her regarding witchcraft from her stepchildren, who were part of the family circle but who did not benefit from her great wealth.

As time passed, her family's financial situation worsened so much that Alice sued her stepson, who was also called Richard de Valle, for withholding her widow's dowry. It was during this period that the stepchildren from her former marriages accused her of witchcraft, the usual accusation made against women who were exceptional in one way or another.

*

The wind was gusty and howling as it bowled over the green hills and fields of southern Ireland. Standing on a hill surrounded by fences and trees was a lone fortress type of building, dark and foreboding. From the third floor a passer-by could see a square of light illuminating the area like a lighthouse. If the passer-by could have come any closer, he would have heard a noisy discussion taking part between several men and a few women, as well as hearing the sounds of drinking, bottles being emptied and glasses being filled.

"It's not right," Le Blund's oldest son said. "William Outlawe has got his filthy hands on all that money and yet we're entitled to it as much as he is."

"You mean because she is our mother as well?" Richard de Valle's youngest daughter asked.

"Of course," Richard Le Blund replied. "Is there any other reason?"

"Well, I've heard that that some people say that she practices witchcraft with those women she employs at the inn, and that the woman Petronella de Meath…"

"What, another one of those Flemish foreigners?"

"Yes, her. Well, she is Alice's chief helper."

"But how much money are we talking about?" the youngest member of the Le Poer family asked.

"I don't know exactly," Richard answered, "but William has spoken about thousands of pounds in the past."

"Thousands?" one of the Le Poer young men repeated. "No wonder the locals hate us so much. They must be so jealous. You know that the village women are calling her the wickedest woman who ever lived in these parts?"

"True, but what can we do about it?" one of the youngest women asked. "It's not as if William is going to have a change of heart and give us any, is it?"

"No, that will never be. We'll just have to force him."

"How?"

"I'm not sure," the oldest son of Adam Blund said, "unless…"

"Unless what?"

"Unless we accuse her of practising witchcraft or something like that."

"You mean that we could go to the Church, to the bishop, and accuse her of poisoning our parents, for instance? You know, say that she killed them so that she could get her hands on the money that should have come to us?" one of the Le Poer women said.

"Exactly. We could charge her with using sorcery and maybe poison. You know, what the judges call *maleficarum*..."

"Witchcraft? That's a very good idea. She is hated so much around these parts I'm sure we'll be able to find a judge or priest who'll believe us."

"Ah, but wait a minute," the oldest de Valle man said, holding up his hand. "The question is where would we make our charges? In the civil or the Church courts?"

"Aren't they the same?"

"No, they are not. They don't always have the same punishments for the same crime. Sometimes the civil courts are stricter and ask for more severe punishments, other times the Church courts, the ecclesiastic ones, are stricter. It depends on who is being charged, and with what crime."

"Yes, you are right," one of de Valle's sons said. "Don't you remember that well over one hundred years ago in England when King Henry the Second was displeased the way the Archbishop of Canterbury...?"

"Thomas à Becket?"

"Yes, him. The king was angry how Becket was always defending the monks and other people in the Church when they did something wrong. Wrong, that was, in the eyes of the king."

"Well, I think that we should go and speak to Richard Ledrede, the Bishop of Ossory. I'm sure that he'll help us.

He's always talking about the Church protecting the poor and the meek. I'm sure he won't be on Alice's side."

"I agree," another of de Valle's sons said. "The bishop is known to defend the Church and its laws, and I've heard that when it comes to charges of witchcraft and sorcery he shows no mercy at all."

*

And so it came about that in 1324, the stepchildren of Alice Kyteler brought their claim to Richard Ledrede. This Franciscan member of the Order of Friars Minor, this 'scourge of heresy and witchcraft', had been a bishop for seven years and was feared by everyone who crossed his path. He had been appointed by Pope John XXII in 1317 and claimed that his own life was in danger from witchcraft. He had a great belief in the powers of the Inquisition – the Roman Catholic Church's much-feared court of enquiry – and he thought that it was his task to root out all forms of witchcraft and supernatural evil.

As a result of the family council, Alice Kyteler was brought before Bishop Ledrede and his ecclesiastic court where she and her followers were charged with:

- *Using potions and sorcery to control innocent Christians*
- *Denying the faith of Jesus Christ and the Catholic Church*

- *Holding secret nightly meetings in churches in order to undermine the Church and also to perform black magic*
- *Cutting up animals to sacrifice to demonic creatures at crossroads*
- *Murdering her four husbands to obtain their finances and their lands*
- *Consorting with Robin Artison, her alleged lover, a man considered to be a lesser demon of Satan*

The bishop tried to have Alice and her close companions arrested. However, he was not able to do so, and it was claimed that Roger Outlawe (Utlagh), her former brother-in-law, used his influence as the Chancellor of Ireland to protect her. In the end this did not stop the bishop from holding an inquisition about Alice in which she was charged with witchcraft, heresy, magic and making sacrifices to demons. Unfortunately for her accusers, she was not present at the hearings when she was found guilty as she had fled to Dublin. As a result, Alice and her witches were excommunicated and it was declared that she when she would be arrested she would be handed over to the civil courts to be punished.

After this, Bishop Ledrede ordered Alice's son, William, to appear in the ecclesiastic court. He was charged with protecting heretics (his mother and her 'fellow-witches') and heresy. But here the bishop's plans came undone.

*

"Your Excellency," the Seneschal Arnold Le Poer leaned forward in his high throne-like chair to Bishop Ledrede, who stood there facing him. "You cannot arrest William Outlawe on these charges of protection and heresy."

"May I ask why not?"

"It is because you are trespassing upon the civil laws of this country, and these laws take precedence over your Church laws. Did you not know that?"

"Yes, my lord, I did. But the crimes that this Master William has carried out are so wicked that he cannot be allowed to remain free."

"That, Your Excellency, is for me to judge. Not you. You have overstepped your authority, and for that I command that you be imprisoned in Kilkenny jail..."

"But, my lord, this is monstrous! I am a bishop. I was appointed by His Holiness, the Pope. And, if I may add, I believe that you are misusing your powers. Just because you are related to Master William Outlawe and his mother, Alice..."

"That is enough! Take him away!"

*

The bishop spent seventeen days in Kilkenny Jail, being eventually released by John Darcy, the Lord Chief Justice, who had ridden the nearly ninety miles from Dublin to Kilkenny to do so. Then Darcy examined the whole case and agreed that Alice had committed major crimes against the Church and its teachings. He commanded that she and her followers were to be severely punished. This was to take the form of being whipped through the streets while tied being to the back of a horse and cart. Then Alice, as the leader, was to be burned at the stake.

In his zeal to arrive at the truth, and since the authorities could not lay their hands on Alice who had fled, her maidservant and chief assistant, Petronella de Meath, was whipped and tortured instead. This was legal according to Church law, but not by secular law. Nevertheless, Ledrede had this sentence carried out and afterwards the poor woman admitted that she and the others had engaged in witchcraft. Bishop Ledrede's report of her confession included the following details:

... [Alice] made an offering of three cocks to a certain demon whom she called Robert, son of Art, from the depths of the underworld. She had poured out the cock's blood. Cut the animals into pieces and mixed the intestines spiders and other black worms like scorpions ... she had boiled this mixture in a pot with the brains and clothes of a boy who had died without baptism and with the head of a robber who had been decapitated...

... Petronella had several times, at Alice's instigation and once in her presence, consulted demons and received answers...

... [Petronella] said that with her own eyes she had seen the aforementioned demon as three shapes, in the form of three black men each carrying an iron rod in the hand. This apparition happened by daylight before the

said Dame Alice and, while Petronella herself was watching, the apparition had intercourse with Alice...

On 3 November 1324, Petronella was flogged and burned at the stake. She was the only one of the women to suffer thus, and Bishop Ledrede never justified his actions. Petronella's daughter, Basilica, like Alice, fled and escaped, while Alice's son, William Outlawe, was accused of heresy, usury, adultery, perjury and clericide. Despite the severity of his crimes, he never had to pay a price like Petronella. According to some records, instead he was commanded to hear three masses daily for a year and to feed the poor. Other records say that he was ordered to make a visit to the Holy Land as soon as possible.

After this, Dame Alice Kyteler disappears from history, and it is thought that she went to England or Flanders. Apart from being known as Ireland's first witch, before Florence Newton (1660) and the eight witches of Islandmagee (1711), she did come back to life some six hundred years later in the last lines of William Butler Yeats' poem, 'Nineteen Hundred and Nineteen':

But now the wind drops, dust settles; thereupon
There lurches past, his great eyes without thought
Under the shadow of stupid straw-pale locks,
That insolent fiend Robert Artisson
To whom the love-lorn Lady Kyteler brought
Bronzed peacock feathers, red combs of her cocks.

Was Dame Alice Kyteler really a wicked woman?

By today's standards she may not have been unless it can be proved that she had murdered her husbands in order to get her hands on their wealth. But as a witch or healer, unfortunately for her, she was living in the wrong period of history. As it says in the introduction to this chapter, women who could cure sickness and whose lifestyle was not that as prescribed by the Church were automatically labelled wicked and in league with the Devil.

Chapter Four

Queen Isabella of England (1295-1358)
The 'She-Wolf' of France

Isabella is one of the most popular female names today both in Britain and in the USA. It comes from the Hebrew name, Elisheva, and means 'devoted to God'. The name has also been linked to the Biblical Jezebel, the wicked wife of Ahab, (Kings 1: 16-22). When Matthew Paris, the medieval monk and chronicler, criticised Isabella of Angoulême, King John of England's wife, for her impious behaviour, he castigated her for being 'more Jezebel than Isabella'.

What is certain is that the Isabella of France who

features in this chapter was not known for her piety. In fact her name became a synonym for manipulation, and the woman herself as a contributor to several murders and other foul deeds. This queen carried out her scheming plots on both sides of the English Channel, in London and in Paris, and many men, both high and low, paid the ultimate price for her adulterous and treacherous actions.

*

"What is it?" the anxious mother asked. "Is it a –"

"It's a girl, *Votre Majesté,* and she looks very healthy, very pretty –"

"Oh, another princess," Queen Joan said, and thinking of her first two daughters, added, "Well, I hope she lives longer than her sisters."

Her two other baby girls had died very young. Margaret had gone to meet her Maker, aged six, while her younger sister, Blanche, had survived for only four years. How long would this one live for?

"Juliet, go and tell the king now, and hurry," the queen commanded the woman standing by the bed. "I'm sure he's anxious to know."

"*Oui, Votre Majesté.*" The servant bobbed and hurried out to tell King Philip IV that he was now the father of yet another daughter. This was in addition to his sons, Louis, Philip and Charles.

"*Oui,*" the queen smiled, looking at the baby girl wrapped up in a soft white blanket and thinking ahead. "*Celle-ci est vraiment très jolie* – This one is *really* pretty.

That will be very useful for getting her a good husband; one who will be good for France. Hmm, I wonder who that will be?"

*

The answer came some ten years later when young Isabella was betrothed to King Edward I of England's son, the future Edward II. The wedding took place at Boulogne-sur-Mer in January 1308, but any initial joy was cut short very quickly as there were problems from the very beginning. These were not due to the fact that Isabella was about thirteen years younger than her husband, but rather that the young, newly crowned King Edward preferred the company of his favourite male courtier, Piers Gaveston, to his pretty wife.

Gaveston from Gascon was a nobleman who was the same age as the king and had originally been introduced to the English court by Edward I. However, when the stern king saw how the relationship between his son and the new courtier was developing, he promptly banished his son's best friend from court. One of the first things the new Edward II did on ascending the throne in 1307 was to have Gaveston returned to the palace. He was given a title, the Earl of Cornwall, which meant that he was now the owner of a vast amount of land in the south-west, Oxfordshire, Berkshire and east Lincolnshire, areas worth millions of pounds today.

While this promotion and kingly generosity to Gaveston must have infuriated the other nobles, it was the special relationship that existed between the king and Gaveston that really offended them. There is no positive proof that the two were lovers, but their public and private behaviour was so repugnant to the leading nobles that they forced the young king to banish Gaveston again.

Gaveston, for his part did nothing to help himself. Mocking the nobles, he called the Earl of Lancaster, 'the fiddler' and the Earl of Lincoln 'burst belly'. He derided the Earl of Pembroke as 'Joseph the Jew', and called the Earl of Warwick 'the black dog of Arden', naming him after a large forest in Warwickshire. It was clear that Gaveston and the leading nobles were on a collision course.

However, like the proverbial bad penny, to the lords' disgust he showed up again and even took a prominent role in Edward's coronation ceremony. It was Gaveston who grabbed the 'top job' of presenting the crown to the king, instead of the premier lord, Thomas, Earl of Lancaster and Leicester.

From here things went from bad to worse. Isabella and Edward crossed over the English Channel from Paris to London, where, according to tradition, on 25 February 1308 they were crowned in Westminster Abbey.

While taking part in his wedding banquet the newly crowned Edward spent more of his time with his best friend than with his new wife. This may be excused by saying that he preferred to chat with his old friend rather than to a twelve-year-old girl, but those present did not accept the king's behaviour as normal. The ecclesiastic chronicler, Adam Murimuth, wrote that Edward 'loved an evil male sorcerer more than he did his wife, a most handsome lady and a beautiful woman'. It was also noted that Gaveston 'was dressed more magnificently' than the king, which was yet one more cause for anger among aristocratic circles.

To make matters worse, Edward preferred to spend his nuptial night with his beloved courtier, a circumstance which caused Isabella to write home to her father saying that her new husband was 'an entire stranger to my bed', and that she was 'the most miserable of wives'.

Despite everything, Isabella did try to pretend that the situation was not as bad as it seemed, but this did not help. The lords put such pressure on the king that over the next three years he was forced to banish Gaveston four times. But every time he left, the persistent 'bad penny' returned.

The last time this happened was when Isabella and Edward were spending their Christmas at Windsor Castle. Suddenly, to the delight of the king, Gaveston appeared. The king and his Gascon favourite immediately started hugging each other as the queen and the assembled nobles looked on with complete contempt for this 'unmanly' show of mutual affection, if not love.

*

"Cannot you stay here and sit with me, my king?" Isabella asked, stepping down from the throne to speak to her husband.

"No, my dear. You know I haven't seen *mon frère* Piers for some time. I must be with him."

"Must you? But I am your wife."

"I know, but I must be with Piers. I'm sure he has much to tell me."

"Well, so have I, and," she said, pointing to her belly, "you seem to forget that I am with child."

"I know, but we must be leaving here soon and –"

"Why? I am in no state to travel. Just look at me."

And saying this, she took the king's hand and placed it on her large, round belly.

"Yes, I know," Edward said, "but I want to leave here soon with Piers before the lords do him harm. I've heard what they've been muttering about him behind my back."

"But I cannot go with you. I cannot make a journey in this condition. Please think of me and your future son," and she put his hand on her belly again.

Edward removed his hand quickly and said, "How do you know it's a son?"

"I don't, but I just feel it is."

"Well, no matter. I am commanding you to come with me. You have no choice. Tell your ladies to pack your trunks because we will be leaving very soon. Pregnant or not."

"But why are you in such a hurry?"

"It's those barons and lords. They are making life impossible for me here in London. All they want is to get rid of *mon cher* Piers again, and that I won't do. Not for them and not for anyone. It's just jealousy. That's all."

"But my dear husband," Isabella said, trying to smile persuasively, "What would happen if you sent him away for a little while? Would that be so bad?"

"Never," was his immediate reply. "Never, and if I did, those lords would see it as if they had beaten me. No! I refuse to get rid of Piers. It would show them that they had won if I did so."

*

As a result, the heavily pregnant Isabella was forced to take a long and uncomfortable journey north. This unpleasant three-hundred-mile ride in a bouncing and swaying padded carriage over bumpy roads and tracks eventually brought her to Tynemouth Priory on the Scottish border. There Edward abandoned her as he turned south to Scarborough on the Yorkshire coast in order to install his favourite courtier in a castle there. Having done so, he left Gaveston behind, as he was planning to deal with the ever-troublesome Anglo-Scottish border. As he rode north again, Edward hoped that his favourite courtier was now well out of the way of his angry and jealous noblemen. However, unbeknown to the king in his absence, a group of top-ranking nobles who had been delegated to do so by their peers, laid siege to Scarborough Castle.

The siege party consisted of the Earls of Pembroke and Surrey as well as Baron de Percy of Alnwick and Baron Robert de Clifford, who despised and hated Gaveston with a vengeance.

Looking out from over his castle's walls and seeing the lords' preparations for a long siege, Gaveston surrendered on 19 May 1312. This surrender was accompanied by the signing of an agreement that Pembroke, Percy and Warenne, the Earl of Surrey, would do him no harm but would escort him to York. There they would negotiate with the king about what should be done with the king's loathsome favourite. The terms of the agreement also stated that if the nobles could not come to an agreement with the king by 1 August, then Gaveston would be permitted to return to Scarborough, a mere forty miles away.

The fateful meeting was held and no agreement was reached with the stubborn king. The result was that the nobles did not keep to the agreement, and that Gaveston found himself being escorted south to London by the Earl of Pembroke. However, when they reached Deddington in Oxfordshire, Pembroke left the group to visit his wife. This was too much for the angry Earl of Warwick who, when he heard about the apparently gentle treatment Gaveston was receiving, raced over to Deddington, took the unhappy Gaveston prisoner and escorted him back to his own castle in Warwick.

When the Earl of Pembroke heard of this, he appealed to the Earl of Gloucester, Gaveston's brother-in-law, and to the University of Oxford to intercede on Gaveston's behalf. Warwick would have none of this. He had the king's favourite brought to face a court led by himself and the Earls of Arundel, Hereford and Lancaster, and there Gaveston was condemned to death. The legal justification for this was that Gaveston had violated the terms of the Ordinances that had been signed the previous year in 1311. These Ordinances designed by the nobles and the Church limiting the king's power were reluctantly agreed to by Edward. It was now that the earls' 'kangaroo court' decided to use its authority, which it did. As expected, they passed a sentence of death on Gaveston.

On 19 June 1312, the twenty-eight-year-old Piers Gaveston, Earl of Cornwall was taken to Blacklow Hill, a few miles north of Warwick, and executed. Since the earls could not do this to one of their own, two Welshmen were employed to run Gaveston through with a sword before beheading him.

And where was Isabella while all this was happening? She was back in London, still pregnant. It was only then that she heard about what had happened to her rival for the king's love and affection.

*

"Your Highness," the Earl of Warwick's messenger said. "You will now have the king all to yourself. That accursed Earl of Cornwall is no more."

"What do you mean, no more?"

The messenger then told her the whole story, ending it with the details of Gaveston's bloody execution.

"What did the king say when he heard this?"

"He went into mourning, Your Highness, and then he swore to have revenge on those who were responsible."

"And has he done so yet?"

"No, Your Highness. Not yet, but in the meanwhile, there have been problems between the various noblemen themselves."

"What sort of problems?"

"It seems, Your Highness, that several of the earls and others have fallen out amongst themselves, and now the Earl of Pembroke, who felt that his honour had been affronted by what the Earl of Warwick had done, is now firmly on your husband's side."

"So does that mean now that the king is in the middle of a power struggle between his earls, some of them on his side and the others not?"

"I don't know, Your Highness. I suppose we will have to wait and see."

*

Isabella's guess was right. An aristocratic struggle for power did occur. It was resolved one year later, in October 1313, when following arbitration led by the Earl of Gloucester, various jewels and horses were returned to the king and the dissenting nobles were pardoned.

After this, Isabella and Edward must have come to a *modus vivendi*, whether out of love, or simply to make sure that there would be a royal heir and a 'spare'. The future King Edward III was born in 1312, and he was followed by: John (1316), Eleanor (1318) and Joan (1321). Naturally, all of them were destined to become aristocrats, or in the case of Joan, queen-consort to King David II of Scotland.

However, despite everything, soon after Eleanor was born, the king found himself a new royal favourite to replace Piers Gaveston.

*

"Edward," Isabella said one evening in the privacy of their bedchamber, "I don't like your new man in court."

"Who, Hugh le Despenser? What's wrong with him? He's most useful."

"*Mais oui*. He is most useful at helping himself. Him and his father."

"But the father showed his loyalty to me during that period a few years ago when I had problems with the lords over that business with Piers Gaveston."

"I know that, Edward, but now the pair of them, especially the younger one, is exploiting his position at court and angering the lords, just like Gaveston did."

"But I need him, Isabella, perhaps even more than I needed *mon cher* Piers."

"I can see that, but if you don't restrain them, you are going to have a civil war on your hands."

"That's not true, Isabella. I only want –"

"But, Edward, I'm begging you, I'm imploring you to send them away before it is too late."

*

Isabella's pleading succeeded, at least for the time being. The two Le Despensers, father and son, were banished from court, to the queen and the leading lords' relief. It was now that Isabella decided to make a pilgrimage to Canterbury. On her way back to London, she planned to stop at Leeds Castle in Kent. This castle was owned by Baron Badlesmere, who had been one of the foremost rebels against the king in the past. When Isabella arrived at the castle, the Baron's wife, Lady Margaret de Clare refused to let her stay.

This was too much for the queen. She ordered her armed guard to force their way in where they were promptly attacked by Margaret de Clare's men. When Isabella returned to London, the king declared that the Badlesmere's behaviour treasonous. The baron was later caught after trying to flee from the king's forces and put on trial. He was found guilty of treason and executed. His wife was given the doubtful honour of being the first woman ever to be imprisoned in the Tower of London, together with her children. They were released one year later, after which she joined a convent, the king paying for her maintenance.

However, despite this generosity on his part, it seemed as if Edward had not learned from his past experience with Piers Gaveston. He allowed the Despensers to return to court, where they immediately alienated the lords, who demanded that they be exiled again. The king refused and the civil war that had been predicted by so many finally broke out. One of the opening rounds was the Battle of Boroughbridge in Yorkshire. There, the royalist forces defeated the rebels with the result that the king had one of their leaders, Thomas, Earl of Lancaster, charged in a show-trial and executed. Thus King Edward II was able to consolidate his rule and rid himself at last of the earl who had caused him so many problems.

But the king's problems were not really over, for now he found that he had to sail to France with Isabella and his army to meet and support his wife's assertive brother, who was now King Charles IV. The recently crowned French king insisted that Edward pay homage for Gascony and that the King of England's officials there carry out new French orders. Tensions rose very quickly, but Isabella managed to defuse the situation and secured a truce with Charles. She also convinced Edward to have their young son, the thirteen-year-old Prince Edward, brought over to Paris to pay homage to the French king.

Now Isabella had the control over the situation that she had planned for. When her husband declared that as there was some sort of peace with France they should all return to England, Isabella refused. And in public, too.

She declared to all who could hear, "I feel that marriage is a union of a man and a woman, holding fast to the practice of a life together, and that someone has come between my husband and myself and is trying to break this bond. I declare that I will not return until this intruder is removed, but, discarding my marriage garment, shall put on the robes of widowhood and mourning until I am avenged of this Pharisee."

On hearing this, Edward took his wife aside. "What is the meaning of this – you're putting on the robes of widowhood?"

"It's true, Sire. I refuse to return to London until you get rid of those despicable Le Despensers. And this time for ever. And not only that, my husband, but I am keeping our son here with me in France until you do!"

"That I cannot do. I need them, and so if you want, you can stay here. We'll see who gives in first. And yes, what's this I hear about you and this man, Roger Mortimer?"

"Mortimer? Nothing. You shouldn't listen to nasty rumours. You know how people love to gossip here at court."

But it was not a nasty rumour at all. A few years earlier, Roger Mortimer, Earl of March, had joined Lancaster and the other dissident earls and had fought against the king at Boroughbridge, where he had been on the losing side. He was condemned to death, but the sentence was commuted and he was sent to the Tower of London instead. He remained there for two years in quarters that were described as, 'less elegant than were seemly' before managing to escape. He did so by using his influential friends, including the Bishop of Hereford. There, in the Tower at the Lammas Day (1 August 1334) celebrations, Mortimer had the wine drugged and while the guards were lolling around drunk, soldiers loyal to Mortimer broke open a wall in his cell which allowed him to escape. Crawling over the roofs of the Tower, he made his way down to the river, where a boat was waiting to take him to France.

It is not known when he first met Isabella, but by the time she was in Paris they had become lovers, although many modern historians think that this may have happened while the queen was still in London. Now, in December 1325, they were seen as such and were protected by Charles IV from any of her husband's men that the Despensers might have sent to harm them. After a while,

68

their affair became such an embarrassment to the French king that Isabella and Mortimer and her son, Prince Edward, were forced to leave his court and move to Flanders. There, the loving couple, together with an army of supporters and mercenaries, planned to invade England and remove the despised Edward from the throne. In the meanwhile, Isabella, in return for the Count of Hainault's support, agreed to the betrothal of Prince Edward to his daughter, Philippa.

On 24 September 1326, Isabella, Mortimer and their forces landed on the east coast of England at the mouth of the River Orwell. There they were joined by more armed men who were against the king and the Despensers. From now on, there was to be two-month chase over England as the king and the Despensers began to feel unsafe wherever they were. By mid-November 1326, the Despensers had been captured. The father, Despenser the Elder, was taken prisoner at Bristol and executed and it seemed clear that his son would suffer a similar fate. All that remained was to see, when and how?

*

"My love," Isabella asked Mortimer that night. "What do you think we should do with the son? I mean, he has led us a merry dance chasing him from London to Gloucester and then to Wales."

"He must be executed soon, and in the most hideous way possible."

"Why so?"

"Because, Isabella, when the word gets out what happened to him, no-one will have the guts to go against us. My dear, if you want to be the queen, you must not only be strong, but you must let everyone see that you are strong. There is no other way."

"Yes, *mon cher*, I suppose you are right. I mean, after all, apart from leading the king by the nose, he did take over lands in Wales which were not his, as well as forcing his sister-in-law to surrender her lands to him."

"And Isabella, what about his pirate activities in the Channel? Ambushing merchants to hand over their goods, or taking money from them instead?"

"*Oui*, that wasn't good for our shipping, was it? And those rumours I heard that he was a sodomite? That's *really* disgusting. At least they didn't say *that* about Piers Gaveston. So, Roger, when do you want him to stand trial, if indeed he is going to be tried?"

"He should stand trial so that justice will be seen to be done. I suggest that we have it soon, towards the end of November, before any of his men can try and rescue him."

*

As a result, Hugh le Despenser the Younger was tried in Hereford on 24 November 1326. His judges included Isabella, Roger Mortimer and their chief supporters. It was clear from the outset that he would be found guilty, and so he was. In order to make sure his humiliation was complete, Despenser was dragged naked through the streets and then hoisted high up onto a tall ladder, where everyone could see what was about to happen to him. He was then hanged, drawn and quartered. Some records claim that he was also publicly castrated beforehand as an extra punishment for allegedly being a sodomite. His body parts were then distributed around the country to 'adorn' the gates in various cities as a warning to other potential criminals and traitors. His head was sent to London to be publicly displayed above the city gates.

The effect of this trial was so great that in 1493, one hundred and sixty years later, Robert Fabyan, a London sheriff wrote:

With ropes wert thou bound and on the gallows hung,
And from thy body thine head with sword was cut;
Thy bowels in the fire they threw and burned long,
Thy body in four pieces with an axe was slit,
Before that by horses wert thou dragged,
none pitying thee.

Two months after Despenser's horrific execution, Parliament declared that Edward would have to abdicate his throne in favour of his fourteen-year-old son, Prince Edward. This was the first time that such a thing had happened in over three hundred years, and so on 25 January 1227, Edward III became the new King of England.

Since he was still a minor, a council was appointed to help Edward run the country. Although Isabella and

Mortimer were not members of this council, they were the ones who were really pulling the strings.

*

"Roger, we have succeeded at last," Isabella said. "We have rid ourselves and the country of Edward. What do you think of that?"

"This is the best news I have heard for a long time, but I'm still worried."

"What about?"

"Edward is still alive and there are those who say we should not have forced him to abdicate."

"So what? It's too late now. What can they do about it?"

"Listen, my dearest Isabella. Do you remember how certain lords, even though they did not agree with Edward when he was king, supported him before the Battle of Boroughbridge? Well, what could stop that happening again?"

"Do you mean, some lords are still supporting Edward, which would mean that we'd have another civil war? But that's impossible, *mon cher*. We've locked him up in Berkeley Castle. He's not likely to escape from there."

"Who says so? Didn't I escape from the Tower, and that prison is much stronger than where Edward is now."

"So have more guards sent to Berkeley. That should solve our problem."

*

It did not. On 21 September 1227, to make sure that he did not become the focus for any royalist opposition, King Edward II was murdered. This may have been done in the traditional way that homosexuals were got rid of, that is, a red-hot poker being forced up his anus. This terrible death meant that no signs of violence were apparent on his face and upper body. It also meant that he could be displayed publicly and shown to have died 'naturally' in the castle. However, his cries of agony were heard throughout the castle and it was impossible to conceal the fact that he had been murdered most violently.

However, even though Christopher Marlowe described this violent assassination in his play, *Edward the Second* (c.1593), this version of Edward II's death is not believed by all modern historians. Among others, Ian Mortimer, a specialist in medieval history (and no relation to Roger Mortimer) claimed in an article in *The English Historical Review* that the deposed king escaped from Berkeley Castle and made his way to Europe. There he became a hermit and as such, lived out the remainder of his days. Mortimer says that there is evidence that in 1331, four years after his abdication and alleged murder, Edward's presence was recorded in the Papal court in Rome.

Whether this is true or not, we do not know. But what we do know is that for the next three years, 1327-1330, although the young King Edward III was England's legitimate ruler, it was Isabella and Roger who controlled the country, if not in name, then at least from behind the scenes. As the years passed, the king's mother and her lover became increasingly unpopular, depriving the nobles of the chance of making a fortune out of war when 'the rulers' signed a peace treaty with Scotland. This was a treaty that many of the nobles considered humiliating and shameful. In addition, Isabella and Mortimer angered King Edward III, who felt that they were usurping his power and not allowing him to reign as he should.

On 15 June 1330, King Edward III's first child, Edward, who would later be known as the Black Prince, was born at Woodstock Palace, Oxfordshire. It was now that the frustrated king felt that he had had enough of his mother and Mortimer's constant interfering, and he struck back.

On the night of 19 October, the king and his men sneaked into Nottingham Castle through a secret tunnel while Isabella and Mortimer were asleep and hauled the surprised Mortimer out of bed. Despite Isabella's cry, "Fair son, have pity on the gentle Mortimer," he was taken to the Tower of London. There he was accused of murdering the king's father, as well as usurping the present king's power. Unlike Gaveston, Mortimer was not tried and not even given a show trial. He was hanged six weeks later, on 29 November, at the newly erected gallows at Tyburn, West London and so became the first nobleman to be executed there. His body was left swinging in public for two days so that Edward III's idea of justice could be seen to be done.

Isabella was spared this grim fate. Instead, she was arrested and forced to give up all her powers, lands and riches that she and Mortimer had accumulated over their three year 'reign'. Fortunately for her, the king must have had a soft spot for his mother, as she was not held for long under house-arrest but was sent out of the way to Castle Rising in Norfolk. She was granted an annual sum of £3000 which was later increased to £4500. However, despite being far from London, she still remained an influential figure at court, although she no longer played any direct part in her son's rule. She died twenty-eight years later at Hereford Castle, on 22 August 1358 aged (about) sixty-three.

Was Isabella of France really a wicked woman?

Even though she, like Henry VI's French wife, Margaret of Anjou, was called the 'She-Wolf of France', she does not seem to have been completely wicked through and through. It is true that together with Roger Mortimer she usurped the throne, exploited her position and amassed a personal fortune while preventing her son, King Edward III, from ruling in his own right. She may have justified this last point by claiming that he was a minor and that having a young teenage boy ruling the country was not a good idea. Not then and not later, as the reigns of Henry III, Henry VI and Edward VI proved.

However, it may also be said that she was at least partly responsible for the executions of Piers Gaveston and of the Le Despensers, father and son, and did nothing to have their death sentences commuted. It should also be remembered that she was an assertive woman living in a man's world. If she had not stood up for herself, she would have been swept along with whatever was happening at the time. It was not in her nature to be a 'rubber stamp', or to be taken for granted – to merely fulfil her role as a docile queen-consort in order to provide a sufficient number of male heirs to the throne was certainly not for her.

Finally, some historians claim that because of the policies she advocated and supported, she was a factor in the outbreak and continuation of the Hundred Years' War, a 116 year long military campaign that led to much death and destruction in France. As Jessica Leggett summed her up in an article entitled, 'Isabella: Traitor, Adulterer, Murderer' in *All About History*, Isabella of France was 'a formidable woman whose bravery changed the course of English history forever'. In *Kings and Queens of England: A Dark History*, Brenda Ralph Lewis sums up Isabella less positively as a rapacious queen who 'plundered the royal treasury… and made huge grants to herself and her lover. She used Parliament to rubber-stamp any laws she wanted'.

Chapter Five

Jeanne de Clisson (1300-1359)
The Avenging Pirate

Execution of Olivier IV de Clisson, 1343, by
Loyset Liédet.

The main thread running through this chapter is that of revenge. The Oxford English Dictionary *defines revenge as 'to satisfy oneself with retaliation, or exacting retribution usually for evil done'. That is certainly the case when dealing with the vengeful actions taken by Jeanne de Clisson, a former Breton noblewoman who became a privateer in order to avenge what she considered the unjustified humiliation and execution of her beloved husband, Olivier de Clisson IV in Paris in August 1343.*

In 1782, Pierre Choderlos de Laclos said in Les Liaisons Dangereuses, *and later more famously repeated by Don Corleone in the 1972 film,* The Godfather, *"Revenge is a dish that tastes best when it is served cold." Jeanne de Clisson would not have agreed with him. She would more likely have agreed with Lord Byron who wrote in his poem* 'Don Juan', *'Sweet is revenge… especially to women'. She would also have probably agreed even more with Pistol, who in Shakespeare's* Henry V *swears that, 'I will most horribly revenge' when he is mocked by his fellow-soldiers before the Battle of Agincourt.*

But what is especially memorable about Jeanne de Clisson's revenge is what she did, how she did it, and the length of time she devoted to doing so before she decided that enough was enough and that her thirst for retribution had been slaked.

*

Jeanne Louise de Belleville, de Clisson, Dame de Montaigu was born in 1300 in Belleville-sur-Vie, a small town in the west of France. Her father, Maurice IV Montaigu was a nobleman who died when she was only three years old. Since he did not leave any sons, this meant that Jeanne de Clisson was the last member of the Belleville family. She was twelve years old when she married her first husband, Geoffrey de Châteaubriant VIII, a Breton nobleman. With him she had two children, Geoffrey IX and Louise. He died in 1326, leaving Jeanne as a rich aristocratic widow.

She remained in this state for two years, then married a widower, Guy de Penthièvre. This was no love-match, and after two years, in February 1330, the marriage was annulled by Pope John XXII.

It was in that same year that Jeanne married Olivier de Clisson IV. He was a rich Breton widower who owned lands and several mansions in north-west France. It seems that they loved each other and that this was not just a marriage of convenience between two noble families – a way in which the nobility kept their land and riches within their own aristocratic circle. They had five children, two girls and three boys. Their happy life was rudely interrupted when, in 1341, Duke John of Brittany died.

*

"How old was he?" Jeanne asked her husband.

"About fifty-two, but now we have a problem. Who of his rival claimants to the duchy do we, that is, our family, support? The duke's half-brother, Jean de Montfort, or Charles de Blois' family?"

"Who do you want to support?"

"The de Blois family of course."

"Why of course?

"Because, *ma chérie*, two reasons. First, de Blois is a much more saintly character and will be a better ruler than de Montfort, and second, he is supported by the French king. De Montfort," he added, "if you don't know, is a lapdog of the English. Their King Edward is using him to extend his control over the north-west of France. De Montfort is nothing but a selfish beast who only thinks of himself and what he will gain. I cannot fight for such a man. He is a disgusting traitor to France."

"But I heard that your brother supports de Montfort."

"I know that, but then Amaury will support anyone who promises him more land and gold."

*

As a result, a local civil war broke out in Brittany. At first, both sides were evenly matched but as the year 1342 progressed, de Montfort's armies began to overcome de Blois' forces in the duchy. By August, de Montfort controlled most of Brittany, including the three key cities of Rennes, Nantes and Vannes. It is true that it took de Montfort, together with his English reinforcements, four attempts to capture Vannes, but when they did, after an extended siege, Olivier de Clisson, as one of the city's most important military commanders, was taken prisoner.

However, for a while, luck was on his side. Instead of being killed, he was held in a castle, and two months later, following a new truce between the two sides, he was exchanged for the Earl Ralph de Stafford, who was being held by the French. But soon after this, Olivier's luck and his wife's joy at seeing him return home was suddenly crushed, and in a way that neither of them could predict.

*

"Jeanne, read this," an excited Olivier said, thrusting a paper at her. "It's from Vannes. I have been invited to come to the city for a tournament, where they are going to celebrate the truce that was signed at Malestroit."

"But isn't that like celebrating your defeat?"

"No, my dear. It's more like celebrating peace. And besides, it says here that they are inviting fifteen other Breton lords to attend. To me it sounds like this is going to be an event that no-one will forget in a hurry."

"And are you going to take part in this tournament, or will you just be a spectator?"

Olivier shrugged. "I don't know, my love. It doesn't say on this invitation. It just says that it is very important that I attend. You know, I never thought that anything like this would happen. It's such a surprise."

*

And a surprise it proved to be. As soon as Olivier de Clisson and his fellow Breton lords arrived at Vannes, they were arrested and held in the castle. There they learned that they had been denounced by Jean, the Lord of France in Guignen, for surrendering prematurely and even voluntarily to the English. The fifteen lords were not held for long in Vannes; soon after, under a heavily armed escort, they were taken to Paris and again imprisoned. There they were informed that they were being held because their superiors had considered that they had not fought bravely enough during the war, and thereby had helped the enemy to win.

"But this is not true," Olivier protested to another lord. "You were with me when we were fighting against de Montfort's men. You were with me on the castle battlements. You saw me leading my men. I wasn't one of those commanders who shout out orders safely from the rear."

"I know that, m'lord, but it seems as if they are determined to put us on trial."

"And what do you think our punishment will be? Execution?"

"Mais non, you are exaggerating. No, they will probably fine us or confiscate some or all of our lands and castles."

"Well, we'll see. I just hope my wife and children won't suffer, that's all."

But Olivier de Clisson IV had hoped in vain. Not only did his wife and children suffer, but he suffered much more. He and the other imprisoned lords held in the Chatelet fortress were brought before a tribunal of their peers to be tried for:

... several treasons and other crimes perpetrated by him against the king and the crown of France, and for alliances that he made with the King of England, enemy of the king and kingdom of France, as the said Olivier de Clisson...

Olivier protested, saying, "I fought as hard as I could against those English soldiers. And as for allying myself with them, that is also not true. This whole thing is a farce, a transgression of justice."

But his and his fellow lords' denial of their accusations did them no good. As the contemporary record shows:

... as the said Olivier has confessed, was by judgement of the king given at Orleans drawn from the Chatelet of Paris to Les Halles... and there on a scaffold had his head cut off. And then from there his corpse was drawn to the gibbet of Paris and there hanged on the highest level; and his head was sent to Nantes in Brittany to be put on a lance over the Sauvetout gate as a warning to others.

In addition, Olivier de Clisson was charged with conspiring with the King of England, who it was said would make the Breton lord an English viceroy in Brittany.

"But this is all lies!" Jeanne screamed when she heard the news. "My Olivier would never have betrayed his country to the English. I will have revenge! My husband won't have died in vain."

"What will you do, *ma mère*?" her oldest son, Olivier, (now Olivier V) asked.

"I don't know yet, but when I decide, it is going to hurt the king very, very much," she replied. "You cannot just try and execute a lord like that – like a commoner – and then display his body in public like he was a peasant criminal. It's just not done."

Soon after this, she took her two sons, Olivier and Guillaume, whom she had by her third husband, Olivier IV, to the ancient city of Nantes, and there she showed them their father's head displayed above the Sauvetout city gate.

"This is supposed to be a warning for the other French lords," she explained as she pointed to the grisly remains of her husband. "But believe me, *mes enfants*, this is going to be the time when the king and his lackey, Charles de Blois, will begin to seriously regret what they did to your dear father. Remember, *mes chers*," she continued as she wiped her eyes, "they called him a traitor and then they murdered him in cold blood. And if that were not enough, they are now publicly humiliating what is left of him. Come, let us go. We have seen enough. But fear not, I *will* have revenge. Of that you can be sure."

*

Now a vengeful and determined Jeanne de Clisson turned her thoughts into deeds. She sold her estates at Clisson: the château, the land, 'her jewels, her pompous attire and precious furniture that decorates her castles' and bought three ships with the proceeds. She had them painted black and their sails dyed red. The flagship of her fleet was aptly named, *Ma Vengeance* – 'My Revenge'. In addition, she raised an army of local Bretons and then set about having her vengeance.

The records show that she attacked a castle owned by one of Charles de Blois' officers, Galois de la Heuse. He was one of Charles de Blois' most loyal supporters and had not heard about what had happened at Vannes. He welcomed Jeanne and her men into his château, and then she in turn plundered the place and killed all of his men except one.

"Madame, why are you going to spare this one soldier?" one of her captains asked.

"So that he will go and spread the word what I have done. But come, this is just one of the castles. There are more."

She then added the garrison at Château-Thébaud to her list, as well as a castle at Touffou, near Bonnes in the south-west. She managed to enter this castle by pretending she was a grieving widow. Once the gates were fully opened, her men rushed in and massacred almost all of the castle's inhabitants. Those who were left alive were told to spread the word about Jeanne de Clisson's revenge.

However, when she saw that her small army's attacks on her larger enemy was not having the desired effect on the king and Charles de Blois, she turned her attention away from the land to the sea. She took her Black Fleet into the English Channel and began to attack French merchant ships, vessels that were bringing merchandise to England and back. There her pirate crews would board the 'enemy' ships, as she thought of them, and kill all the crew except a few lucky souls. As before, they were spared so that they could spread the word that they had been attacked by *La Lionne Sanglante* – The Bloody Lioness. She gained this reputation as it was reported that, despite the fact that she could have made money ransoming the nobles she found on board, she preferred to have them beheaded with an axe before casting their headless bodies into the sea.

In addition to these acts of piracy and murder, Jeanne and her fleet are reported to have attacked several coastal villages in Normandy. Here her men killed the locals and set the villages ablaze. This angered the king for many reasons, not least because of the loss of his tax revenues from the villagers.

"But this is not enough," the avenging Jeanne de Clisson declared to her children. "We must hurt the French king even more."

"How, Mother?"

"We will use our fleet to help the English transport their supplies," she replied. "We will carry the English soldiers, horses and guns, their bows and arrows and cannon from England to France. Ha! That will show King Philip what I think of him and what he did to my dear Olivier. Oh, yes my children, that evil king will live to regret that terrible day at Vannes."

Although King Philip was known as 'The Fortunate', in 1340 his luck ran out when his fleet was completely defeated by King Edward III's English navy at Sluys (on today's Belgian coast).

While the English lost only two ships, the French lost almost two hundred, with most of them being captured and towed back to England. After this, the French coast was undefended, allowing the English army to invade France. One of King Edward's major victories was in August 1346, when his smaller army routed the French at the Battle of Crécy. The English lost about three hundred men

86

and King Philip over ten times that number. What made this battle so important was that over fifteen hundred nobles were killed or taken back to England to be ransomed. Jeanne de Clisson must have felt very pleased that day, knowing that she and her ships had contributed to this English victory.

Jeanne de Clisson's campaign of revenge, both on land and sea lasted for thirteen years. In a way, it ended with an anti-climax. On her last expedition, her flagship was sunk and as a result, Jeanne with her two sons, Olivier and Guillaume were cast adrift. They spent five days floating in the English Channel until they were rescued by de Montfort's supporters, who took her to Morlaix on the coast of Brittany. However, in the meanwhile, the younger son, Guillaume, had died of exposure in his mother's arms.

Unlike many of the stories in this book, this one ended peacefully and happily. Deciding to bring her campaign of revenge to an end, Jeanne de Clisson married for the fourth time in 1356, this time to an English knight, Sir Walter Bentley. He had been one of Edward III's commanders and had been rewarded with many French lands and castles. Jeanne and Sir Walter settled down at Hennebont on the Brittany coast and there in 1359 she died aged fifty-nine after a brief, three-year marriage.

However, the name of Clisson did live on. Jeanne's son, Olivier V, after two marriages, two attempts on his life and a stormy and warlike career, became the Constable of France (1380-1392), the highest honour a French nobleman could receive. Like his mother, despite his action-filled life, he died peacefully in bed in 1407 aged seventy-one, a great age in those turbulent times.

Ironically, Charles de Blois, the nobleman who had Jeanne de Clisson's second marriage annulled by the Pope, later became extremely pious and declared a saint, and this despite the fact that he had had fourteen hundred townspeople massacred after the siege of Quimper. The original proposal was put forward in 1368 but, owing to the deaths of various popes and the passage of time, he was not beatified until 1904, well over five hundred years after the initial request. Charles de Blois-Châtillon, Duke of Brittany, then became the Blessed Charles de Blois, his Saint's Day being 30 September.

Was Jeanne de Clisson really a wicked woman?

It is true that she deliberately set out to kill as many of the enemy as she could, as well as plundering their property. However, this was, as she saw it, the only way to right the wrong she felt had been carried out against her beloved husband. She knew that she could not seek justice in the courts, and so a long campaign of violence and premeditated murder on land and sea was, as far as she was concerned, her only alternative. However, her acts of revenge, which may have seemed justified to her, that is, the killing of tens, if not hundreds of soldiers and sailors who were only carrying out their duties, certainly puts her in the ranks of a wicked woman.

Chapter Six

Elizabeth Báthory (1560-1614)
The Aristocratic Hungarian Serial Killer

Elizabeth Báthory painted in 1585 (artist unknown)

The best-selling book, Guinness World Records, *originally known as* The Guinness Book of Records *(1955-1999) grew out of the desire to have a book of facts which would solve arguments in pubs. From its simple beginnings sixty-seven years ago, it has become the most authoritative source for establishing the record for being the biggest, the longest, the fastest, etc.*

One of the grimmest facts noted in this ever-popular annual publication is that Elizabeth Báthory, a Hungarian noblewoman who lived some four hundred and fifty years ago, was the world's most prolific female serial killer and also one of the most prolific murderers in the Western World. Báthory easily outranks some other infamous female serial killers, such as the Russian noblewoman, Darya Nikolayevena Saltykova (1730-1801) who was accused of killing 138, mainly female, serfs; the English baby-farmer, Amelia Dyer (1836-1896), who killed about four hundred babies and young infants; "Jolly" Jane Toppan (1854-1938), from Boston, USA, who confessed to thirty-one murders and who possibly killed more, as well as the Mexican murderer, Juana Barraza, (b.1957) nicknamed 'La Mataviejitas' – the Old Lady Killer. In 2008 she was sentenced to 759 years in prison and is now sitting in Santa Martha Acatitla Penitentiary, Mexico for having killed up to forty-eight people.

*

Born on 7 August 1560 in Nyirbátor, Hungary, Elizabeth Báthory had it all. Her high social standing came from the fact that she was the daughter of Baron George IV Báthory and his wife, the Baroness Anne. Her uncle was Stephen Báthory, the King of Poland, Duke of Lithuania and the Prince of Transylvania. She was raised as a Calvinist Protestant and was well-educated, studying Hungarian, Greek, Latin and German. However, what she sorely missed was good health. It is this factor that may possibly explain the rest of her life. As a young girl she suffered many seizures which may have been caused by epilepsy.

These attacks would not have been helped by the then held belief that her condition could be cured by rubbing the blood of someone who did not suffer from epilepsy on her lips, or by other strange, contemporary alleged cures.

Other speculative stories about her youth say that she was forced to witness members of her family and army officers administer cruel and brutal punishments to local peasants and servants. These included the use of witchcraft and Satanism. In addition, she is reputed to have given birth by the time she was thirteen or fourteen, the father being a peasant who worked on her father's huge estates. It is said that the unfortunate father was later torn to pieces by dogs and that Elizabeth's child was given away to a local woman in order hide the family's shame.

On 8 May 1575, when she was fifteen, Elizabeth Báthory was married in a huge ceremony to Count Ferenc Nádasdy. This marked the end of a five-year engagement, a political arrangement in order to link two powerful aristocratic families together. The Nádasdy family gave Elizabeth the Castle of Csejte in the Carpathian Mountains together with seventeen villages and a country house.

Three years after their marriage, Ferenc Nádasdy was promoted to become the commander of Hungary's army in the country's fight against the Ottomans. This was to become an extended drawn-out campaign known as the Long Turkish War (1593-1606), and the Báthory estates covered a strategic area to the east of the Austrian capital, Vienna. This meant that Elizabeth was left to manage the family's estates and business affairs while her husband was away fighting. In addition, it was during this period that Elizabeth gave birth to three girls: Anna, Orsolya and Katherina, and also to two boys: András and Paul. As their mother was busy managing the family's assets, the children were raised by a governess in a way similar to that by which Elizabeth herself had been raised.

On 4 January 1604, Ferenc Nádasdy died after suffering for three years from severe pains in his legs. He and Elizabeth had been married for nearly thirty years. On his death he willed the running of the estate to György Thursó, an important Hungarian aristocrat, a man who six years later would investigate the many accusations of brutal murder brought against Elizabeth Báthory.

It was during the latter part of her husband's absence, from 1602 until 1604, that rumours about Elizabeth's bestial treatment and torture of her servants and others began circulating. Many poor local girls, aged between ten to fourteen who had been lured to the castle looking for work, began to disappear. Then wealthy daughters of the gentry similarly began to vanish. They had been sent there by their parents in order to be educated and learn courtly etiquette from the countess in her women's apartments.

These rumours about the missing girls and women spread so fast and became so widespread that the authorities, led by István Magyari, a royal minister, began complaining about Elizabeth's allegedly terrible behaviour in public and also at the royal court in Vienna. As a result, in 1610 King Matthias II ordered György Thurzó to see if there was any truth in the stories that he kept hearing. He in turn appointed Mózes Cziráky and András Keresztúry to investigate the situation.

*

András Keresztúry asked Elizabeth, "Countess Bathory, unfortunately it has come to our attention that great harm has come to some young ladies…"

"Young ladies?"

"Yes, Countess, young ladies, that is, the daughters of various noblemen who have been sent here, as well as to several servant girls who came looking for employment here in your castle."

Elizabeth Bathory shrugged, "What a lot of nonsense! I too have heard these vicious rumours. But I must tell you, and of course your fellow investigator, Mózes Cziráky, that these rumours, these nasty untruths are completely, and I repeat, completely unfounded."

Mózes interjected, "But my dear Countess, I am afraid to tell you that we have gathered evidence from some three hundred witnesses who said –"

"Then they were all lying! And you can go and tell György Thurzó that, even if he is the king's minister and the Palatine of Hungary."

"But my dear Countess, how can you explain it that three hundred people are telling us the same stories of your terrible treatment and torture of these people who have come to your castle?"

"Well, all I can say is that they are all liars. That's all."

András asked, "But why should they spread all these lies about you?"

"Huh! That's easy enough to answer. They are all

93

jealous of me and my wealth. I mean, look about you. Look at this hall. Look at my tapestries, statues and jewellery. Wouldn't *you* be jealous if you were a young girl? Yes, of course you would."

Mózes said, "But we believe it is more than that, more than mere jealousy, Countess Báthory. We can believe that looking at your great wealth might turn the heads of some young girls, but here we are talking about many and repeated tales of horrifying torture."

"Yes, and these rumours which you deny are so widespread. You should know, madam that they have even reached the ears of the king and the royal court in Vienna."

"Well, it doesn't matter how far they have reached. They could have reached Paris and Madrid for all I care. All I know is that they are utterly untrue and that they have been started by stupid ignorant and jealous peasants."

"But, my dear Countess –"

"And so, if these rumours are true, what are they saying? That I've eaten all these poor girls for supper?"

András and Mózes looked at each other. The content of some of what they had heard was not too far from Countess Elizabeth Báthory's last statement.

"Madame, do you really wish to hear the terrible reports that have come to us during these investigations? They will fall like blows on your gentle ears."

"I don't care and yes, I do want to hear them. I want to hear all the rubbish these stupid people have been saying about me behind my back. And after all I have done for them. Fed and entertained them, provided them with money and employment and… Tell me, how ungrateful can people become? Tell me that."

"Yes, Madame, I am sure that is all true, but this is what we have heard." He took out a large piece of paper, paused to clear his throat and then began to read in a clear voice. "Madame, they say that you have beaten young girls to death with clubs; that you have burned your victims with hot irons; that you have stuck needles under their fingernails and that you have poured either ice cold water or scalding hot water over their naked bodies... need I continue reading this list, madame?"

"Yes, yes, do go on. I would like to hear the rest of this pack of lies. Why, I did not know that people could be so imaginative. Yes, please continue."

András looked at Mózes, shrugged and continued to read: "That you covered your servants and other people's bodies with honey and live ants and –"

"Why should I do that?"

"Because as it says here, their honey-covered bodies were then attacked by all manner of bugs and insects that bit them, causing them great suffering and hurt. And yes, it is claimed that you even sewed your victims' lips together and bit great chunks of flesh off their faces and breasts."

"What! Are you saying that in addition to all of the lies you have just read out that I am a cannibal as well?"

András Keresztúry did not answer, but just handed the list over to his fellow investigator, who said, "My dear Countess, we are merely reading what has been reported. That is all. But unfortunately, we have not come to the end of this terrible list. As it says –"

"What, there are even more lies? You haven't finished yet?"

Mózes cleared his throat and continued: "We have on record, madam, that you enjoyed torturing your victims with scissors. That you would cut off their noses, their hands, and even their, er, how shall I say this? Er, their lower parts."

"What, with scissors? This shows that all these stories have been made up by ignorant people who hate me and are jealous. How can you cut up a body with scissors? Tell me that. Huh! With scissors? Don't you know, sir, that scissors are meant for cutting thread and pieces of material? They are used by seamstresses and spinsters. Not by me. *You*, sir, you try cutting a body, even a piece of meat with scissors and you'll see how far you get. Scissors! Huh!"

"And then, Madam, at the end of this list it says that one of your favourite ways of inflicting pain on your victims was to use these scissors –"

"Huh! These scissors again. Yes, what else was I supposed to have done with them?"

"That you used to cut open the skin between your victim's fingers."

"Now supposing that these preposterous and ridiculous stories are true, how are you going to prove them? And remember, sir, I am a countess in this country. I am related to some very important people... very important."

*

But the gruesome list was not the end of the charges laid against Countess Elizabeth Báthory. In addition, some of the witnesses claimed that she had sex with the devil, and that she had become known as the 'Blood Countess' because of her vampiric tendencies. These stories said that she would bathe in the blood of her young victims, and this was her attempt, at the age of about forty, to preserve or restore her youthful appearance.

Once András Keresztúry and Mózes Cziráky had completed their investigation, they handed over the results to György Thurzó, who then charged Countess Báthory with the murder of eighty girls. The Palatine of Hungary was able to reinforce his accusations, as one witness claimed to have seen the countess' record book in which she listed the details of her victims' terrible tortures and deaths. This witness stated that this book, which was never found, contained a list of six-hundred and fifty names. Two other witnesses, court officials, Bendek Desŏ and Jakab Szilvássy, stated that they had personally watched the countess torture and kill some of her servant girls. In addition, shallow graves were found in the vicinity of her castle and when they were opened, they were found to contain the scarred and mutilated bodies of some of her victims.

At the end of the trial, all of Countess Elizabeth's accomplices, including Ilona, her wet-nurse, who looked after her mistress' children, were accused of witchcraft. There was only one punishment for this – to be burned at the stake. As for the instigator of this incredible catalogue of evil, Countess Elizabeth Báthory, she claimed immunity, but this did not help. There was simply too much evidence against her in terms of oral and written reports, as well as physical proof in the form of the mutilated bodies found in the nearby shallow graves.

Owing to her aristocratic status, she was not burned at the stake as a witch, but in 1610 she was bricked up in her room at Csejte Castle. She remained there for four years until she died, unlamented, 24 August 1614, aged fifty-four. She was buried in the Csejte church the following day, but the local villagers would not accept this. They forced the authorities to dig up her body and move it to where she was born at Ecsed. Here she was reinterred in the Báthory family crypt.

Was Elizabeth Báthory really a wicked woman?

After reading this gruesome tale of mass mutilation, torture and murder, the question today is, can we believe it? Did it really happen? Two Hungarian academics have suggested that Elizabeth Báthory's name was unfairly besmirched. They claim that many other Hungarian aristocrats were jealous of her great wealth and of her ownership of considerable swathes of land. They say that this wealth and power made her a potential threat to her contemporaries, and that blackening her name was a very good way of getting rid of her permanently. It also did not help her that during this period of Hungarian history there was much rivalry for power between the most important aristocratic families. Proof of this may be found in the fact that after Elizabeth Báthory had been arrested, King

Matthias had a huge debt owed to her cancelled.

Other ideas regarding the authenticity of this story refer to the question of religion. The original complaints against Elizabeth were made by a Lutheran minister, István Magyari. The Countess was a Calvinist Protestant. It is no coincidence that this story, whatever the truth of it, happened in Europe when the continent was undergoing a long series of religious wars and local hostilities, so did the question of religion influence Elizabeth Báthory's behaviour? As a background to the following, it should also be remembered that while she was alive, the Hundred Years Croatian-Ottoman War (1493-1593) was being fought, a war to decide which religion would prevail in Eastern Europe – Christianity in one form or another, or Islam.

However, there were flaws in the evidence against the Blood Countess, or Countess Dracula, as she has sometimes been called. Most of the witnesses based their testimony on hearsay and not any verifiable evidence. As stated earlier, there were vested interests in painting her in a bad light, in that various other aristocrats did not want to repay their debts to her and once she was convicted as a cannibal and a witch, this absolved them from doing so.

Therefore, perhaps the truth is to be found somewhere in the middle. Perhaps she did act pitilessly and possibly very cruelly towards her servants, but during this period of history, that attitude was considered acceptable. In addition, in terms of numbers, the original number of people she was said to have murdered was whittled down to only eighty (!) and this terrible number may have been nearer the truth.

However, if there is any truth in this story, Elizabeth Báthory, who was naturally a very vain woman and who was said to have changed her clothes at least five times a day, probably made a major mistake in acting too harshly with the young aristocratic girls who came to stay at her castle. It was this as well as several financial issues that turned the rest of the aristocracy against her. That, and also being jealous of the wealth and power that the widow wielded. Spreading stories about her evil ways would be guaranteed to make sure that she would never be able to raise her head in 17th century Hungary's high society ever again.

Chapter Seven

Guilia Tofana (c.1620-c.1651?)
The Italian Mass Poisoner

Since biblical times when Cain murdered his brother, Abel, people have always wanted to permanently rid themselves of other people. Over the passage of time, the individual murderer's temperament and the means available have meant that the way they have done so has varied. Perhaps before the invention of gunpowder and the use of firearms, poison and bladed instruments such as daggers and swords were the most common methods. Then on 13 November 1535, Robert Pakenton (or Packington) was shot by a handgun as, according to John Stow in his

Survey of London (1598), this London merchant was 'going to morrow mass'. From then on, people saw that they were able to kill from a distance and hopefully get away with murder.

Another aspect of this murderous activity often depended on whether the murderer was a man or a woman. It seems that men often preferred to use daggers or swords, and later, firearms, whereas women chose gentler, less violent means including poison. Such poisons included Deadly Nightshade, venom from snakes such as asps (Cleopatra) and arsenic which the women in the Italian Borgia family were supposed to have used.

One of the most infamous female poisoners of all time was Guilia Tofana, a woman who allegedly caused the deaths of hundreds of men during the 1630s. What makes her story even stranger is that she hardly knew any of her victims and that none of them had personally done her any harm.

*

It is thought that she was born in about 1620 in Palermo, Sicily. When she was a young girl, her mother, Thofania d'Adamo was executed on 12 July 1633 for killing her husband. It seems that her parents were involved in the business of concocting poisons, and so with what she had learned at home, young Giulia Tofana fled and moved to Rome. There she mixed with apothecaries – pharmacists – and improved her knowledge about potions, cosmetics, perfumes and medicines. Despite being a woman in the male-dominated world of trade, she set up her own pharmaceutical business. This was very successful and she opened more branches in Rome and Naples.

Her best-selling product was 'Aqua Tofana', a poison which she sold attractively packaged and disguised so that it looked like bottles of perfume or holy oil. Some of these bottles were supposed to have been labelled, 'Manna of St. Nicholas of Bari', a well-known healing oil for blemishes of the skin. The deadly poison contained arsenic, lead and belladonna as well as some genuine perfume so that it would have the correct smell if anyone became too curious as to inspect what was in the bottle. The actual liquid itself was tasteless, colourless and odourless.

The first dose would cause physical weakness and exhaustion and the next dose would cause vomiting, dysentery and stomach pains. These symptoms would not have aroused any suspicion in Renaissance Italy due to the generally poor standards of public health. If a third or more doses were necessary, then these would be fatal, the *coup de grâce*. In addition, this poison was so concocted that it did not show up in any post-mortem that may have been carried out after the victim's untimely demise. It sold so well that later Giulia later became known as the 'Queen of Poisons'. She made sure that when she sold it, she knew something about her customers' backgrounds and that both sides, Giulia and her customer, had vested interests in not divulging their wicked secrets. Her business was so successful, that in the end it ran for about twenty years.

One morning while Giulia was sitting in her shop near the Colosseum in Rome, a well-dressed lady entered. After looking around to make sure that there was no-one else in the shop she asked, "Excuse me, but are you Signora Tofana?"

"*Si.* Why are you asking?"

"And are you the lady who makes and sells Aqua Tofana?"

"*Si,* do you want to buy a bottle?"

"*Si.*"

"And you've heard of course that this is a special perfume and that it has extra qualities as well?"

"*Si, si.* My friend who lives in Naples had told me all about this."

After hearing this, Giulia sold the lady a bottle together with instructions on how to use it, and yet another satisfied customer left the shop. Giulia was sure that this lady would use her 'perfume' to kill off her husband. From her own bitter childhood she knew that many women in Italy were forced into loveless marriages. This was often done as a way of making sure that the family's fortunes remained in the family, or to preserve a certain social or aristocratic status, and Giulia knew that many of these unhappy and abused wives wanted nothing more than to discreetly rid themselves of their husbands.

According to *Chamber's Journal*, a 19th century weekly magazine, if Aqua Tofana was:

... administered in wine or tea or some other liquid by the flattering traitress, [it] produced a scarcely noticeable effect; the husband became a little out of sorts, felt weak and languid, so little indisposed that he could hardly call

in a medical man... After the second dose of poison, this weakness and languor became more pronounced [and the wife] who expressed so much anxiety for her husband's indisposition would scarcely be an object of suspicion, and perhaps would prepare her husband's food, as prescribed by the doctor, with her own fair hands. In this way the third drop would be administered and would prostrate even the most vigorous man. The doctor would be completely puzzled to see that the apparently simple ailment did not surrender to his drugs, and while he would still be in the dark as to its nature, other doses would be given, until at length death would claim the victim for its own.

Therefore, the powerful Aqua Tofana in their wine or soup would do the trick, as five or six drops of this harmless looking liquid were 'sufficient to destroy a man'. Afterwards the poor grieving widow had several alternatives, which may have included demanding a post-mortem to prove that the death of her dear husband was merely an unfortunate act of fate. As *Chamber's Journal* noted:

To save her fair name, the wife would demand a post-mortem examination. Result, nothing – except that the woman was able to pose as a slandered innocent, and then it would be remembered that her husband died without either pain, inflammation, fever or spasms.

She could remarry in the hope that her next husband would treat her better, or she could remain single and become a prostitute, governess or servant of some sort. It was often very much a question of luck of what the future held for women in this patriarchal society.

Incidentally, because the poison took a few days to work, it allowed the victim to put his affairs in order and in a deeply religious country such as Italy he would have had the time to repent of his sins. As a side benefit, the wife did not have to feel too guilty, as she knew that her dear departed husband was going to meet his Maker with a pure soul.

Some historians claim that it was not Giulia who invented this potent poison, but her mother, who then passed on the secret to her daughter. It is also thought that Giulia passed this grim recipe for death onto her own daughter, Girolama Spara. However, what is definitely known is that Giulia was so successful that she organised an underground network to distribute the poison, and it is thought that about two hundred people from all levels of society were involved.

However, it seems that this whole business venture collapsed over a simple and innocuous domestic situation which was completely out of the control of the Queen of Poisons.

*

Picture the scene. Marco and Rosa Mancini are sitting down in their humble home just about to have their evening meal. Marco is a large muscular fellow who works in the local market, while his petite and gentle wife carries out all the traditional duties associated with being an obedient and passive housewife.

But all is not well. She hates her husband, who is constantly beating and raping her, and when he is not doing that, he is forever complaining about her cooking, the clothes she wears and the cleanliness of their home. After he had beaten her black and blue last week after attending mass, she decided that she had suffered enough. That last beating was the straw that broke the camel's back.

The day following the beating she met her old friend, Francesca Rossi, in the town square.

"My dear Francesca, if I may say so, you look so good even though your poor husband died last month."

"Grazie, amica mia," Francesca replied, "but come over here behind the wall as I have a secret to tell you and I don't want anyone here to overhear me."

Francesca then told Rosa how she had killed her faithless husband after she had found out that he had been having a long-time affair with a young woman on the other side of town. She told Rosa how she had obtained a small bottle of Aqua Tofana and that now she was looking for a new husband.

Armed with this knowledge and the details of where to obtain some of Giulia's Tofana's poison, Rosa Mancini sought out an old apothecary and bought a bottle of the liquid that would also buy her longed-for freedom.

"Rosa, woman. Where is my soup?" Marco demanded that evening, banging his huge hairy fist on the wooden table. "I'm hungry."

Rosa hurried over holding a steaming bowl of vegetable soup and carefully placed it in front of her impatient husband. Little did he know that blended in among its ingredients were several drops of Aqua Tofana.

"This is too hot, woman," Marco growled. "How d'you expect me to eat it now?"

But just then, for whatever inexplicable reason, Rosa had second thoughts. She did not want to become a widow like her friend, Francesca. Better the devil you know, she thought and began to remove the bowl of hot soup.

"Hey, what are you doing now, woman? I want that," and Marco reached out for the pale blue bowl.

"No, no, you can't," a panicked Rosa said. "It's… it's…"

"It's what, woman? Speak up."

"It's poisoned," Rosa blurted out.

"It's what? What are you babbling about? Tell me!"

And Rosa did so. She told the whole story, and after he had given his wife the most vicious thrashing ever, Marco grabbed his jacket and went to report the whole affair to the authorities. It did not take long for them to act. However, luck was on Giulia's side. According to some sources, she was warned that the long arm of the law was looking for her, so she fled to a convent where the constabulary could not touch her.

*

From here on, that is, from when she ceased her poisonous activities until her own death, there are several versions of what happened. One account claims that word got out that she was hiding in the convent and a mob appeared at the convent's gates. The nuns felt that they had no alternative, especially as it was rumoured that she was responsible for poisoning the local drinking water, and frightened, handed her over to the authorities. Under torture, Giulia is alleged to have confessed that between 1633-1651 she was responsible for the deaths of six hundred men. After this she was executed, together with her daughter and three employees, and her body was dumped back in the convent.

Another version states that she was never caught and continued to concoct and distribute her poisons to the needy. She is said to have died peacefully of natural causes in bed in 1659, and that her daughter, Girolama Spara, took over the family business. But this date too is suspect, as some historians who may have mixed her up with other poisoners claim that she died in 1709, aged about eighty. A highly improbable third version is that Giulia died peacefully in about 1730. If this is true, that meant that she would have been one hundred and ten years old! A rare event today and very unlikely then.

But however long she did live, her story and her well-known poison lived after her disputed demise. On 5 December 1791, the 35-year-old composer, Wolfgang Amadeus Mozart, died in Vienna. While on his deathbed, ironically while composing his fantastic *Requiem*, he is recorded saying, "I feel definitely that I will not last much longer; I am sure that I have been poisoned. I cannot rid myself of this idea… Someone has given me Aqua Tofana and calculated the precise time of my death." However, the official records claim that this musical genius died of *hitziges Frieselfieber* – severe military disease – which caused him great pains, swelling and vomiting... just like the Italian men who had died one hundred and fifty years earlier. In addition, there were theories that Mozart's bitter rival, Antonio Salieri, poisoned him, but this has since been disproved.

Was Giulia Tofana really a wicked woman?

I think the answer is definitely yes. Although she did not administer her poison herself to the victims, she concocted her Aqua Tofana for a profit and knew exactly what the results would be if someone drank it. Add to this the fact that an unknown (probably large) number of men died because of her, there is no way, whatever her motive was apart from making money, that she can be considered anything else but wicked. In a way, Giulia Tofana may be compared to a modern-day hitman. Such a person is paid to kill someone who he is not emotionally involved with, the only difference being is that the hitman, unlike Giulia Tofana, has to see his victim when he kills him.

Chapter Eight

Mary Read (1685-1721) and Anne Bonny (1697-1721?)
& Other Wicked Women of the
High Seas

The classic image of pirates includes sailing ships under full sail, their masts topped by a black and white skull and crossed-bones flag flying bravely in the wind while scruffy bearded pirates bury or uncover a treasure chest on a sandy beach. This is one image. Another one is of a full-blown battle on a ship's deck between rival gangs of pirates, or of pirates fighting the king's naval officers as muskets flash, cutlasses are thrust and thrills and excitement are in the air.

This romanticised version of the truth has been current since 1724 when Captain Charles Johnson wrote his General History *of the Pyrates. His descriptions were later reinforced by such books as* Treasure Island *by Robert Louis Stevenson (1883) and* Peter Pan *by J.M. Barrie. (1911). Later, various action-packed films, some of which were based on these books, strengthened these images even further.*

However, the 'Golden Age of Piracy', of which the first paragraph of this chapter describes a fantasy version, actually only lasted for about eighty years, from 1650-1730. Pirates, often called buccaneers, plied their 'trade' mainly in the Caribbean. But that is only part of the story. Piracy – violent robbery at sea – dates back to the 14th century BCE on the Aegean and Mediterranean Seas. It also took place in other areas that were important centres for trade such as the South China Sea, the Gulf of Aden and the Arabian Sea. Today, this last-named area is still a centre of piracy, as so too are other areas, including the Gulfs of Mexico and Guinea and south-east Asia.

But now is the time to forget your image of a black-bearded tricorn hat-wearing pirate brandishing his cutlass on board the Jolly Roger. Today's pirates, probably wearing torn T-shirts and jeans, attack oil tankers and bulk-cargo ships using powerful motorboats, machine-guns, assault rifles and hand-grenades. It has been estimated that modern piracy is costing the world over $70 billion per annum.

However, this description of contemporary pirates is far away both in terms of people, methods and targets from the two pirates who feature in this chapter. So grab your sea-legs and prepare to meet two female pirates: Mary Read and Anne Bonny.

*

The clouds were grey and threatening as the high winds caused the ship, *Ranger*, to roll badly from side to side in the high seas of the West Indies. The decks were rising and falling so much that the pirate on the foredeck was knocked backwards as a huge wave crashed down just a few feet away from him. Putting out his hand to steady himself, he reached out for the top part of the body of the man behind him and was immediately surprised. He had not touched the hard chest of a fellow-pirate, but instead something soft and yielding.

"Hey, you're not a man!" he shouted over the sound of the roaring winds. "What are you?"

"Ssh!" the other shouted back, put his finger to his lips and pulled the first pirate down a short flight of steps to the shelter of the deck below. There the pair of them caught their breath.

"So you're not a man, are you?" the first pirate repeated. "So what are you? A woman?"

The second pirate nodded. "Aye, like you."

"What d'you mean, like me?"

"You're also a woman, and don't deny it. I saw you tie up your blouse last night and push your tits back in again."

The first pirate touched the top part of the other one's body again and felt that it was as soft as it had been a few

113

minutes earlier on the upper deck.

"And so are you, and if you're not, you're a very fat man."

"Meet Anne Bonny," the second pirate smiled. "And who are you?"

"Mary Read," the other replied, "although I often answer to the name of Mark. And who and what are you?"

"Me, Anne Bonny?" the red-headed pirate grinned. "I've been known to answer to the name of Andy, but yes, you're right," she said, untying the top part of her blood-red blouse and showing her deep cleavage for a moment, "I'm as much a woman as you."

"So what are you doing on board the *Ranger*?" Mary asked. "Are you a pirate as well? I see you've got a pistol stuck in your belt, so I don't s'pose you're some sort of passenger."

"No, lass, I'm no passenger, I'm the captain's girl."

"So why aren't you wearing a dress?"

"Because you know what sailors and pirates think about having a woman on board…"

"You mean, they bring bad luck?"

"Aye."

"Ah, so I was right," Mary said. "I thought there was something strange about you and him. Now I understand, but tell me, how did that come about?"

Anne shrugged. "Easy enough, I suppose. I was in a tavern in Nassau when I met Captain Calico Jack Rackham, and we liked each other and sort of fell in love. That's all."

"But you're not English," Mary said. "You've got some

114

sort of accent. Like you're Irish or Scottish."

"Right first time, lass. I was born in Ireland, near Cork to be exact, and then when I was young my family moved to London. My pa wanted me to marry some friend of his, but I didn't want to, so I married this sailor fellow, John Bonny his name was, and we sailed to the Americas."

"So where is he now? Dead?"

Anne shrugged. "I don't know, and to tell you the truth, I don't rightly care."

"Why not?"

"'Cos that stinking rat turned out to be an informer for the governor."

"Which governor?"

"The Governor of the Bahamas. You know, Master Woodes Rogers 'imself. So one night I snuck out of the house and went to this tavern on the quayside in Nassau. There I met Calico Jack and I've been with 'im on board ever since."

"And no-one here knows you're a woman?"

Anne shook her black curly head. "No, no-one, that is until you came along. They just think that I'm a good friend of the captain. So don't you ever say anything, 'cos if you do…" and Anne pointed to the butt of the pistol sticking out of her belt.

"Fear not," Mary said, putting a hand on Anne's shoulder. "I know when to keep my trap shut."

"So now you know about me," Anne smiled, "tell me about yourself."

"Huh, there's not much to tell. "I was born in England the year the second King Charles died."

"Where? In London?"

Mary shrugged. "Dunno. Just England. An' anyway, we was dirt poor, so my mum used to dress me up as a little boy an' sent me out to beg."

"Didn't your pa work?"

Mary shrugged again. "Didn't have one, or at least a bloke tha' I knew was my pa. Anyway, when I was abou' thirteen my ma sent me to work, all dressed up of course, as a footman. I didn't like that very much, so I ran away and joined the army. There, I thought, at least I'd 'ave a roof over me head and food in me belly."

"Did you do any fighting or anything like that?"

"Yes, I did some fighting in Flanders and then I fell in love with this Flemish bloke. I didn't wan' anyone else but 'im to know of course tha' I was a woman, so I jus' made sure that I kept my tits covered up good an' made him swear to keep his mouth shut."

"How did you do that? You know blokes like to boast about what they've done with women."

"Don't I know it! I told 'im tha' if he opens 'is big mouth, it's over between us. No tits and no nothin' else."

"And did it work?"

"Oh yes. What bloke d'you know who wants to give up the chance to 'ave free tits and the rest? Besides, I 'ad to stay in the army, didn't I? I mean otherwise I'd 'ave been without ev'rythin'. If they'd 'ave found ou' tha' I wasn't a bloke they'd 'ave chucked me out, no? And then I'd 'ave been without anything. No food, no shelter and no money. And in a foreign country, to boot. So I kept my trap shut and so did he. Then one day we ran off together, deserted,

116

and got married."

"So that was alright then, no?"

"Yes and no, I s'pose. We put whatever money we 'ad together an' bought this little tavern called *De Drie Hoefijzers…*"

"What does that mean?"

"The Three Horseshoes, but then he died on me. Just like that," and Mary clicked her fingers. "So seein' tha' I didn't wan' to get' married again an' I needed money, I dressed up again like a bloke and joined the army again. Then when the fighting was over between the Dutch and the French, I left the army and then took a ship to the West Indies."

"Yes, but how did you end up here, on Jack Rackham's ship?"

"Well, when we was near the Bahamas, some pirates attacked our ship and they forced me to join them."

"What, you as a woman?"

Mary nodded. "Aye, but then my life turned upside down again"

"How?"

"Well, y'know tha' the king issued a pardon las' year, tha' if any pirate was willing to surrender they wouldn't be punished?"

"Yes, I heard about that. I was thinking of surrendering myself, but I didn't in the end."

"Well, all the men on the ship I was on did and so we sailed back to por' and I 'ad to think wha' I was going to do next."

"And?"

"I became a privateer once again, and 'ere I am."

"Tell me, Mary, or should I call you, Mark? Does Cap'n Jack know you ain't a bloke?"

Mary shook her head. "No, and don't you tell 'im neither. I'll tell 'im in my own good time."

Anne Bonny kept her secret and the two female pirates continued with their illegal careers, fighting His Majesty's soldiers and sailors, plundering merchant ships and living a noisy life while in port, selling their loot, drinking the proceeds and generally keeping quayside tavern-owners very happy.

One day while they were in a waterfront tavern after successfully plundering a French merchant ship, Mary asked Bonny why when they fought the king's men or another pirate ship, she always had her blouse half-open.

"Oh, haven't you guessed, lass?" she laughed. "When I'm fighting some bloke and he sees my tits, that's all he can think about. 'E's so busy looking at them that he can't fight right and then I beat him. You try it. It works very time. Oh, yes, I forgot to tell you. Me and Jack sort of got married."

"But no' in a church."

"No, Mary. We swore an oath between us to be faithful and 'until death do us part' and stuff like that."

Rackham, Anne and Mary and the rest of the crew continued to strike out at merchant ships in the waters of the West Indies. Sometimes they did poorly and managed only to capture £10 worth of loot, but other times they were more successful – especially when using the Revenge, a captured ship, they seized goods worth over

£1,000 (£120,000 approx. today).

However, Rackham and Anne's marriage, together with their piratical career, were not destined to last for long. On 15 November 1720, Captain Jonathan Barnet, a Royal Navy officer who had been dispatched to the West Indies to help put down the piracy there, captured Captain 'Calico' Jack Rackham. This happened off the west coast of the Bahamas at Negril Bay, now known as Bloody Bay.

While Barnet, who had been informed about the whereabouts of Rackham ship, was lying in ambush, Rackham and most of his crew were half-drunk, having consumed all the wine they had recently stolen from another ship. The only two members of the crew who were sober were Anne and Mary.

Barnet's ship approached Rackham's *Revenge* in mid-morning. He called on the pirates to surrender but they refused. "We will give nor take any quarter," Rackham shouted in reply, but as soon as Barnet's men had fired a volley disabling the *Revenge*, Calico Jack Rackham ordered his men to hide below decks. According to contemporary accounts, only Anne and Mary remained on the top deck. It seems that Mary was so angry at the way the rest of the crew were behaving that she fired her pistol into the hold and killed one of her fellow-pirates who was hiding there.

Swarming aboard, brandishing their cutlasses and firing their pistols, the king's men, no doubt to their great surprise, found themselves facing two women. Naturally Anne and Bonny were quickly overcome and after that the rest of the crew was soon rounded up, arrested and taken to Port Royal. From there they were transferred to Spanish Town where they were imprisoned before being put on trial.

Piracy was seen as one of the most serious crimes that could be committed against the state and the standard punishment was death by hanging. Captain Jack Rackham was the first to die, on 18 November 1720. Before the noose was put round his neck he asked to speak to his 'wife', Anne Bonny, to seek some comfort from her. He received none. Believing that she was the next to be hanged, or at least serve a long spell in prison, all she said to him was, "If you had fought like a man, you need not have been hanged like a dog." He was hanged at Gallow's Point, a low rocky spot later renamed Rackham's Cay.

When the rest of the crew were hauled before the judge, they all pleaded 'not guilty'. It did not help. Of the nine-man crew, three were hanged at Gallows Point, Port Royal on 17 February 1721, and four of the remaining six were hanged at Kingston, Jamaica. It is not known what happened to the other two.

When it was Mary and Bonny's turn to be sentenced, they were asked if they had anything to say in their defence. "No," they both replied defiantly, and thus they too were sentenced to be hanged. Now there was a surprise. Both of the female pirates stated that they were 'quick with child' – pregnant – and so according to the law, their executions were postponed. They were both sent to prison and while there, according to the records of St. Catherine's Church, Jamaica, Mary Read died, probably of gaol-fever, today known as typhus, at the end of April

1721. She was about thirty-five years old. There is no record of what happened to her baby.

As for her fellow-pirate, Anne Bonny, what happened to her remains a mystery. Somehow she avoided being hanged and it has been thought that she returned to her first husband. Others believe that piracy was so much in her blood that she changed her identity and continued as before. A third theory is that she returned to Charleston, married, had children and lived out the rest of her life there as a respectable southern housewife. However, recent research has shown that the name Anne Bonny appears in the parish records of St. Catherine's Church, Jamaica and that this Anne Bonny lived only until she was thirty-four, before dying in 1731.

But whatever happened to her, the exploits of these two female pirates has supplied the writers of stories and songs, as well as filmmakers, with much exciting material.

As stated earlier, the first description of their escapades appeared in Charles Johnson's history of pirates in 1724. While much later history books and historical novels include *Bold in her Breeches*; *Women Pirates Across the Ages* by Jo Stanley (1996), *Anne Bonny* by Chloe Gartner (1977) and *Sisters of the Sea: Anne Bonny & Mary Read* by Sandra Riley (2003).

An Italian film, *Le Avventure di Mary Read* was produced in 1961, while a TV film, *True Caribbean Pirates*, featuring Mary Read as a character, made its debut in 2006. The two female pirate 'stars' of this chapter also appeared in an animated film, *Jolly Roger in the Deep Azure* which was released in Japan in 2007.

In addition, two modern ballads dedicated to Anne Bonny and Mary Read were written by Jane Yolen (1998) and Steve Parmelee (2018).

Another artistic tribute to these two female pirates consists of a pair of statues sculpted by Amanda Cotton. These were first exhibited at Exhibition Dock, Wapping, by the River Thames, where many pirates were hanged in the past. The statues are now to be found at Burgh Island on the south Devon coast, a place where pirates sailed from in their pursuit of illegal fortunes in the Caribbean. Some of the local Devonshire population objected to these statues being erected, saying that they blackened the name of the area. Other citizens thought that the two pirates may have been lesbians as well as outlaws and thus, from their point of view, doubly discredited their part of Devon.

Finally, Anne Bonny and Mary Read were not the only female pirates to sail the seven seas. One hundred years before our 'heroines' set off to find fame and fortune, Mary Wolverston (before 1525-after 1587), alias Lady Killigrew, the wife of Sir John Killigrew, was not only the daughter of a pirate, but her husband was also one! Queen Elizabeth I had appointed him to put an end to the piracy that was threatening Her Majesty's revenues, but instead of doing so, he, together with his wife, changed sides.

Eventually Mary was captured in Cornwall and sentenced to be executed. However, at the last moment, the queen must have had some pity on her because she was pardoned just before she was due to meet her Maker. Her husband had died a few years before, in 1584.

Another female pirate who linked her career to a man

was Sayyida al-Hurra (1485-1561). This Arab woman became a pirate leader as well as the consort to her husband Ali al-Mandri, the governor of the city of Tétouan, Morocco. She was well-educated, spoke several languages, but had never got over the fact that at the age of seven she had had to flee Granada, Spain.

She turned to piracy as a way of wreaking revenge and linked up with the famous Algerian admiral, Hayrettin Barbarossa. As a successful pirate in the western Mediterranean near Gibraltar, it was recorded that she took 'much booty and many prisoners', and she was known for releasing her Spanish and Portuguese captives. After reigning thirty years as *hurra* – queen – being the last Moslem woman to hold this title, she was overthrown and lived quietly for the next twenty years until she died, aged seventy-six in 1561.

Although the United States has had to deal with many gangsters, robbers and bandits during the past two hundred years, it has had very little trouble with female pirates. However, Rachel Wall (1760-1789) was one of the few. Like Anne Bonny and Mary Read, she ran away to sea from home in Pennsylvania when she was a teenager and married a fisherman. When the couple came in dire need of money, they began robbing ships off the New England coast.

They attracted their victims as a spider attracts a fly. They pretended that they were in distress at sea, and when a ship came to rescue them, they killed and plundered the unfortunate crew. In all, this husband-and-wife team captured twelve boats, stole $6000 (well over $120,000 today), a fortune in jewellery and killed two dozen sailors. All of this happened between 1781-1782. After her husband and the crew were accidentally washed overboard, Rachel returned to Boston and used her dubious talents on land. However, she was captured and on 8 October 1789, executed, her death being the last time a woman was hanged in the State of Massachusetts.

Chapter Nine

Jeanne de Valois-Saint Remy (1756-1791)
French Con Artist

Some con artists hit the headlines as the result of a single con; others achieve their dubious glory due to having duped their 'marks' over a long drawn-out period. The subject of this chapter belongs to the first category. Jeanne de Valois-Saint Remy, together with her husband, initiated such a remarkable con that many historians agree that it became one of the leading causes of the fall of the French monarchy and the French Revolution at the end of the 18th century. It was during this tumultuous period that the king and the queen of France, as well as many of the nobles –

both men and women – who supported them, lost their lives, actually their heads, to 'Madame Guillotine'.

Perhaps the great irony of this enormously pricey con was that the person responsible for it did have a tenuous connection to the French royal family. Although she did not live at Versailles or at any other royal palace, this did not stop her from having some very regal ambitions.

*

Jeanne de Valois-Saint-Rémy was born on 22 July 1756 in Fontette, a small village some one hundred and ten miles south-east of Paris. Seeing that her name included 'Valois', you would be correct in thinking that she had royal connections. This is true. Her father Jacques de Valois was the Baron de Saint-Rémy, though several generations removed from the viciously anti-Protestant French King Henri II. This king had reigned from 1547-1559 and died as the result of being fatally injured in a tournament. During this test of skill and honour he wore the colours of his mistress even though his wife was looking on as a spectator. Even though Jeanne's father had such an illustrious past, this did not prevent him from becoming an impoverished drunkard while her mother, Marie Jossel, was a servant of some sort.

Two of Jeanne's bothers, Joseph and Jean, and one of her sisters, Marie Marguerite, died in infancy, leaving Jeanne to grow up with her brother and sister, Jacques and Marie-Anne. Despite any claims the family may have had to royalty, the children were brought up in great poverty.

They often had to beg for food, went about barefoot and spent much of their time looking after the family's animals.

However, in the end they were lucky. Somebody, perhaps a Madame de Boulainvilliers from Boulogne, took the young children in and looked after them. It is possible that it was this woman who established their past ties officially to the French royal house of Valois, which enabled them to receive stipends from the royal purse. This meant that Jeanne's brother was sent to a military academy where he was assured of an education, bed and board, while the two girls were sent to a boarding school in Passy, near Paris, to be educated as nuns. Neither Jeanne nor her sister wanted this to be their future, and so they went to live with the Surmont family instead, a family with its own distant claims to the nobility.

Jeanne lived with the Surmont's for four years in Bar-sur-Aube, a small town south-east of Paris. Then at the age of twenty-four, an eight-month pregnant Jeanne married Monsieur Surmont's nephew, Marc-Antoine-Nicolas de la Motte, an officer in the gendarmes.

On 7 July 1780, Jeanne gave birth to twins who both died soon after. There were questions about who the father was, some saying that it was her husband, while others that it was the Bishop of Langres, who had officiated at the young couple's rushed wedding. It was also during this period that, despite their lack of high-class education and riches, Jeanne and her husband decided to give themselves aristocratic titles. He was to be known as the Comte de la Motte and Jeanne was to be his *comtesse.* In addition to

127

successfully pulling off this con, Jeanne managed to become one of the many courtiers who used to hang around the royal palace at Versailles.

However, despite this climb up the social ladder, it was not long after this that Jeanne's relationship with her husband began to break down. Although they continued living together, she took one of her husband's fellow officers in the gendarmerie, the Marquis d' Autichamps, as a lover. This short-lived affair caused such a scandal that her husband had to resign his commission. As a result, money which had already been tight, now became even more scarce.

*

"You know," Jeanne began one evening. "I cannot stand living in this penny-pinching way. It's so miserable and humiliating, especially when I know I am connected to royalty. Is this the way we should be living? I mean just because my family is descended from Henri II's mistress, Nicole de Savigny, and not his wife, does that mean that we should suffer?"

"Tu as tout à fais raison," Marc-Antoine replied. You are absolutely right. "But what are you going to do about this?"

"Listen," she began, her eyes, shining. "I've had an idea. I'm a Valois, aren't I? I'm of royal blood, and that's been officially established. And not only a French Valois, but the Valois family were also important in England."

"They were?"

"*Bien sûr* – Of course they were. Wasn't it a Valois, Catherine, who married England's King Henry V? Wasn't she the mother of Henry VI and the grandmother of Henry VII? So why shouldn't I approach the queen and ask her to help me? I'm sure that she'll do so. After all, I'll petition her, woman to woman, and as royal women as well."

And so Jeanne de Valois-Saint Rémy made the first of several trips to Marie Antoinette's palace at Versailles in the hope of attracting the queen's attention. But all of Jeanne's plans came to nothing. The queen had heard about her would-be petitioner's lifestyle and refused to have anything to do with her.

If her first husband, Marc-Antoine, was not too serious about supporting Jeanne's ideas, her next one certainly was. His name was Louis Marc Antoine Rétaux de Villette and he was a childhood friend of her husband. What probably attracted Jeanne to him even more was that he was a minor noble. He was good-looking and made his money through his connections with various brothels in Paris. Jeanne lived off him for a while, and then a dramatic change happened in her life; a change that would influence her forever and thereby secure her place in history.

In about 1783, her old guardian, Madame de Boulainvillers, introduced Jeanne to Cardinal Prince Louis René Édouard de Rohan. This distinguished gentleman not only had connections to the royal family, but he had served as his country's ambassador to Austria. When he first met Jeanne de Valois, he was a cardinal, a member of the Académie Française and also the Prince-Bishop of Strasbourg. However, despite his exalted status, the Queen of France, Marie Antoinette, was his enemy. This was because when he had served as an ambassador to Austria – the queen's home-country – ten years earlier, he had annoyed the queen's mother, the Empress Maria Theresa, by interfering with her plans for an Austro-France alliance. In addition, Marie Antoinette both disapproved of Louis de Rohan's corrupt lifestyle and took personal umbrage that he had tried to prevent her from marrying King Louis XVI. However, for Jeanne, de Rohan was perfect: rich, powerful, and not bound too strictly by his priestly vows of chastity.

*

One day, Jeanne returned home from a late-night romantic tryst with her latest lover.

"Marc-Antoine, I have some good news for you," she began.

"Oui, what is it and where have you been all night?"

"I've been with Cardinal de Rohan and he's going to help us."

"How?" Jeanne's angry husband replied. "Apart from giving you a good time, what else can he do for us?"

"He is going to obtain for you the post of being a bodyguard for the Comte d'Artois. Isn't that good?"

"Comte d'Artois? The king's brother?"

"Oui. You are to go to the palace tomorrow and then you will start soon after that."

As a result the de la Motte's family finances improved, though not enough for the ambitious Jeanne.

One day she contacted her former lover, Antoine Rétaux de Villette.

"Antoine," she said, allowing him to look down the front of her low-cut bodice. "Do you remember that you told me once that you were very good at copying other people's signatures?"

Antoine raised his eyes to look at Jeanne's persuasive eyes. "*Oui, c'est vrai*. Yes, that's true enough. Why, what do you want me to do? Whose signature do you want me to forge?"

"The queen's."

"The queen's? Whatever for? You know that's not just a simple crime. If I am caught doing that, I would end up in the Bastille."

"I know that, my love," Jeanne replied, smiling sweetly and stroking the back of his hand, "but I need you to forge her signature on a letter that you will write for me. Just this once."

"And what will this letter say and who will read it?" Antoine replied, enjoying her company.

"It will be from the queen to the king and they'll say that Cardinal de Rohan is to increase the allowance that she is getting from him."

"What, doesn't she get enough?"

Jeanne shrugged. "I don't know, but if Her Majesty knows that I was responsible for her receiving an even larger allowance, she will be my friend. *Tu comprends*? And of course, I won't tell her how."

"*Oui, je comprend*. And when do you want me to write this letter?"

131

"*Aussi vite que possible*. As soon as possible," the impatient Jeanne replied and gave Antonie Rétaux a kiss on the lips.

*

Antoine Rétaux forged the necessary letter and Marie Antoinette received well over one hundred thousand francs from the king. A huge sum at the time.

Although the queen began to look with favour on Jeanne de Valois-Saint-Rémy, it was not enough for the new courtier. She wanted more. Much more. As far as she was concerned, as there was money and power at court, why should she not have a larger share? The question was how? She was not the only ambitious person, smiling and fawning at her superiors at the royal palace at Versailles.

Then soon after this Jeanne, she of the attractive figure, fashionably pale skin and rich chestnut-brown hair, bumped into the famous Parisian jeweller, Monsieur Charles Auguste Boehmer at court. He was looking very down in the dumps.

*

"Monsieur Boehmer, why are you looking so sad?" Jeanne began. "How can a man who designs such exquisite pieces of jewellery look so forlorn? Has anyone died in your family? Has there been a robbery?"

"*Non, non*, Madame. Nothing like that. It's just that Monsieur Bassenge –"

"Your partner?"

"Yes, my partner and my friend as well. So, *ma chérie*, the story is like this. About fifteen years ago we began working on this beautiful diamond necklace for the former king, Louis XV, as a present for his mistress –"

"Madame du Barry? Who was banished from court by the present king?"

"Yes, that's the one."

"So what's the problem? Doesn't she like it?"

"*Non, non*, Madame, that is not the problem. She likes it very much," Monsieur Boehmer explained. "It's just that, as you know, the old King Louis died of smallpox and now the present king doesn't want to buy it. Not for her and not for anybody."

"So, *Monsieur*, why don't you sell it to someone else?"

"I can't, Madame. You see, we made it for the previous king, and it is so expensive that hardly anyone else can afford it. If we can't persuade the new king or queen to buy it, then we, that is, me and Monsieur Bassenge, will be bankrupt. You see," he added unhappily, his eyes near to tears, "we both invested a fortune in it – all those diamonds and other jewels as well as all those long hours of work."

*

Leaving Monsieur to think about his future and what to do with his diamond necklace, Jeanne hurried over to the palatial home of the cardinal de Rohan. She had an idea, one that in the end would cause one of the greatest scandals to hit the country. However, to carry out her scheme she would again need the skills of her sometime lover and master-forger, Antoine Rétaux, as well as the co-operation of Cardinal de Rohan.

Once she arrived home, she waited for her husband to arrive. When he eventually did so, even though it was late at night, she told him of her plan.

*

"Why are you still awake?" he asked, leaning his rifle against the wall and taking off his uniform jacket. "You are usually asleep by the time I get in."

"I know but I have something important to tell you. I've had an idea that might make us rich, but to do so, we have to use the skills of your officer, Rétaux."

"As a forger or a lover?"

"As a forger of course."

"So what do you want from him? A letter saying that the king owes you five million francs?"

"No, not exactly, but something similar. So here, listen to my plan," Jeanne hurried on, thinking of all of the sacks of francs she would soon be able to enjoy. "Do you remember me telling you yesterday about this fantastic necklace that Monsieur Boehmer made for the queen?"

"*Oui*. What about it?"

"Well, *mon cher*, first, we ask Rétaux to forge a letter from the queen to me saying that she wants to buy the diamond necklace that Boehmer and Besange made but that the king doesn't want her to buy because it is too

134

expensive."

"Then what?"

"Then in the letter it will say that she hopes that the Cardinal de Rohan –"

"Your lover?"

"Oui, my friend, will secretly lend her the money and that I will act as the intermediary who passes on the money from the queen to the agent."

"Jeanne, why can't the queen give the money directly to the Cardinal? They both move in the same circles."

"Oh, you are so slow. Perhaps because it's late at night, but don't you remember? The queen doesn't like or talk to the Cardinal and so there's no way she will give him a fortune to buy this necklace," Jeanne explained. "And besides, if I'm to be the intermediary here, I will also make some money for my services, *non?"*

*

The next day, de la Motte persuaded his officer to write the letter Jeanne had described and he promised the forger that it would be well worth his while to do so. "You'll get your share once we have completed this business," Jeanne's husband promised. "So make sure that this is the best forgery that you have ever written. Remember, it will have the queen's signature on it."

Rétaux played his part and wrote the most convincing letter that he could. It looked so genuine in fact, that Jeanne was really impatient to show it to de Rohan the next day.

On the following evening when he had returned home

135

from carrying out his duties at Versailles, Jeanne went to see him.

Once she had gained admittance to the Cardinal's opulent home, she asked him whether there was a room where they could talk without being overheard by any of his family or servants.

*

"Of course there is," he answered. "We'll go and talk where I always go on such occasions, to my orchard at the back of the house. There'll be no-one else there and you will be able to tell me absolutely anything you like."

Five minutes later found Jeanne de Valois and her aristocratic clerical lover and patron hidden among the apple and cherry trees in de Rohan's spacious garden.

"Now what is it that is so important and secret," de Rohan began, "that we have to talk about it here outside instead of being in the warmth of my *château*?"

"Your Eminence, I would like to…"

De Rohan put a caressing hand on Jeanne's exposed shoulder. "*Non, non*, Jeanne, here where we are alone, you may call me Louis. Now what do you want?"

"You know you wish to regain the queen's good favour and to become one of the royal ministers? Well, I have a letter with me from the queen that should do just that."

"But the queen doesn't like you," Rohan said. "She won't even talk to you. She –"

"No. Louis, she will now."

"Why? How?"

136

Jeanne put her finger to her lips. "Women, my love. We women have different ways of solving our differences."

"*Bien*, so let me read this letter… Hmm, it looks genuine enough and I'd recognise her signature anywhere. I mean, I've seen it on many documents in the palace. So, my love," he said, "Your idea is that I would buy this necklace for the queen and then I would be back in favour, *oui*?"

"*Oui*. But are you sure you have enough money to do so?" Jeanne asked, knowing that he had.

"But of course I have. So, my love, my little pigeon, I will write to the queen and tell her that I will buy this necklace for her, but secretly of course."

*

This signalled the beginning of a series of genuine letters written by a genuine cardinal and a false queen. The tone of the letters grew more affectionate, and in the end, Cardinal de Rohan believed that Her Majesty, Queen Marie Antoinette, was in love with him. Such a love affair was nothing unusual – it was the norm for royalty and the *aristos* to have lovers and mistresses. This was nothing. Had not the past king, Louis XV, been known to have had half-a-dozen *maîtresses-en-titre*, chief royal mistresses, as well as dozens of *petite maîtresses*, who he replaced almost every year?

The next time Jeanne met with de Rohan, it was his turn to ask for a favour. As before, they met secretly in his orchard at the back of his mansion.

"Jeanne, my love," he began. "I have something to ask you. I believe Her Majesty is in love with me, or at least is deeply enamoured with me, and I would like you to arrange a secret nocturnal liaison between us. Do you think you could do this?"

Within herself, Jeanne was thrilled when she heard this, but she did not let de Rohan know. Her plan seemed to be working but she did not want him to guess how great a part she had played in this latest development.

"I will try my best, Louis," she replied quietly. "I will speak to Her Majesty when I next see her and try to arrange a meeting between you."

De Rohan bent forward and hugged his lover. "Oh, you are so good for me," he said as he buried his face in her curly hair. "And in more ways than one."

"Where would you like to meet her?" Jeanne asked once she had disengaged herself from his embrace.

"I was thinking somewhere in the gardens at Versailles. Perhaps near in or near *Le Petit Trianon*. She has complete authority there and no-one can go in there without her permission."

*

Jeanne promised that she would do her best and began organising the next stage in her plan. She hired Mademoiselle Nicole Le Guay d'Olivia, a prostitute who looked remarkably like the queen, and arranged for her to meet the delighted de Rohan one evening in the shadows behind *Le Petit Trianon*.

"How was your meeting?" an impatient Jeanne de Valois asked de Rohan a few days later. "Did she greet you graciously? Has she forgiven you?"

"My dear, it was wonderful," the Cardinal gushed. "Not only did she say that she would forget and forgive me for the past, but that she would be delighted if I contacted Boehmer, the jeweller and to arrange to buy the necklace and give it to her."

"So in other words, my dear Cardinal," Jeanne said, "you want me to see the jewellers?"

"*Oui, oui*, as soon as possible."

This Jeanne did, and after refusing to accept a commission at first, she appeared to change her mind and received a goodly amount for her work from the thankful jewellers. She then had several forged letters, apparently signed by the queen, sent to de Rohan commanding him to buy the necklace, with the injunction that this is to be done as secretly as possible.

As a result, de Rohan bought the necklace for two million livres (well over £10 million today) which he paid for in instalments. At first Boehmer and Bassenge were suspicious, but when the Cardinal showed them his authorisation from the queen, they agreed on the sale.

De Rohan then took the necklace to Jeanne's house, from where she delivered it to one of the Her Majesty's personal valets. Only he was not. He was another criminal who was involved in the gigantic swindle.

As a result, the beautiful diamond necklace, the fruit of Boehmer and Bassenge's devoted expertise, was picked apart. The jewels were sold on the black market in Paris and London. Naturally Jeanne de Valois made sure that she benefitted from these illicit sales.

The next stage in this incredible story unfolded soon after, when Cardinal de Rohan was arrested after the jewellers had complained to the queen that they had not received the agreed payment for the necklace.

"But, *messieurs*, there must be a mistake," the queen told the unhappy jewellers. "I have never received this necklace and neither did I order de Rohan to purchase it for me."

In the ensuing investigation, not only was de Rohan held in custody, but so too were Jeanne de Valois and her lover, the forger Rétaux de Villette, as well as Nicole d'Olivia and Count Alessandro Cagliostro, an Italian adventurer who claimed that he was a holy man who was supported by the Cardinal. The only reason Jeanne's husband was not arrested was that he was in London at the time.

"He was the man, my husband, who persuaded the Cardinal to buy the necklace," Jeanne de Valois claimed at the inquiry, doing her best to shift the blame. "Myself, I had nothing to do with this. I don't even know why you have arrested me. I tell you, I am completely innocent." And saying that, she allowed a tear or two to roll down her beautiful cheeks as she took a lace handkerchief out from the top of her low-cut bodice.

King Louis XVI and his wife, Marie Antoinette decided

to publicise the whole matter. "In that way," the queen said to her complacent husband, "the public will see that we had nothing to do with this sordid affair."

But this plan backfired. The publicity that the trial generated added fuel to the anti-royalist flames that were beginning to burn in France. Marie Antoinette, who was often derogatively referred to as *L'autrichienne* – the Austrian, a reference to her country of birth and France's enemy, and whose name included the word, *chienne* – bitch, was seen as an unthinking grasping woman who only thought about her own riches while much of the country was poverty-stricken and starving.

In the trial that followed, Nicole d'Oliva, the prostitute who had played the fake Marie-Antoinette who had duped de Rohan, was acquitted. She died aged just twenty-eight. Alessandro Cagliostro, who had played a minor role in the scandal was held in the Bastille for nine months and then left France and moved to England. Cardinal de Rohan was found not guilty and acquitted but was ordered to leave Paris and to live in one of his houses in the south of France. This he did, spending some time in the abbey at Chaise-Dieu before later returning to Paris. Rétaux de Villette was found guilty of forgery and exiled to Italy, where he wrote a book about the affair and died in poverty in 1797 aged thirty-nine.

And what happened to Madame Jeanne de Valois-Saint-Rémy de La Motte, the initiator of the *Affaire du collier de la reine* – the 'Affair of the Queen's Necklace'? She was found guilty and sentenced to be branded, whipped and imprisoned. However, public opinion was on her side, not because the people thought she was innocent, but because the royal family was so unpopular. This saved her from being executed but she was sentenced to spend the rest of her life in the combined prison and hospice, the Salpêtrière in Paris. There she disguised herself as a boy, and with help of some friends, escaped and fled to London in 1789, the year the French Revolution broke out.

While she was in London she published her memoirs, *Mémoires Justificatif de la Comtesse de Valois de La Motte* in which, as can be seen from the title, she insisted on using her aristocratic title while justifying her part in the 'con'. In addition to blaming the unpopular Marie Antoinette for everything she claimed that the queen and Cardinal de Rohan had been lovers. It is also possible that she met her husband again in London, but this has never been proved.

She died on 23 August 1791 in the act of fleeing from several debt collectors. As they were banging on the door of her hotel room, demanding to be let in, she ran to the window and accidentally fell to her death below. She was buried, aged fifty-five, in St. Mary's Churchyard, Lambeth.

Was Jeanne de Valois-Saint Rémy really a wicked woman?

Does this grasping and scheming woman deserve to be placed in a book mainly devoted to female pirates, murderers, poisoners and serial-killers? In comparison with their crimes, was hers so wicked?

It is true that she did not wound, maim or kill anyone, but the French Revolution that broke out just four years after the Affair of the Diamond Necklace was certainly used as ammunition by the Parisians against the royal family, and especially against the hated queen, Marie Antoinette. It is true that there was more than one factor behind the outbreak of the Revolution, but it must be remembered that this 'affair', which Jeanne de Valois started and the revolution which followed did cause the deaths of thousands of people throughout the whole of France over a period of several years.

Chapter Ten

Zheng Yi Sao (1775-1844)
The Chinese Pirate Chief

Our reading and studying of history tends to be selective. If we believe in the 'people make and influence history' theory or the theory that 'history is a process of events that makes and influences people', we will be inclined to concentrate on European and North American people and events that are close to or of concern to us. Therefore in the West, history usually focuses on events and people such as two world wars, the French, Russian and other European revolutions, or people such as Napoleon, Churchill, Stalin, Washington, Shakespeare, Einstein and

Freud, who are part of every European and American citizens' 'cultural baggage'. Stop the 'person in the street' and ask them a question about one or more of the above and they will probably know at least one or two things about them, if not a lot. Ask that same person about the Chinese Opium Wars or when Algeria or Bolivia gained their independence and you will probably draw a blank.

The same is true regarding crime and criminals. Ask about British, American or European criminals and what they did, you will probably receive some sort of reply. Many in the West have heard of Jack the Ripper, Al Capone or the Kray Brothers, but now ask about South American, Asian or Chinese criminals and again you will probably draw a blank.

This is also true when it comes to pirates. Most Brits have at least heard of Captain Kidd, Henry Morgan and Blackbeard, but which British citizen has heard of any Asian or Chinese pirate leader who sailed the South China Sea? And who in the West has heard of Zheng Yi Sao, the female pirate chief who controlled thousands of pirates and hundreds of pirate ships? She made the English pirates named above seem like amateurs, but her fantastic exploits are virtually unknown in the English-speaking world. However, now is your chance to read about this woman who was an active pirate for nine years, and a pirate chief for four of them.

*

Zheng Yi Sao was first known as either Chingh Shih or

Mistress Ching. She was born as Shih Yang in 1775 in the poverty-stricken area of Xinhui, Guangdong, China and all we know about her early life is that she worked in a 'flower boat', a floating brothel as a prostitute or a procurer. When she was twenty-six, in 1801, she married a well-known pirate, Zheng Yi, and changed her name to Zheng Yi Sao, meaning Zheng Yi's wife. We don't know how this partnership came about, but whatever the circumstances, not only did her social status change, but so did her lifestyle. From working in a brothel, she now became an active pirate.

Apparently she got on well with her husband, at least for a while, a privateer who had fought for the Vietnamese. However, later, he took a young man, a Tonkin fisherman called Cheung Po Tsai, to be his close companion. It was fashionable then for pirate chiefs to train such a person to become a chief later who would follow in their footsteps.

One year after their marriage, in 1802, Zheng Yi's cousin, Zheng Qi, was captured and executed by their enemy Nguyễn's forces. Zheng Yi then took over Zheng Qi's pirate fleet, and after a period of infighting between the various pirate fleets, managed to become their leader.

In order to establish a united pirate confederacy, he made each of the local chiefs give up some of their privileges. From this, six individual but co-operative fleets were formed, each one being known by its coloured flags: red, yellow, black, blue, purple and white. Zheng Yi was the commander of the Red Fleet, which was the largest. This pirate confederacy consisted of four hundred junks – ships with a high projecting bow that could carry up to five square sails made of linen or matting flattened by bamboo strips.

The combined fleets worked in harmony for five years. The smaller ships would raid the coastal villages, while the larger ones would set out to sea and attack and pillage passing merchant ships and government vessels. They were so successful fighting the emperor's fleet that they destroyed nearly half of his 135 ships.

Then in November 1807, Zheng Yi Sao experienced another major change to her life. Zheng Yi either fell into the sea during a storm or was pushed overboard, probably by a rival captain. Zheng Yi Sao had to make a quick decision: leave the life of piracy or continue as a woman in a man's world. She chose the latter.

She and her dead husband's protégé, Cheung Po Tsai, became lovers, and he became the active captain of their huge fleet, while she remained in the background pulling the strings. They kept their ranks as the leaders of the Red Fleet while she and her future second husband, Zhang Bao, strengthened their rule by imposing a strict code of behaviour on the thousands of pirates under their command. This included the following rules:

• No pirate may go ashore without permission. First punishment for breaking this rule: to have one's ears slit. Second punishment: execution.

• Captured goods are to be registered before being shared out.

• An individual ship that captures a cargo ship keeps one fifth of loot; the rest is for the whole fleet.

- Townsfolk must be paid for their provisions.
- There is to be no abuse of women, captured or not, without permission from the quartermaster.
- A pirate may buy a captured woman for his wife for the equivalent of $40 (if she is not to be held for ransom).
- If a woman agrees to have sex with her captor, the man is to be beheaded and the woman is to be thrown overboard with a weight attached to her legs.
- A pirate caught disobeying orders or stealing from the common treasure is to be beheaded.
- A pirate caught deserting or going absent without leave is to have his ears cut off.
- A pirate caught concealing plundered goods is to be whipped the first time and executed if he repeats this offence.

However, Zheng Yi Sao's success in maintaining such a well-ordered and disciplined fleet became the reason for her ultimate undoing. In the end, the Chinese government and foreign countries trading with China began to employ their own navies to combat what they saw was an expensive disruption of international trade. In addition, other Chinese pirate fleets began to attack and nibble away at Zheng's power.

In March 1809, Sun Quanmou, one of her commanders, attacked a rival pirate fleet and called on Zheng's Red and White Fleets for support. They beat the enemy fleet, but Liang Bao, the leader of the White Fleet, was not destined to enjoy his victory for long. He was killed that July by the Qing navy, along with another senior commander in an action that destroyed his fleet by sinking twenty-five of the pirate confederation's ships.

Zheng wanted revenge. One month later she carried out a massive raid on the pirate enemy which lasted for six weeks. The fighting took place along the Pearl River and its many tributaries and about ten thousand people were killed. She followed this up in the September with another attack, her raiding parties killing an additional two thousand people living in coastal villages. Later that same month Zheng took her fleet of five hundred ships and raided the town of Shating. They captured four hundred civilians and then went on to raid Sanxiongqi village on the Shunde Shuido River. However, after this, Zheng's luck turned and her commander, Sun Quanmou, was defeated in battle on 21 October.

Now that it seemed that Zheng's fleet was not invincible, the Chinese government, together with foreign fleets, decided to attack the pirate confederation again. The Portuguese were particularly interested in crushing Zheng's maritime power. In September her fleet had captured the brig belonging to the Portuguese fleet's governors, Antonio Botelho Homen, and the Portuguese were thirsting for revenge.

Over the next three weeks, both fleets, Zheng's and a Sino-Portuguese navy, manoeuvred against each other, trying to gain an advantage. In the end, seeing that he was not getting anywhere, Sun Quanmou turned forty-three of his own ships into fire-ships (as Drake had done when he fought the Spanish Armada in 1588) and set them off towards the enemy.

Unfortunately, at this point the wind changed and two fire-ships were blown back in the direction of Sun Quanmou's own fleet, though they did not cause any damage. By the end of the battle, the pirates had not lost any ships and the enemy had lost three.

Despite this success, the 'Pirate Queen' Zheng Yi Sao now faced a mutiny. By now it seems that the leader of the Black Fleet, Guo Podai, had had enough. He refused to send reinforcements to Zheng during her battle with the Sino-Portuguese navies, having decided to surrender to the imperial authorities instead. For this he was made a sub-lieutenant by the Chinese navy.

On top of this, the British decided to help the Sino-Portuguese forces by sending a ship called the *Mercury* to join a combined sixty-ship anti-pirate fleet. They began to be successful, which caused Zheng, in February 1810, to meet with her enemy with the aim of bringing the whole wartime situation to an end. At first, the negotiations failed as neither side would compromise. However, this stalemate was broken when Zheng saw ten large British Indiamen warships sail past her fleet, a sight which caused her to surrender.

So it was that on 17 April 1810, Zheng officially surrendered and did so in style. This proud, unrepentant woman sailed her entire fleet with all their flags flying into Canton harbour, marched up to the authorities and demanded a pardon. But not only for herself. She demanded that over seventeen thousand of her pirates be pardoned, and when her terms were accepted, she handed over 226 ships and thousands of cannon and other weapons to the Chinese government. She was made a lieutenant and allowed to keep between twenty to thirty ships. Her crews also received money, pork and wine.

But this would not be the end of her pirate days. Before retiring completely, she fought and defeated the Blue Fleet, then accompanied her husband to Min'an, Fujian where she gave birth to a son.

She died peacefully in 1844 aged 68 or 69, after becoming involved in politics and running an infamous gambling house.

If we compare Zheng Yi Sao and her fleet to those of Blackbeard and Sir Francis Drake, Zheng had control over fifteen hundred ships as opposed to Blackbeard's twenty and Drake's five, and she had approximately eighteen thousand pirates under her command, whereas Blackbeard had five hundred men and Drake a mere seventy. While it is not difficult to judge her as a wicked woman – after all, she had caused thousands of sailors and coastal villagers to die – it cannot be denied that Zheng Yi Sao was the most powerful and successful pirate ever to set sail.

Chapter Eleven

The 'Mad' Queen Ranavalona of Madagascar (c.1788-1861)

One of the most fascinating aspects of reading history is that it is filled with hundreds of controversial people. Very few human beings are pure saint or pure sinner, and many of those in the past who were held up for their good deeds have since been condemned for their nefarious activities and/or immoral behaviour. A classic example is Edward Colston (1636-1721) who until recently was revered as a philanthropist. However, because he based his financial success on shipping slaves to America, his reputation has since been ruined. So much so, that his statue in Bristol

was pulled down and thrown into the harbour as part of a 'Black Lives Matter' campaign. In addition, the Colston concert hall was renamed the Bristol Beacon.

On the other side of the Atlantic Ocean, statues of American Confederate leaders and victorious generals such as Jefferson Davis and Robert E. Lee have also been defaced and/or removed. The same has happened to statues of Christopher Columbus who, despite his successes as an explorer, has been attacked as a man who brought large-scale death and disease to the Americas.

Another example of a man whose reputation has been changed through revisionist history is King Henry VIII. When I was a pupil in school in the fifties, this king was presented to us as a jolly tubby fellow who, although he executed two of his six wives, was not really such a bad man. Since then, in 2015, television's History Channel has reported that in a recent poll, a group of historians thought that he was England's worst king ever. Apart from executing two wives and many nobles and opponents, he had seventy-two thousand other people killed during his thirty-eight-year reign. He was also constantly at war against the French and the Scots, and he wasted the fortune that his father, King Henry VII, had saved up for him.

Famous people like this in a limited way may have become controversial during their lifetimes, whereas others, such as Abraham Lincoln and the Confederate leaders and generals of the American Civil War, as well as figures such as Karl Marx, Martin Luther and Joan of Arc certainly stirred up strong feelings during their own

153

lifetimes. In short, it all depended on which country you lived in or what your beliefs or politics were. Or, in other words, judging people about their degree of wickedness often depends on who is doing the judging. Did they agree or not with their subjects religious, political and other beliefs? Did they think that the subject of their remarks acted wisely or not?

To many people, Stalin was a great leader. He saved Russia from Nazi Germany, he industrialised a backward country and modernised the Russian economy. However, millions of Russians died to bring this all about and the agricultural system was completely overhauled as well. Or take Napoleon; if you lived in 19th century England, he was the worst enemy ever. But if you lived on the other side of the English Channel in France, he was a national hero who, apart from saving the country after the French Revolution, introduced the Napoleonic Code system of law and enacted some much-needed civil legislation.

Another 19th century ruler who was responsible for killing thousands of people but who rigidly enforced her country's independence was Queen Ranavalona I of Madagascar. Until recently, her name was synonymous with her being an extreme dictator. As you will read, to achieve her aims, she caused thousands of her subjects to die. She killed off many of her own family and she threw out almost all the foreigners and Christians living in her country.

However, since the 1970s, some historians have begun to see her in a new light. They say that she acted as she did in order to expand her empire while protecting

Madagascar's independence. It was during her reign (1828-1861) that both France and Britain were hoping to make her country one of their new African colonies, but she absolutely refused to go along with such schemes.

Was she wicked? You can be the judge. Here is her story.

*

Queen Ranavalona I (née Ramavo) was born in the royal palace in Ambatomanoina, Madagascar in 1778, but it was not thought at the time that she would ever become the future queen of her country. This only came about when her father warned the king that his uncle was planning to assassinate him. This was because the uncle had been usurped by Ramavo's father and now he wanted revenge and his throne back. In order to show his gratitude, the king betrothed the teenage Ramavo to his son, Prince Radama, who was designated to be the next king. In addition, any child that Ranavalona had would be next in the line of succession after King Radama.

Unfortunately, Ramavo did not have any children, but when the king died in 1810, Prince Radama did become king. He promptly executed several potential rivals for the throne, including some from his wife's family. This did nothing to improve their loveless relationship, and it is possible that Radama, who may have been suffering from syphilis, was the cause of the marriage remaining childless.

This put Ramavo in a dangerous position. She had not

been born into a royal family, and despite what her father-in-law had decreed, Prince Rakotobe, the well-educated son of the king's oldest sister, was the rightful heir to the throne. The prince therefore had a vested interest to move quickly to remove any opposition. However, he did not move fast enough. Several officers who supported Ramavo's claim to the throne hid her in a safe place. Then after making sure that there would be enough officials, judges and men of religion to support her, she rounded up a sufficient number of soldiers who then occupied the palace. Anyone who resisted her *coup d'état* was given the choice, surrender or be killed. Among those who were eliminated, Prince Rakotobe was speared to death while his mother was starved into her grave. This meant that on 1 August 1828, Madagascar had a new ruler, Ramavo becoming the country's first female leader since it was founded in 1540.

Queen Ramavo changed her name to Ranavalona, and in keeping with the national tradition, promptly executed her potential and political rivals. Despite her later enacting many anti-European actions and laws, her coronation ceremony, which was held ten months later in June 1829, was very reminiscent of those held by European monarchies. In his biography of her, Keith Laidler writes that the newly crowned Queen Ranavalona proclaimed:

"Never say she is only a feeble and ignorant woman, how can she rule such a vast empire? I will *rule here, to the good fortune of my people and the glory of my name! I will worship no gods but those of my ancestors. The ocean*

shall be the boundary of my realm, and I will not cede the thickness of one hair of my realm!"

As events were to prove, her prediction came true, although perhaps not in the way her subjects were expecting. As soon as she came into power, she quickly cancelled many of her predecessor's reforms and ended the trade agreements that he had struck with England and France. She also repelled a military attack by the French navy which had come to reinforce France's influence in the country. In addition, she brought back some of the traditional ways that had existed in Madagascar before various European powers had made their influence felt. Anyone who resisted these changes became subject to the dreaded age-old *tangena* loyalty test.

*

"Your Majesty," a minister said one day after being allowed to approach the throne and speak. "You know the minister for the navy, the one who –"

"Yes, yes, what does he want?"

"Well, I don't want to say something behind his back, but yesterday after our meeting when you said that we should –"

"Yes, man, what do you want? Spit it out and stop shaking. I'm not going to eat you."

"Yes, Your Majesty, well, anyway, yesterday he said that he disagreed with your policy of throwing the English and the French out and –"

"Oh, he did, de he? Well then, go and tell the captain of the palace guards to have him brought here, to me. Now! Do you understand?"

"Yes, Your Majesty," the minister bowed and made off as quickly as he could to find the captain of the palace guards.

An hour later, the unfortunate minister for the navy was kneeling on the polished marble floor facing his royal mistress.

"Stand up, you miserable man," the queen commanded.

"Yes, Your Majesty. What do you want of me?"

"Tell me, did you speak to anyone yesterday about what you thought about my ideas for dealing with the English and French representatives in this country?"

"Er, yes, Your Majesty," the minister muttered. "I just thought that perhaps we should change –"

"*We are not going to change anything*!" Queen Ranavalona thundered. "But you may be changed, soon and permanently. Guard," she called, "have this man subjected to the trial by ordeal, the *tangena* test."

"No, no, Your Majesty, anything but that!"

It was too late. The unfortunate minister was escorted out into the courtyard and made to eat a *tangena,* a poisonous nut. This nut was to be found inside the plum-like fruit that flourished in Madagascar.

"You will swallow the nut now," the queen's officer said, "together with three pieces of chicken skin. You know what the next thing is?"

"Yes, yes," the shaking minister replied. "When I vomit after eating the nut, if I vomit out the three pieces of chicken skin, then I am innocent. If not, then I..." He left the rest of the sentence unsaid. It did not matter. Everybody present knew what would happen to the minister if he failed to vomit the necessary three pieces of chicken skin. After his death his family would not be allowed to take his body and bury it in the family tomb. Instead, he would be buried far away and he would be declared a sorcerer.

"Count yourself lucky," the minister's friend whispered to him in his last minutes of agony. If you had survived, the queen would have had you progressively amputated – first one leg, then the other, then..."

"Enough," murmured the dying minister and collapsed.

*

But those who were forced to undergo the eating of the *tangena* nut were not the only ones to endure Queen Ranavalona's wrath. Many of the native population suffered as the queen exploited the traditional rules of forced labour – *fanompoana* – in order to pay taxes on the purchase of goods. She then conscripted these unfortunate people to join the army so that she could carry out her expansionist foreign policy and be able to rule the whole of Madagascar, the fourth largest island in the world, an island even larger than France. Experts have estimated that under the queen's regime, between 1833-1839 the country's population was halved from five million to two-and-a-half million.

In addition to carrying out these genocidal measures,

the queen decided to rid the country of its European, that is, its mainly French and British diplomats. At the same time she began increasing her restrictions on the Christian missionaries who had arrived in the country to spread the 'good word'. She banned Christian church services, marriages and baptisms for the local population who were studying in the London Missionary schools, and in December 1831, extended this ban to the whole of her country. This meant that those Christians who remained practiced their religion in secret. Four years later, in 1835, in order to close down the missionary press, but without drawing any unnecessary foreign attention to her policy, she forbade the local population to work for them, though somehow the press continued printing its materials and distributing them around the country.

However, despite the above, it seems that Queen Ranavalona still had a complicated way of dealing with the English, French and Christian organisations who wished to play their part in Madagascar. In February 1835 in a *kabary* – an important speech delivered in public – she declared that while her own subjects were forbidden to practice Christianity, she acknowledged the benefits that Western technology had brought to her country:

"To the English and French strangers: I thank you for the good that you have done in my land and my kingdom, where you have made known European wisdom and knowledge. Do not worry yourselves, I will not change the customs and rites of our ancestors. Nevertheless, whoever breaks the laws of my kingdom will be put to death –

whoever he may be… Concerning you, foreigners, you can
practice according to your own manners and customs.
Nevertheless, if skilled handiwork and other practical
skills exist, which can profit our people, exercise these
skills that good will come."

Then later in 1835 the devoted Christians who looked after the souls of half the country's population were ordered to leave – or face the consequences. To underline her seriousness, in 1836 she had fourteen Christian missionaries massacred. Her plan succeeded, and within a year virtually all the country's foreigners, Christian or not, had left. As a result, to increase Madagascar's policy of self-reliance, she employed the *fanampoana* tradition of forced labour to get the work done that the foreign population had previously carried out.

However, despite the queen's anti-European policies, she was still fascinated by French culture. She would have her courtiers dress in French fashions, but in the end, when it came to an attempted joint French and English invasion of her country in 1849, she fought back with everything she had. When the attacking forces landed on the beach, they were pleased to see that there was apparently only a poorly built fort to stop them. But as they advanced they discovered that this structure concealed a much more substantial fortress, and by the end of the day the colonial forces were in retreat. To remind them of their failure, the queen had twenty-one European skulls mounted on poles displayed along the shoreline, a grim reminder to discourage any future invasions.

However, there was one European who managed to survive Queen Ranavalona's actions. And not only did he survive them, but he flourished.

Jean Laborde was born in France in 1805. Trained as a blacksmith, this future engineer emigrated to India and was later shipwrecked off the east coast of Madagascar. Instead of being sent back to Europe, the queen recognised his talents and promoted him to become one of her most important engineers. She granted him large tracts of land, an unlimited number of forced labourers and enough money to carry out any project she wanted from him.

He established an arms and munitions factory in addition to a full-scale industrial complex. This manufactured iron and steel, glass and bricks, cement and textiles – while the queen did not want Europeans in her country, she was certainly less dismissive of the products of European industrialisation. In addition, Laborde also built a summer palace for the queen and was responsible for other engineering projects, including roads and bridges.

Despite this exception to the rule, Queen Ranavalona kept strictly to her 'Madagascar for the Madagascans' policy. She sent her army of twenty to thirty thousand mainly forced recruits to expand her territory, and anyone who resisted was harshly dealt with, often being enslaved. It is estimated that between 1820 and 1853, one third of the population was made up of captured slaves. The historian, Gwyn Campbell, estimates that between 1816 and 1853, about sixty thousand people died as a result of the queen and her predecessor's expansionist military expeditions. Famine and a scorched earth campaign caused another estimated 160,000 people to die, in addition to those who died from malaria and other diseases.

Another example of Queen Ranavalona's extreme behaviour occurred in 1845. She ordered a buffalo hunt to take place in which every single nobleman was to participate. Each of them was commanded to bring a full retinue of slaves and underlings, which meant that some fifty thousand people were involved. No preparations regarding food and other essential supplies were organised for this massive expedition and the 'hunters' were ordered to live off the land. As a result they were forced to buy or steal their food from the villages they passed and it was recorded that the villagers charged exorbitant prices for their rice and other foodstuffs. This hunting party also included slaves and road builders. When they died from exhaustion and hunger, their corpses were cast aside and new builders were conscripted along the way. Biographer Keith Laidler described the royal route being:

... littered with corpses, most of which were not even buried, but simply thrown into some convenient ditch or under a nearby bush. In total, ten thousand men, women and children are said to have perished during the sixteen weeks of the queen's hunt. In all this time, there is no record of a single buffalo being shot.

Eventually, as a result of her unpredictable and capricious behaviour, several plots were formed to get rid of Queen Ranavalona. In 1857, her son, Prince Rakoto, who succeeded her as King Radama II, together with Jean Laborde conspired with the French to overthrow his mother.

One evening in a royal apartment on the far side of the palace courtyard, two men, the swarthy heir to the throne, Prince Rakoto and Jean Laborde, were deep in conversation. The prince had sent all his servants out for the evening as he did not want any ears to catch what he and his guest discussed and then report back to the queen.

*

"Monsieur Laborde," the prince began. "First of all, do have a glass of this cognac. It is one of the best I have ever drunk."

Laborde drank off a little and raised his thumb. "Prince Rakoto, you are absolutely right. It is certainly a superb cognac. But now, please tell me, why have you invited me here tonight? Usually when we meet it is in daytime and there are always plenty of people around."

"I know that, *mon ami*, but this time, no-one, and I mean no-one must hear this conversation."

"*Pourquoi pas?*"

"Why not? Because it concerns my mother, the queen. Now, before we begin, have you heard any, er, let us say unflattering remarks about her recently?"

Laborde threw back his bearded head. "Some, you say? I've heard hundreds. Remarks made by unhappy lords, nobles, and of course also from workers in the palace and slaves. Why do you ask?"

"Because, my friend, I am thinking of planning a *coup d'état* and getting rid of her. That's why."

"But is that wise? You should know that she has ears and eyes everywhere, and I for one don't want to undergo that *tangena* test."

"Yes, that I understand, but what I want to know is if you will support me? I know you have been very unhappy about how my mother has been ruling the country recently, so I hope you will support me."

"Oh, that I will, but my prince, my support will not be enough."

"I know that, and that is why I would like you to make contact with the French and see if they will help us. Ah, yes, have another glass of cognac."

Laborde drank another glass and promised that he would contact his French connections and report back to the prince as soon as he could. Two weeks later, the two men had another evening meeting, but this time it was in Laborde's house.

"Prince Rakoto," Laborde began. "Please forgive me for not speaking to you sooner about this matter, but after I spoke to the various French diplomats who I know, they told me that they would have to speak to their British counterparts."

"And have they?"

"*Oui, mon ami*," Laborde replied, "and the news is not good. The French won't join us unless the English do, and the English are not prepared to take part in such a *coup*."

"Are you sure?"

"*Absolument*. There is no way that the French will help without English support and the English are quite adamant about not helping. I am sorry, my prince," Laborde shrugged, "but that's the way it is."

*

In the end, the prince and Laborde did attempt to carry out their *coup,* but it failed. This was probably because the queen had her spies planted among the conspirators. However, instead of killing her opponents immediately as expected, Queen Ranavalona delayed their deaths. Apart from her son, she sent them on a forced march through malaria-ridden swamps which ended the lives of many of them. Laborde somehow survived and fled the country.

Two unforeseen results of the queen's harsh and unyielding rule were that when Rakoto did ascend the throne four years later, he invited Laborde to return and continue with his various projects. However resentment against the queen and her family was so widespread that within two years the new king was assassinated.

On 16 August 1861, Ranavalona, who was now aged over eighty-two, died in her sleep after appointing Rakoto to succeed her. To make sure that there would be no last minute 'surprises', he had his residence surrounded by hundreds of loyal troops.

The queen in her typical grandiose manner had commanded that her funeral be a grand event. Twelve thousand zebu cattle were slaughtered and their meat was distributed to the population. However, not everything went according to plan. A stray spark accidentally ignited a barrel of gunpowder near the coffin. This caused a massive explosion. Several mourners were killed and three royal residences were seriously burned.

Ironically, following Radama II's assassination, Madagascar was ruled in turn by three queens, including Queen Ranavalona I's cousin, and Ranavalona II who Christianised the court. None of these three queens could resist France colonialising the country, and when the monarchy was abolished in 1897, Madagascar became a part of the French colonial empire, only regaining its independence in October 1958. The country is now officially known as the Malgasy Republic.

Was Queen Ranavalona really a wicked woman?

Was she simply a mad tyrant or simply a queen who loved her country so much that she would do anything to prevent foreign influences dominating her national culture?

Her foreign contemporaries definitely thought that she was mad, cruel and extreme. Her actions were those of a xenophobic despot. Thousands of her subjects, noble and peasant, paid for her policies with their lives, but on the other hand, despite non-stop French and British pressure, she did manage to preserve Madagascar's native culture and way of life.

Perhaps, if you think that she was wicked, the real question is, was the price that the country paid to keep its national and cultural independence worth it?

Chapter Twelve

Mary Willcocks alias Princess Caraboo (1792-1864)

Princess Caraboo (Mary Baker), from an engraving by N. Branwhite

Many people have conflicting attitudes concerning con artists. On the one hand they are often impressed by their gall and effrontery, but on the other, they despise their power to dupe the more gullible people in society. Usually, such con artists, often referred to as 'grifters' and 'hustlers', use their charms and tricks to cheat and steal. They rely on their powers of persuasion and on the fact that their 'marks', their victims, often go along with them because they too wish to make some extra money without working too hard.

Mary Baker was one such con artist, except that she did not set out to fool people for financial gain. However, what she did do was to tell her lies in such a dramatic and outlandish way that in the end very few people doubted the veracity of her words or who she claimed to be.

*

This story starts on Thursday, 3 April 1817. The Napoleonic wars were over and Britain was in the throes of the Industrial Revolution. This meant that fewer people than previously were involved in agriculture, as this aspect of the economy had become increasingly mechanised. Those who did not remain to work on the land moved to the big cities in the hope of finding employment there. Rural poverty was also exacerbated by the recent Enclosure Acts. This meant that the commoners now had no or limited access to the land which they had previously used for grazing animals and collecting firewood.

This was the situation when a local village cobbler from Almondsbury, Gloucestershire was walking along a country road and suddenly spotted a strange-looking woman walking along the same road on her own. Being a friendly soul, he tried to speak to her, but all he received in return was a whole lot of words in a language that he did not understand.

*

"Oh, I didn't know you was a foreigner," he said, and indicated that she should come back with him to his own home. There, after a quick consultation with his wife, they decided to take the exotically dressed woman to see Mr Samuel Worrall, the local magistrate and Overseer of the Poor at his house at Knole Park.

"What shall we do with her?' the magistrate's wife, Elizabeth, asked her husband. "The cobbler cannot put her up."

"Yes, I know that, my dear, and apart from that, we don't know anything about her. She doesn't speak English and she didn't say anything when I tried my few words of Welsh and French on her."

"Yes, I heard you, and isn't she wearing such strange clothes? I wonder where she's from. I mean, look what she's wearing," Mrs Worrall continued. "This long black gown, a red and black cotton shawl and this wide black sheet thing around her head. Now who wears clothes like that?"

As an educated man, the magistrate went off to consult with the local vicar to see if he could find the answer. They went into his library and looked in several of the latter's books before the magistrate returned home.

"Did you have any luck, Sam?"

"No, my dear. We couldn't find anything that would tell us where she is from. I think –"

"Do you think that she is Greek or something like that?" Elizabeth asked. "Just look at her face. She doesn't look English. She's too dark for that. And look at her hands.

They don't look like the hands of a woman who's had to work hard on a farm or as a servant girl."

The magistrate looked at the slender stranger's hands and agreed.

"You know what, my dear?" Elizabeth Worrall asked. "I suggest that we send her to the pub with our maid, and hopefully they'll be able to put her up there for the night…"

"Aye, and perhaps get a meal as well if she's lucky."

*

And that is what happened. Elizabeth Worrall's maid accompanied the strange visitor to the local pub. There the kind-hearted villagers arranged for her to spend the night and enjoy an evening meal. The next morning, the curious magistrate's wife went to the pub hoping to learn more about this mysterious stranger who had suddenly appeared in their village. Elizabeth and the other people present tried everything they could in order to communicate with the woman. After trying unsuccessfully to talk to her, someone suggested that perhaps they give her a pen and paper and that she write something. This they did but they had similar results.

*

"'ere, what's she written? That ain't no English. It's scribble," one of the villagers said looking at the page he was trying to read.

"Maybe you're holding it upside down," his friend suggested, and turned the page the other way. "No, that don't help, neither. I wonder what it says?"

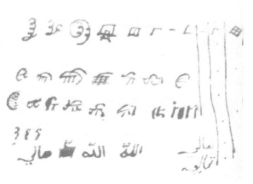

From page showing Princess Caraboo's writing

Just as everyone there was debating what to do next, the centre of their attention, the black-turbaned young lady suddenly pointed at herself and said, "Caraboo."

"Caraboo, what's that?"

"It's the name of some sort of reindeer."

"No, it's not. This must be a different sort of caraboo."

Just then the woman pointed to herself again. "Caraboo," she said.

"Ah, I know. That's her name. Mistress or Mrs Caraboo."

"Well that's not a local name. I've never heard of anyone around these parts called that."

"*Nanas! Nanas!*"

"What's that? Who said, 'Nanas'?"

"She did, Fred. She just pointed at that picture of a pineapple on the wall and said, 'Nanas'."

"Well, I suppose that's what pineapple means in her language, but I wonder what that is."

"Here, look what she's doing now. She's lying on the floor."

"Whatever for?"

"Search me. Maybe she wants to go and sleep. Perhaps that's how they do it where she comes from."

"You know what, I think the best thing for 'er is if someone took 'er back to the magistrate's 'ouse. 'e'll know 'ow to deal with 'er."

*

And so it was. The Worralls' maid returned to the pub and took 'Mistress Caraboo' back with her. While she was staying there, a well-travelled acquaintance, Captain Palmer, came to see Mr Worrall and while they were there in the parlour, Samuel Worrall naturally began to talk about his new houseguest.

*

"Captain, you've travelled around quite a lot, haven't you?" he began. "Europe, America, even the Far East. So come and see this lady who is staying with us. If I understand her correctly, she calls herself Caraboo, but that's about all I know of her. From your experience, tell me what you make of her."

"All right, but I suggest that you allow me to sit with her here in your parlour, just her and me. That way she may be more inclined to talk, you know, without so many people about."

The Worralls agreed and Elizabeth indicated to their new guest to come and sit in the parlour with their other guest. Half an hour later, Captain Palmer emerged smiling.

"This is what I've learned," he said. "I showed her a map of the Far East and she pointed to China and from that I understood that she was born, or at least, somewhere near there. Anyway, she claims that she is a princess and –"

"But how did she end up here?" the impatient Elizabeth asked.

"Yes, I was coming to that," the captain said. "She says that she came from an island called Javasu and that her father was Chinaman called Jessu Mandu and her mother was a Malay woman. She said she was a princess and if she wanted to go anywhere she would be carried around on men's shoulders on some kind of covered litter and –"

"But how did she end up here?" Elizabeth asked again.

"Wait a minute, Mistress Worrall, I'm coming to that. One day while she was in the garden of her palace some men broke in and carried her off. They were pirates and their chief was called Chee-min."

"You mean she was kidnapped?"

"Right, and then these men sold her to the captain of a ship called the *Tappa Boo* and he took her off to sea with him. To Europe."

"And how long was she on that ship?"

"From what I can understand, Samuel, she was there

for nearly three months."

"How did they treat her?" Elizabeth asked. "I mean, did they treat her like royalty, or did they lock her up or use her as some sort of slave?"

Captain Palmer shrugged. "She didn't say. But what she did say was that once she saw that the ship was near land, that is, it must have been England, she jumped overboard."

"So that means that her ship must have sailed up the Bristol Channel?"

"Yes, I suppose so."

"And then she swam here?"

"Well, yes, that's the logical answer. I mean Gloucestershire does have a coast and we are only about five miles away from the sea from here, aren't we?"

Samuel Worrall looked somewhat suspicious when he heard this. "So now I'm going to ask a question like a magistrate. Why is it that her clothes don't look as if they've been soaked in seawater?" he asked. "They look too clean for that."

"Yes, Sam, I also thought that and so I asked her, delicately at first. I mean, one hesitates to ask young ladies, especially if they are princesses, about their clothes and…"

"And, Captain, what did she say?"

"She said that when the cobbler met her, she had already been wandering around the countryside for well over a month and that she had managed to get herself some new clothes."

"How?"

"I didn't ask her, Sam. As I said, I didn't want to dwell on the subject, also because I thought that if I did so, she might clam up and stop talking to me."

"Do you think her story is true, Captain?" Sam asked as he poured him a glass of port.

"I'm not sure, my friend. I think that it's possible, but I have no way of proving or disproving it."

"Well, she certainly behaves and looks like a princess to me, although I admit I've never met any live princesses in my life before," Elizabeth said. "I mean, look at her clothes and how she holds herself. She doesn't look like a milkmaid in disguise, does she?"

"Yes, I tend to agree with you," Arthur said. "And as you pointed out, her hands are very smooth and look very well taken care of. But you know, I did notice that they do have some strange marks on the back of them. While we were talking I made a special point of looking at her nails carefully. I'm telling you, it's really puzzling but they are not all broken and dirty as you would expect a servant's or someone like that to be."

"Well, if that's the case," Elizabeth said, "and if she is a princess, we had better start treating her as such. I mean, can you imagine what would happen if we treated her like some common working girl and it turned out that we were wrong? We could go to jail for that, no?"

*

The others were not sure if they would end up in jail, but from then on, they decided to address their guest as

Princess Caraboo and to treat her as royalty.

From that moment the exotic Princess Caraboo put on quite a show for the locals. She showed them that she was quite adept with a bow and arrow and she would walk around with feathers and flowers in her hair. She wore a gong on her back and she demonstrated that she was familiar with a *kris*, a Far Eastern form of dagger that Captain Palmer showed her. A few times, some of the villagers even caught her swimming at night naked in a small lake nearby.

*

"Is she a Christian of sorts?" someone asked Elizabeth Worrall one day.

"No, my dear. I don't think so. Every night before she goes to sleep she prays to this god of hers. Allah-Tallah is his name. I can't understand what she says or what she's praying about, but she sounds very serious about it."

"Maybe she's thanking this Allah-Tallah for saving her life?"

"Perhaps, but I can't tell you any more than what I've told you."

*

Of course it was impossible to keep the story of this exotic and colourful woman a secret and soon the word got out. Tens if not hundreds of visitors descended upon the hitherto peaceful village of Almondsbury to see the foreign Princess Caraboo, and she in her turn obliged them by looking and behaving as outlandishly as possible.

She would answer questions in fractured English, just enough to satisfy some of her listeners' curiosity, but no more. A few linguists turned up and after a several minutes' conversation with her, they declared that they had no idea which language she was speaking. In addition, several craniologists and physiognomists came to the village to try and solve the mystery of who this woman really was. However, after delicately running their hands over her face and skull, they were still none the wiser. Any local cynics who doubted her story had their questions squashed when a Dr Wilkinson stated quite authoritatively that while not giving it a name, the language she spoke was referred to in *Pantographia*, a learned book written by that most eminent man of letters, Edmund Fry. In addition, the respected doctor said that marks on the back of Princess Caraboo's hands were definitely those made by oriental surgeons.

*

"Well, if Doctor Wilkinson says she's genuine, then it must be true," was the opinion of most of the village.

But another doctor, Dr William Mortimer, had other ideas.

One day the Worralls called Dr Mortimer to come and examine their 'princess'. She had gone out for a walk and had returned late in the evening, her clothed spattered with mud. She did not say what had happened but that soon afterwards she had fallen ill.

"You know, sir," the doctor said to Mr Worrall after he had examined her. "I don't believe that your Princess Caraboo is really from the Far East."

"Why not?"

"Well, for a start," Doctor Mortimer replied, "her skin is white and not yellow and so I am sure that she is European. But to be sure, I'll come back later with another doctor if that's all right with you?"

Mr Worrall said it was and Doctor Mortimer returned soon after with a colleague. As they and a maid were standing next to the 'princess's' bed discussing the case, Doctor Mortimer's colleague said that she was dangerously ill.

"How long do you think she's got?"

The colleague shrugged. "I can't tell, not long, but I'll ty and do my best for her… but look, her face has suddenly gone bright red! I'm telling you, this young lady understands what we are talking about. I tend to agree with you, William, your patient is a fraud. She's no foreigner."

"But she's had these red flushes before," the maid said. "Why, only yesterday she…"

"Well, I'm still not convinced," Doctor Mortimer interrupted, and looking at his colleague said, "If you won't be offended, I'll ask Dr Charles Wilkinson from Bath to see what he thinks. I know him and I respect his opinion. I'm sure that way we'll get to the bottom of this matter."

*

Doctor Wilkinson arrived soon after and examined the sickly princess. Then being impressed by her, he wrote an article which was published in the *Bath Chronicle*. The result was that the Worralls were soon flooded with letters from all sorts of people giving their theories about where their Princess Caraboo came from.

By this time, the Worrall's houseguest had regained her health and one day went for a trip to Bath. She was spotted there by someone who had read the article in the *Bath Chronicle* and he contacted Dr Wilkinson. They arranged to meet at the Pack Horse Inn, where Princess Caraboo was visiting. They took her back to the Worrall's house in Almondsbury where she broke down.

"I'm so sad," she said in her broken English. "I want to go home to Javasu. I want to see my mother and father. Oh, I am so sad."

Elizabeth Worrall managed to calm her down and later told her that they would be going to Bristol where the well-known artist, Mr Edward Bird, would paint her portrait. The idea of being the subject of a portrait pleased the 'princess' and so a few days later, they made the eight-mile journey to Bristol. But Elizabeth Worrall was not telling the truth. Instead of taking her guest to the artist's studio, she took her to Dr Mortimer's house. There, Elizabeth met Mrs Neale, the owner of a lodging house in Lewin's Mead, Bristol.

*

180

"That's not no Princess Caraboo," Mrs Neale told Elizabeth once she had seen her. "I'll tell you who she is. Her name is Mary Baker and she's from Devon. I'd know her anywhere."

"Excuse me," Elizabeth asked, "but how do you know about our Princess Caraboo?"

"Me, I've seen her at my boarding house, I have, and I must add, it's a very respectable place it is. *That* I can tell you." Mrs Neale continued. "And this is what I can tell you about that lady who calls herself Princess Caraboo. Her real name is Mary Baker and your so-called princess comes from Witheridge, near Tiverton, in Devon. And not only that, but her father is a cobbler and that young lady is nothing but a servant girl – a trumped-up servant girl."

"But she doesn't have the hands of a servant girl."

"Well, I don't know about that," Mrs Neale shrugged, "but I know she is."

"So you know what we'll do?" Dr Mortimer said. "We'll call her in here and confront her with what you have just told me. Hopefully, this way we will learn the truth."

Elizabeth got up, opened the door and invited the 'princess' to join them for tea. As they were sitting there, Elizabeth started asking her houseguest some very direct questions.

"Mrs Neale here says that you are not really a princess at all."

"But I –"

"She told me and Doctor Mortimer that your real name is Mary Baker," Elizabeth Worrall said. "Is this true?"

181

"Well, I –"

"And that you are really a servant girl and that you are from Devon."

"No, no, this is not true. I come from Javasu and –"

"That's a lie," Mrs Neale interrupted. "I've seen you at my boarding house. You was there some time ago. You pretended you was a foreigner then, but I overheard you talking English like you was born here."

At that point Princess Caraboo raised both her hands in the air. "I give up," she said. "I'm not Princess Caraboo."

"So who are you, and what's your story?" Doctor Mortimer asked.

"So now I will tell you," the red-faced imposter replied. "My real name is Mary Willcocks and I come from Witheridge in Devon –"

"You see," the triumphant Mrs Neale burst out. "I told you she was no foreign princess. I said that she –"

"Please be quiet, Mrs Neale, so we can hear her story," Doctor Mortimer said. "Please continue, Mistress Willcocks."

The demoted princess took a deep breath, looked around and continued her story. "So as I said, I come from Witheridge in Devon and from when I was a small girl I worked as a wool-spinner. Then I left home when I was sixteen and began working for a family, that is, looking after their children and doing odd jobs on their farm. But I didn't like it there and they paid me very badly. So I left and went to Exeter. I thought that if I'll be in a big town, I'll find a better job, you know, with more money."

"And did you?" Elizabeth asked.

"No, I couldn't find any regular work and I had to beg and scrounge for my bed and board. In the end, after two months I left. And you know, I was so hungry and unhappy that I seriously thought of hanging myself and putting an end to my misery."

"So why didn't you?" Doctor Mortimer asked.

"Because just then I remembered something that I'd heard in church," Mary replied quietly. "Something like, 'Cursed are they that do murder and sin against the Lord'. I got so frightened and just carried on walking down that country road. Then soon after that I met this nice man and I told him how miserable I was. He gave me five shillings and told me not to sin or even think of doing so. I suppose he meant by hanging myself."

"So what did you do next?" Elizabeth asked.

"I went to Taunton and used the five shillings on lodgings. Then I went to Bristol and started begging for money there to find lodgings and –"

"Ha," Mrs Neale interrupted again. "That's when I saw you. I knew –"

"Please, Mrs Neale, let Mary continue with her story," Doctor Mortimer said. "It is so fascinating."

"Yes," Mary said. "One day when I was begging in a village just outside Bristol, the local constable arrested me. He took me to the lock-up and said he was going to take me to the magistrate in the morning. I was scared that I'd be sent to prison I escaped through the window. Then I started walking east as far as I could, to stay away from the law."

"How far did you get?" Elizabeth asked.

"I'm not sure, but I think I was quite near London, and then I fell ill. I hadn't eaten properly for days and all the time I kept walking. Sometimes I was lucky and managed to scrounge lifts in farmers' carts, but that didn't happen very often. Then one day I fainted from weakness and these two kind ladies took me to the nearest hospital."

"Where was that?" Doctor Mortimer asked.

Mary shrugged. "I don't know. All I know is that one day after I got better I walked into a brothel thinking that it was a convent. I'd heard that I could get a bed and a meal there, but once I saw where I was, I left immediately and kept going east. I got to London and ended up taking lodgings with a Mrs Hillier. She was a fishmonger."

"Did you find work in London?" Elizabeth and Doctor Mortimer asked together.

"I was just coming to that," Mary replied. "One day while I was shopping for this Mrs Hillier, this posh-looking man came up to me. He looked a bit foreign and I found out that he was half-English and half-Malay. He said his name was John Henry Baker or something like that and he said that he had once been a sailor. We became very friendly and after a few weeks we got married. For fun he taught me a few words in Malay, but we could never find any regular work. So that seeing life wasn't easy in England, my new husband went to Calais, y'know, in France hoping he'd find work there. The idea was that if he did, then I'd come over and join him. But I never heard from him again, and then I discovered that I was with child. His child –"

"Oh, you poor dear," Elizabeth said. "So what did you

184

do then?"

"I worked for a bit at the Crab Tree coaching inn and then I went to this hospital to have my baby. It was a boy and as I couldn't look after him, y'know, no money and no home of my own, I gave him up to the foundling hospital. I used to visit him every week, but he was so weak that he died soon after. After that I decided I'd had enough of wandering around and begging so I made my way back home."

"To Witheridge?" Mrs Neale asked.

Mary nodded. "That's right, and then I went to Bristol, and that's where you saw me. And while I was staying in your lodging house, one day I dressed up in a long dress and a turban I made out of winding a long piece of cloth around my head and went begging. I made more money that way so I did it some more. Then one day, I met this ship's captain – I've forgotten his name – and he said he'd take me to America, but that it would cost me five pounds. And that's the time that you, Mrs Worrall, saw me in my muddy clothes when I became ill and you called in Doctor Mortimer here."

"Why what happened? You never told me or my husband at the time."

"Yes, I know," Mary gave a quick smile. "I was Princess Caraboo then, wasn't I?"

Elizabeth nodded and Mary continued: "That night I had left your house to go to Mrs Neale's to collect my trunk. I was going to meet this sea-captain after that in the harbour in Bristol, but I got there too late. He had already left for America. So after that I came back to your house,

Mrs Worrall, but now I was all dirty from my trip to Bristol and back."

For a moment everyone was silent in that room absorbing the tale Mary Willcocks, alias Princess Caraboo, had told. Was it true? Her listeners were thinking. It was so fascinating, far-fetched and foreign to them all. Princess Caraboo, China, half-Malay sailors, Calais, London, voyage to America. How much could they believe her?

*

Mrs Worrall was not fully convinced. Mary had fooled her once before. What was to stop her doing so again? So she asked Captain Palmer to investigate for her, and he went to Witheridge and contacted the vicar in nearby Tiverton. He said that he had known Mary's parents for twenty-five years and together the two men went to speak to them in Witheridge. They said that the first part of Mary's story was true, but were upset when they heard about their daughter's wanderings between the West Country and London, and about how she had had to give up her baby boy.

Captain Palmer then reported back to Mrs Worrall, who offered to pay for Mary's passage to America. Mary accepted, and accompanied by three other women, set sail for Philadelphia. However, this time she took yet another name. Now she was Mary Burgess, as her other names were too well-known.

"Why do you want to go to America?" the local

villagers asked her when they heard of her plans. "To become rich?"

Mary nodded. "You'll see. One day, when I return, I'll be coming back with a carriage and four horses."

In America, Mary appeared as 'Princess Caraboo' at the Washington Hall in Philadelphia, but her performances were not a commercial success. Seven years later, in 1824, she returned to London, without a carriage and four horses, and took lodgings in New Bond Street. She tried to make money by dressing up again as Princess Caraboo and charged one shilling per person to see her. She was as successful here as he had been in America and so she returned to Bristol. After this, little is known of what happened to her. It is recorded that she married, had a child and spent much of the remainder of her life selling leeches for medical purposes to the local hospital. She died on Christmas Eve, 1864 and was buried in an unmarked grave in the Hebron Road Cemetery, Bristol.

Was 'Princess Caraboo' really a wicked woman?

Is it fair to include her in a book full of truly nasty and wicked women – women who had tortured others, poisoned and murdered their children and other people, as well as female thieves and outlaws? It is true that Mary Willcocks did not kill anyone, and she did not con people out of their hard-earned savings. However, for a period of about one year (1817-1818) she successfully fooled a lot of gullible souls and 'deceived the world with ornament', as Shakespeare says in *The Merchant of Venice* (III.ii).

And as the Bible says, 'Let no man deceive you with vain words' (Ephesians 5:6), and for having done this, 'Princess Caraboo' was certainly very guilty.

Chapter Thirteen

Sarah Rachel Russell (1814-80)
Victorian Cosmetician, Blackmailer & Con Artist

Throughout history, women have used cosmetics to beautify themselves and adorn their faces. Evidence for this even appears in the Bible. In 2 Kings (9:30) we read that the wicked Queen Jezebel 'painted her face and tired (adorned) her head' as she waited for Jehu, her military commander. Later, in the Book of Jeremiah (4:30), the prophet castigates women who paint their faces 'in vain shalt thou make thyself fair, thy lovers will despise thee'. In the Book of Esther (2:12), the young future Queen of Persia uses 'oil of myrrh and perfumes and feminine

cosmetics' in order to beautify herself for an audience with King Xerxes. It is thought that she may also have used henna, as well as oils of spikenard and frankincense.

Centuries later, the Romans used cosmetics and there is also proof that these allegedly beautifying materials were used during the Middle Ages. During this period, it was fashionable for upper-class women to whiten their faces. Queen Elizabeth I used an unhealthy combination of white lead and vinegar to whiten her face and also to cover the small pits that were a result of the bout of smallpox she had suffered in 1562. Three hundred years later, Queen Victoria declared that the use of cosmetics was vulgar and inacceptable, but by the 21st century few would agree.

Today, every year women in Britain spend about £10 billion on cosmetics and hair products at 41,000 cosmetic businesses. In the USA, the cosmetics industry is worth over $62 billion dollars, while according to one study, the average American woman spends over $300 per month on making herself beautiful. Moral of the story: cosmetics are big business.

Sarah Rachel Russell, the 'heroine' of this chapter, decided to defy Queen Victoria's proclamation denigrating the use of cosmetics by making her fortune from doing just the opposite – selling them, and as many as possible.

*

London in the mid-1850s. Queen Victoria has been

monarch for almost twenty years and Elsie and Agnes, two middle-class ladies, are discussing their own health and beauty.

"Listen, Agnes, I've been thinking. I think it's about time I did something with my face."

"What do you mean? Have some sort of operation?"

"No, no, my dear. I think I should start investing a bit of money on improving it – you know, making me look a bit younger and more attractive."

"How?"

"I've been thinking about trying some of those cosmetics they've been selling. Y'know, the ones that I've seen in the advertisements in the newspapers."

"How do you know that they're not a lot of rubbish? Like water with some colouring stuff in it?"

"No, Agnes, I'm sure they're not. Here, just look at this advertisement that I saw in this morning's paper. It's by this lady called Madame Rachel. Look, she's selling this 'Desert Water' and 'Liquid Dew' and –"

"And what are they for and how do you use them?"

"You put them on your face. Here, listen. 'Madame Rachel had the honour of supplying and furnishing the Elegant Cabinet of Her Majesty, the Suntana, by whom her costly Arabian preparations and cosmetics have been so fully appreciated that another order has been received by Madame R'."

"So?"

"So I'm telling you, Agnes, if these cosmetics were no good, this Suntana queen wouldn't be ordering any more, would she?"

191

"Yes, I suppose you're right. But Elsie, show me that advertisement again. Hmm, it says that her make-up is free from 'deadly leads' and 'other injurious matters' and that they are the 'purest, rarest and most fragrant productions'. Well, my dear, if that's the case, let's go and buy some."

*

And so Elsie and Agnes joined the hundreds, perhaps thousands, of Victorian women who helped Sarah Rachel Russell make a small fortune out of some very dubious cosmetics, products which used such ingredients as lead carbonate, prussic acid, and of course the age-old aid to beauty, arsenic.

Who was this Sarah Rachel Russell, this purveyor of such dangerous cosmetics? She was born in London's poor East End in about 1814 to a theatrical family. Her poverty and illiteracy made her think that if she were to make her way in the world, she would have to resort to crime in one form or other. This meant that sometimes she would spend time in prison for minor offences. An example of this was when she appeared as a witness to prove an alibi for a violent character called David Belasco. He was charged with manslaughter while Sarah Russell was sent to Newgate prison for three weeks for having committed perjury.

In 1844, she married Jacob Moses, a chemist in Manchester, but two years later he walked out on her. She then moved in with a Philip Levinson or Leverson, changed her name to Sarah Levinson/Leverson and the couple had six children. It was during this period that she began dealing in second-hand clothes as well as running a stall where she sold hot baked potatoes and fried fish. However it seems that this did not make enough money and so she began to think about making more through dubious means. It has also been noted, but not proved, that at this stage in her life she also worked as a procuress for a brothel.

It was also at this time that she became ill and her black hair began to fall out. Naturally this disturbed her and so she tried all sorts of remedies. Eventually she found one tonic which was successful, which gave her an idea. Why not go into the business of making and selling hair restoratives? However, due to her lack of education, reputation and specific knowledge about such restoratives, she decided to link herself with the French actress, Elizabeth Félix, who was also known as Mademoiselle Rachel.

Like Sarah Russell, this actress was born poor. Her father was a pedlar and her mother dealt in second-hand clothes. However, she was determined to succeed in life and began singing on the streets of Paris. Somehow she managed to raise enough money to take drama lessons, and she became romantically involved with the director of the Paris Opera. It was also during this period that she became the mistress of both Napoleon III and Prince Napoleon, Napoleon Buonaparte's younger brother. Such connections must have aided her career because by 1841 she was singing in London, as well as many other European cities including St. Petersburg. However, all of this was too much for her and she contracted tuberculosis as a result. After a long fight with the disease, she died in 1858 aged thirty-six.

Although the two women never met, Sarah Rachel Russell exploited her alleged connections to the famous French singer, that is, they both shared the same name and began trading on the French woman's famous reputation. In an advertisement she placed in the *Morning Post* of 3 March 1859, for her new business, she wrote:

Madame Rachel's Blanchinetta *and* Arab Bloom Powder *can only be obtained at Madame Rachel's residence, 480, New Oxford Street (opposite Mudie's library). All preparations notwithstanding there may be bear Madame Rachel's names and labels, if obtained elsewhere than at the above address, are spurious and decidedly injurious.*

Although this sounds like Sarah Russell now had a prestigious address, Oxford and New Oxford Street in the mid-19th century were renowned for cheap shops, prostitutes and con men. However, despite this, and probably due to advertisements like the above in many newspapers and magazines, together with the London women's desire to appear younger, she succeeded in carving out a good name for cosmetic products.

This success was built on lies – there were no laws about 'truth in advertising' in Victorian England. Seeing that she had a ready market, two months later in May 1859, the new 'Madame Rachel' asserted that she was selling her cosmetics to some of the most famous people in Europe and she reinforced her claim stating that she was connected to the French singer of the same name. Sarah Russell's advertisement said that she was 'a near kinswoman of the late lamented Tragedian of that name'.

Cashing in on the same name, and referring to herself as 'Madame R', she publicised her cosmetics saying that the French singer:

... who so fully appreciated [her products] that another order has been received by Madame R., whose success in restoring and beautifying the complexion, imparting a bewitching brilliancy to the eyes, removing all defects from the skin and teeth, and adding fresh grace and luxuriance to the hair, has been acknowledged by most of the crowned heads of Europe and the Aristocracy of this country.

Apart from telling the gullible public what her cosmetics could achieve, Sarah Russell also claimed that they were the 'purest, rarest and fragrant productions'. Her customers would receive everlasting youth and see tremendous changes in their skin, especially as the products were made out of pure and unpolluted ingredients. This was, of course, one big lie. Her 'Herbs of the Earth' and 'Liquid Flowers' for a soothing and cosmetic bath were made out of nothing but bran and water. In addition, her 'Armenian Liquid' and 'Magnetic Rock Dew Water' were guaranteed to remove wrinkles, while her 'Circassian Powder' allegedly worked wonders on her Victorian clientele's hands and nails. And if the above were not enough, 'Madame Rachel's' 'Chinese Leaves' and 'Indian Coal' were sure to rejuvenate your lips, cheeks and eyes respectively. Sarah Russell obviously realised that if she connected her cosmetics with exotic place names, her sales would increase.

As Geri Walton writes in *Unique Histories from the 18th and 19th Centuries*, fashionable Victorian women loved to have pale complexions. Therefore, Sarah Russell claimed that her products, which were of course exclusive, would 'enamel' the face and give the fortunate wearer the porcelain-looking skin they were striving for. Madame Rachel's oils and cosmetics would remove any hair through *'the use of Arabian Baths, composed of pure extracts of the liquid of flowers, choice and rare herbs, and other preparations equally harmless and efficacious'.*

Nothing could have been further from the truth. These alleged aids to beauty were cooked up at home and had no cosmetic value at all. Although the creams may have disguised ugly scars and pits in the face, because of their poisonous ingredients, they were dangerous to use.

One problem that Sarah Russell faced was that Victorian women wished to hide the fact that they were using make-up. 19th century standards equated painted faces with actresses and prostitutes and, as we have seen, this idea was reinforced by Queen Victoria's statement that skin cosmetics were vulgar and unladylike. In other words, if you wanted to be a stylish woman, you had to be discreet. Sarah Rachel Russel was the solution to the problem. In addition to her advertisements, she ran a salon.

There she could sell her products and also go one farther –
seeing that her customers wanted to buy her 'Royal
Arabian Toilet of Beauty', oils and creams anonymously,
'Madame Rachel' began blackmailing them.

"You don't want me to publish who my customers are,
do you?"

"No, no, of course not."

"Then that will cost you an extra…"

Exploiting her customers' weaknesses and desires to be
beautiful, Madame Rachel would persuade them to return
to her shop to buy more. Then after being presented with
an outrageous bill, the customer would discontinue from
buying any more cosmetics. This did not seem to faze our
'heroine', as there were always more gullible ladies
willing to part with their husbands' or lovers' hard-earned
money, paying several pounds a time for Madame's exotic
products.

All was going well until Sarah Rachel Russell
(sometimes called Levinson/Leverson after her second
husband) began selling her cosmetics to a Mrs Mary
Tucker Borradaile. This lady, the widow of a colonel,
wanted to recapture her youthful looks, was well-off and
extremely gullible. In other words, she was the perfect
victim for Madame Rachel.

Mrs Borradaile first met the 'promiser of eternal youth'
in early summer 1864 and bought some cosmetics. On
learning that her new customer was wealthy, 'Madame
Rachel' persuaded her to return later for more. Over the
next two years, she fleeced the old lady, who bought even
more of her cosmetician's beautifying and exotic powders,

soaps and creams. None of them, of course, made any difference to Mrs Borradaile's face, and if anything, their continuous use may have harmed her skin.

At the end of two years, Mrs Borradaile came to the conclusion that she had been wasting her time and a lot of money and she wanted to end the relationship.

*

"Good afternoon, Madame Rachel. How are you today?"

"I am fine, thank you," Madame Rachel smiled and curtsied a little. "I must say that your skin is looking so much better today, far better than when I saw you last week. Now, madame, what would you like to purchase today? Another bottle of Moroccan Rock Dew or some Royal Arabian Bath Oil?"

"I don't want to buy anything this time."

"What? Nothing? Nothing at all?" Madame Rachel replied, quickly hiding her shock at hearing this.

"No, Madame Rachel, I have decided that your creams and other things haven't made any marked difference at all, and I have come here today to tell you that I no longer wish to be considered as one of your customers."

"Ah, My dear Mrs Borradaile, that is such a shame that you are saying that, because I was just about to tell you that apart from the improvements my cosmetics have made to your complexion, that a certain gentleman who I know has expressed some – how shall I phrase it? – yes, some romantic interest in you."

"And who is this gentleman?"

198

"Lord Ranelagh, my dear, a very good man, and one who is very rich as well."

"But how do you know this? I have never met him, and as far as I know, I have never been in his presence."

"Ah, Mrs Borradaile," Madame Rachel replied, tapping the side of her nose. "Those of us in the business know such things. Although you may never have met him, as you say, he has been looking at you from afar and now that you are looking so beautiful and attractive, he would like to marry you."

"But he doesn't know me."

Madame Rachel shrugged. "Huh, that is no problem. I'll arrange for him to meet you. Would it be in order if he came to your residence tomorrow for afternoon tea?"

*

And so it was. Sarah Russell contacted Lord Ranelagh, who promptly went to visit the colonel's widow the following day. This was to be the first of several visits, and in the meanwhile, not only did the naïve Mrs Borradaile change her mind about stopping paying Madame Rachel for more cosmetics, but she began to buy even more. Much more. Madame Rachel persuaded her to spend £1,000 to beautify herself for His Lordship, and in order to do so, the widow began selling off some of her stocks.

Mrs Borradaile must have been extremely trusting, for she went along with Madame Rachel's instruction that, at least for the beginning of the wooing, the matter was to be carried out completely by mail. After this, Madame Rachel explained, the marriage would be by proxy.

Thus, Mrs Borradaile began receiving love-letters from her 'William' (whose real name was Thomas Heron Jones, 7th Viscount Ranelagh) addressed to 'my only dearly beloved Mary'. He expressed all the correct sentiments about love and courtship, while also advising her to listen to whatever 'Granny' Madame Rachel told her. Naturally, some of this advice included instructions that she should continue buying cosmetics at Madame Rachel's salon.

The lovelorn widow did as she was told, not realising that she was in fact reading forged letters penned by Madame Rachel herself. In order to cover herself, the crafty purveyor of hope and beauty kept copies of all of the letters: those she had written in the name of Lord Ranelagh and those that she had sent under her own name to Mrs Borradaile.

The wooing progressed and through one of Madame Rachel's letters Lord Ranelagh proposed marriage to the gullible widow. Mrs Borradaile accepted and the bride-to be paid Madame Rachel money for carriages and lace, in addition to making over £1,600 (more than £200,000 today) in bonds for the groom. The beloved William told Mrs Borradaile to hand over all her jewels to 'Granny', justifying this by saying that once they were married, he would buy her even finer ones. Madame Rachel then sold the jewels and kept the money.

By this time, the future Lady Ranelagh had been stripped of all her worldly goods, but this was not enough for the avaricious Sarah Rachel Russell. She threatened her client over the £1,600 in bonds and this proved to be the straw that broke the camel's back. Now Mrs Borradaile, supported by her family, realised that she had been thoroughly duped and went to the Marlborough Street police station to lodge a complaint.

As a result, Madame Rachel was accused of obtaining money by false pretences and conspiracy to commit fraud. Mrs Borradaile now sued her for a sum between four and five thousand pounds.

It was probably at the ensuing trial at the Central Criminal Court in London, the Old Bailey, that the yellow-haired and heavily made-up Mrs Borradaile met her hoped-for future husband perhaps for only the third time. There the suave, heavily bearded 7th Viscount Ranelagh was questioned.

*

"How well, my lord, do you know Mrs Mary Tucker, Borradaile?"

"I don't know her really, Your Honour. I may have met her in the past, and if so, only on very short occasions."

"And apart from that, Viscount Ranelagh, have you had any other direct dealings with the lady in the past?"

"No, Your Honour, None."

"Have you ever expressed any intention of marrying the aforementioned Mrs Borradaile, verbally or in a written form?"

"No, never. I am perfectly happy with my own bachelor status."

Murmuring and laughter was heard in court at this

point, an acknowledgement of Ranelagh's philandering with famous women, married or not.

"Viscount Ranelagh, did you know anything about the financial arrangements between Mrs Borradaile and the accused, Mrs Sarah Rachel Russell?"

"No, Your Honour, I have not been involved in any of their financial dealings."

"Viscount Ranelagh, have you ever written her any love-letters?"

"No, Your Honour. Any lady I communicate with, I do so directly, not through Her Majesty's postal services."

More murmuring was heard in court on the subject of Ranelagh's well-known affairs.

"Viscount Ranelagh, have you ever asked the defendant, Mrs Borradaile, for any money?"

"No, Your Honour."

"Not even a small sum?"

"No, Your Honour. Nothing. Not even a brass farthing. As you may know, I am affluent enough to be able to stand on my own two financial feet without needing to ask anyone for help."

*

After hearing this series of denials and listening to what 'Madame Rachel' had to say in her defence, the judge ordered the jury to reach a verdict. Then came the surprise of the day. After deliberating the proceedings for over four hours, the jury declared that it was deadlocked and was unable to come up with a verdict. A retrial was called for.

This second trial took place one month later and lasted four days, starting on 22 September 1868, and was again held at the Old Bailey. The prosecution, among other accusations, charged that Sarah Rachel Russell was a procuress and 'a woman of loose habits, who was willing to prostitute herself'. As proof, they submitted the letters Mrs Borradaile had written at Madame Rachel's dictation. In defence, Mrs Borradaile admitted that she had indeed written such letters, but that she had never been in league with her supposed husband-to-be in order to defraud anyone.

Again, Viscount Ranelagh was questioned *vis-à-vis* his relationship to Mrs Borradaile and Madame Rachel. He repeated that he had never had any intention to marry the colonel's widow and that he had no need to defraud her of any money. He said that he had not worked in tandem with Madame Rachel, but that he had, on occasion, visited her salon out of curiosity.

*

"Viscount Ranelagh, and why did you do that?"

"Because I wanted to see at first-hand who this Madame Rachel really was."

"And for no other reason?"

"You don't suppose I went there to get enamelled, do you?"

Tittering in court followed this remark.

"And do you know who this 'William' is who is mentioned in the alleged correspondence between yourself and Mrs Borradaile?"

"No, Your Honour. I have no idea at all."

*

Again the judge, Mr Commissioner Kerr, ordered the jury to come up with a verdict and this time they did so. It took them only fifteen minutes to find 'Madame Rachel' guilty. They declared that Madame Rachel, alias Sarah Rachel Russell, was guilty of using 'false and fraudulent means' to defraud Mrs Borradaile of a large amount of money and property. The maker of 'pure and rare' cosmetics was sentenced to serve five years of penal servitude, beginning at Millbank Prison.

Two interesting aspects of this trial were the testimony of Mrs Borradaile and the fear of several of Madame Rachel's patrons that their names as such would become known to the public. As the *Cardiff Times*, (3 Oct. 1868), one of the many newspapers which reported on this trial, noted:

Each day the court has been crowded with listeners expecting to catch a glimpse of aristocratic depravity or middle-class folly.

Even though Mrs Borradaile won, the *Morning Post* (23 September 1868) noted that in a way, she did not get away from this sensational trial scot-free. The newspapers mocked her for having paid one thousand guineas so that she could be made 'beautiful forever', as Madame Rachel had promised. They also laughed at her for saying, "I should be made beautiful for ever before I was married to the rich and good man she had introduced me to... Lord Ranelagh. I did take more than a hundred baths by her direction... She always said that I must do as she told me."

But this was not the end of the road for Sarah Rachel Russell. She was released from Brixton prison in 1872 and without wasting too much time, established herself in a new salon in the West End, and from there she went back to selling cosmetics of a dubious nature. Unsurprisingly, the name of her new business boasted a sign saying, 'Arabian Performer to the Queen'. Naturally Sarah Rachel Russell did not define the name of this particular queen.

However, what was perhaps even more surprising was that, despite the massive publicity her trial had generated, more and more ladies queued up to buy the proven fake, allegedly curative oils, face-powders and creams, and very soon business was booming. All of these cosmetics of course came from supposedly exotic locales, and in order to impress her new customers, Helen Rapaport writes in *Beautiful For Ever: Madame Rachel of Bond Street*, 'Madame Rachel' would greet them decked out in lush robes, dripping jewels and with crystal talismans around her neck. When any of her customers had the temerity to ask her about her trial and imprisonment, she would say that she had been 'the victim of a vile conspiracy'. She would then add that the Right Honourable Henry Bruce, the Liberal Home Secretary himself, had cleared her name.

During this period she was arrested for fraud a few times, but somehow managed to stay out of prison again that is, until she met Mrs Cecilia Pearce. This woman paid Madame Rachel a small fortune to cure her skin problems, including giving her cosmetician some jewellery. Nothing helped. In fact, Mrs Pearce's skin broke out in a painful rash and the poor woman demanded the return of her jewels. Sarah Russell refused, and when Mrs Pearce insisted, the latter told her that she 'would make the city ring' with all that she knew about Mrs Pearce's affairs.

Unfortunately, Mrs Pearce was nothing like Mary Tucker Borradaile. She was a much tougher character and she had a husband to support her claims. Together they called Madame Rachel's bluff and obtained a warrant for her arrest. She was charged with intent to defraud.

The trial took place in 1878, and many of Sarah Russell's secrets were exposed to the public.

*

"Is it true, Mrs Russell-Leverson, er, that is your full name, isn't it?"

"Yes, Your Honour, except that I rarely use the Leverson bit."

"I see, and so is it true that you used only pure ingredients in your cosmetics?"

"Yes, Your Honour. That is indeed the case. I would never –"

"Then why is it that the forensic officers have found that you have used such dangerous materials as arsenic, lead, starch and hydrochloric acid in your products?"

"Well, Your Honour, it is like this. I may on occasion

have used –"

"And why if your creams etc. are so beneficial, why, as has been claimed in this court, have you not used them on yourself?"

"Your Honour, I believe at my stage in life, that they would not be so beneficial. You see, I am now eighty-five years old and I have no need to make myself look any younger."

The judge paused and looked at his notes. "Excuse me, Mrs Russell, but according to what I have written here before me, you were born in 1814 or thereabouts. This means that you are now merely sixty-four years old, some twenty-one years less than what you have just claimed."

The trial continued and at last the judge ordered the jury to go into their room and come up with a verdict. The question was, would this jury act in a similar way as the first jury had done ten years earlier? The answer was no. Within ten to fifteen minutes the jury walked back into the crowded and hushed courtroom to resume their places.

"Have you reached a verdict?" the judge asked.

"Yes, Your Honour," the foreman replied. "We have."

"And what is it?"

"Guilty, Your Honour."

*

Mrs Sarah Rachel Russell was convicted for a second time, this time for 'unlawfully obtaining from Mrs Cecilia Maria Pearce two necklaces and other articles by false pretences'. She was sentenced to serve another five years and was sent to Woking Prison. There she became very ill and was taken to hospital. It was found that she was suffering from catarrh and later this illness was compounded by rheumatism, dropsy (the old word for edema, an inordinate amount of fluid in certain parts of the body) and heart disease. She died in Woking Prison on 12 October 1880, having served less than half of her sentence. She was sixty-six years old. The *Illustrated Police News* reported that the coroner said that she had died of various illnesses while a later jury claimed that the dropsy and her other fatal ailments were a 'visitation from God'. She was buried in a cemetery in Willesden, north-west London, near where Sir George Lewis, one of the prosecutors against her in 1868, was also buried.

However, what may be considered strange is that, even while Madame Rachel was serving her second prison sentence, and despite all the negative publicity her second trial had generated, there were still women who wrote to her for advice about how to be 'beautiful forever'.

Not much is known about her descendants except that her daughter, Helene Crossmond-Turner, became an opera-singer. In 1888, following an argument with the producer over a contract to sing at Covent Garden, she shot herself in the back of a cab in central London and died soon after.

Ninety years later, Glyn Jones wrote a play, *Beauty For Ever – A Play for Women* based on the grasping Madame Rachel's deal made with the foolish Mrs Borradaile. In the drama Madame Rachel is supported by her daughter,

Leontine, and both use their knowledge of chemicals that they had learned from one of Madame Rachel's husbands.

Was Sarah Rachel Russell really a wicked woman?

She did not murder anyone or cause anyone to die, but it may be said that her deliberate and mass deception of Victorian ladies who just wished to improve their looks was certainly an immoral act. Perhaps the question to be asked here is not one about just fooling people and taking their money, but rather the scale of her crimes and her duping of so many gullible women. She defrauded Mrs Borradaile of a sum amounting to about £5,000 (about half a million pounds today) and even after she had completed her first prison sentence, she did not express any remorse. In fact, she continued with her old lifestyle and went on to steal jewellery and 'other articles' from Mrs Cecilia Pearce and probably from several other women as well. If Sarah Rachel Russell was not wicked, what was she?

Chapter Fourteen

Mary Ann Cotton (1832-1873)
Serial Killer

County Durham in the north-east of England can sometimes be a very grey and dreary place (I should know because I lived there for four years), but it was probably even more so in the 19th century when the landscape was dotted with coalmines and slag heaps and nothing was done to control the pollution in the air. At the same time, the major rivers of the area, the Tyne and the Wear, were the sites of the important shipbuilding industry centred around Newcastle and Sunderland, the latter being known as the world's largest shipbuilding town.

One of these coalmines was to be found at Murton, County Durham, eight miles east of the historic city of Durham. Until the first coal-pit was sunk in 1838, Murton had been one of the many agricultural villages which had made up much of the north-east of England. After this date, coal overtook agriculture and, at one point, the Murton colliery employed one thousand men. As well as completely changing the local economy and landscape, the coalmines brought dirt and disease with them. However, the grim reality of working in the mines was surpassed by the tale of a local lass, Mary Ann Cotton.

*

If you look at the iconic photo of Mary Cotton, you will see the Victorian image of a woman aged about forty wearing a bonnet over her hair, which is parted in the middle. On her unremarkable face there is a not too intelligent expression and she is wearing a checked coat or shawl. If you had passed her on the village street in Murton, County Durham, you would probably not have noticed anything unusual about her as she looked typical of the time and the place.

Mary Cotton was born Mary Robinson on 31 October 1832 at Low Moorsley, County Durham to a staunch Methodist family. Her father, Michael, worked in the new coalmine and her mother, Margaret, was a housewife. She had a sister, Margaret, who was born two years later but who died soon after and a brother, Robert, who was born in 1835.

When she was five (or eight), the family moved to Murton, and at some point while she was a young girl, her father died, falling three hundred feet to his death down a mineshaft. This meant that Mary, who had been described by the school superintendent as 'a most exemplary and regular attender of school', and a pupil who was of 'innocent disposition and average intelligence', had to leave school and become a nurse in order to supplement the family's income. Her father's unexpected death cannot have been made any easier when his body was handed over to her mother for burial in a sack stamped, 'Property of the South Hetton Coal Company'. The immediate result was that the family had to move, as their cottage was owned by the coalmine.

Fortunately, domestic finances improved within a year or two, when Mary's mother married George Stott, another coalminer. When Mary was sixteen, in 1848, she left home and went to work as a nurse in the nearby village of South Hetton. Four years later the attractive twenty-year-old Mary married William Mowbray, another coalminer. He was to be the first of her four husbands and several lovers.

The couple moved to Plymouth on the south coast and had five or six children in quick succession, but four of them died of 'gastric fever'. After this they returned to County Durham, where William worked as a fireman on a steamship. In the meanwhile, they had three more children, of whom either two or all of them died. The reason for the vagueness here is that during this period deaths were not always recorded when they were supposed to be. It was not until 1874 that the law concerning the registration of deaths was strictly enforced.

When William Mowbray died in Sunderland in 1865 of an intestinal problem, Mary received £35 (over £3,400 today) from their life insurance policy. As a result, she moved to Seaham Harbour in County Durham, where she fell in love with Joseph Nattrass. For some reason this relationship did not develop into marriage, and so she moved to Sunderland, where she worked as a nurse at the local infirmary. There she met her second husband, engineer George Ward. It was during this period that her daughter died of typhus, which meant that of the nine or ten children she had borne, only one was still alive. Death seemed to follow Mary. George died one year after they were married from a form of paralysis and intestinal problems. Apparently he had not been well when they had 'tied the knot', but it meant that again Mary received money from the family's insurance company.

Now Mary had to look for work again, and she found a job as a housekeeper for James Robinson, a Sunderland shipwright. His wife had recently died and soon after Mary joined his household, the Robinson baby son too died of gastric fever. So too did Mary's daughter, Isabella Mowbray, as well as James Robinson's two other children. As Isabella was her own daughter, Mary received yet another insurance payment.

While living with her new employer, Mary became pregnant and gave birth to his daughter, but she too died early after Mary married James Robinson in 1867. In the same year, death also claimed Mary's mother. Two years later, Mary and James Robinson had a second child,

George, born in June 1869. This meant that by the time Mary was thirty-six, at least ten of her children had died. It was during this period that James Robinson became suspicious of Mary's insistence that he should insure his life.

*

"Why?" he asked.

"Well, my dearest," Mary replied, putting on a winning smile. "You wouldn't like to leave me penniless, like what happened to the wife of our neighbour, would you?"

"No, but –"

"And think of our dear baby, George Robert, you don't want him to be brought up in poverty, do you?"

"No, no, of course not, but there's another thing I want to talk to you about –"

"What's that, my dear? Don't you like my newest bonnet that I bought yesterday?"

"No, no, it's nothing to do with that. It's to do with this." And James slid a pile pf papers over the table towards her.

"What are these, my dear?" Mary asked, already guessing the answer.

"They are bills," he replied. "Bills for £60, that's what they are. Bills that you have run up without me knowing anything about them until today."

"I'm sure there must be a mistake, James," Mary said, getting up. "But now I must see about young George's supper. It's going to burn."

"*Let it burn!*" the angry James Robinson shouted. "I want some answers. And yes, what happened to the £50 I gave you at the end of last month? Where is that?"

"What £50, James?"

"The £50 I gave you to bank, Mary. It's not there. I spoke to the bank manager this morning and that's how I learned about your debts and the missing £50. Now what do you have to say about this? We are talking here about £110 altogether (approximately £15,000 today). Now out with it, woman. What have you got to say for yourself?"

"Well, James, you know I needed a new hat and also the price of food has gone up a lot recently and –"

James slammed his huge fist down on the table, making the cutlery jump. "Stop it with these stories and tell me the truth!"

"But, James, I am. I –"

"And another thing. What's this I hear about you making my older children pawn some of their mother's jewellery and knick-knacks?"

"It's not true."

"So, my children are liars, are they?"

"No, James, it's just that –"

"Yes, it's just that I couldn't find my dearest Hannah's necklace yesterday. When I asked Robert if he had seen it, he broke down and told me the truth. Now what have you got to say to that?"

"Nothing, I –"

"That's right. You have nothing to say. Go and pack your bags and make sure that you are out of this house within the hour. I'm going out. If you are here when I return, I will send for the police. Now woman, get out of my sight!"

*

That night Mary was penniless and without a husband again. James had retained custody of their son, George, and the desperate woman needed a bed and board immediately. Fortunately, her friend, Margaret Cotton was at hand.

"How about moving in with my brother, Frederick?" she suggested. "His wife died recently and I know he needs a housekeeper to help him look after his two children, Charles and Frederick Junior. The poor lamb," Margaret sighed. "I do feel for him so. Apart from his wife dying, two of his other children also died. I would take them in myself, but my house is far too small."

*

Soon Mary had a roof over herself and a new man in her life. She became pregnant yet again, and she and Frederick Cotton were married bigamously at Newcastle-upon-Tyne. Their son, Robert, was born in 1871.

Mary's life continued in its regular way. Frederick Cotton, who was a sick man, died within two years from 'gastric fever' and Mary collected on the insurance while she was living with her former lover, Joseph Nattrass, some thirty miles away in West Auckland, County Durham. She had moved in with him when she had found out that he was no longer married.

Officially, Nattrass became Mary's lodger, and to make some more money she also worked as a private nurse to a John Quick Manning. (This may not have been his real name, which may have been Richard Quick Mann.) She had her thirteenth child with him. Meanwhile, Frederick Cotton Jr. died in March 1872, and was soon followed by his younger brother, Robert. Very soon after this, Nattrass became ill with gastric fever and just before he died, he changed his will in Mary's favour. As before, Mary cashed in on her dead husband's insurance policy.

Up until this time, apart from losing most of her children, four husbands and at least one lover, financially Mary had done well out of life. But now she came under suspicion. Perhaps she had avoided such a situation so far by constantly changing her address within County Durham.

Thomas Riley, a parish official, asked Mary to help one of the local villagers suffering from smallpox. She agreed, but on the condition that her last surviving son, Charles Cotton, could move into the local workhouse.

*

"I'm sorry, Mrs Cotton," Riley replied. "As West Auckland's assistant coroner, I cannot agree to that."

"But I insist."

"I'm sorry, madam, but it can't be done."

"Well, I could have been married to my late husband's brother," an aggrieved Mrs Cotton said. "Anyway, as for the boy, he won't live long. He'll go like all the rest of the Cotton family."

"You don't mean that a healthy boy like him will die?" Riley asked, not really believing what he was saying.

"Oh, yes."

*

Five days later, Mary's prediction came true. Charles was dead and Mary said she was ready to take on the nursing post. Instead of employing her, Riley went to the police and convinced the local doctor to delay writing out a death certificate until Charles' death could be investigated more fully. This angered Mary as she could not claim the insurance money until a valid death certificate had been issued.

An inquest was held in which Mary said that she had used arrowroot to cure her stepson's illness. She also claimed that Riley had brought the matter up because she had rejected his romantic advances. Mary won and the jury returned a verdict that young Charles Cotton had died of natural causes.

However, this was not the end of the case. A story concerning an alleged but unproved murder and the desire to claim the insurance money soon appeared in the local press. The local authorities began to ask questions and soon found out that Mary had lived in several different towns in County Durham where three of her four husbands, her mother, her lover and several of her children had died. Not only that, but they had all died of various forms of gastric fever.

A Doctor William Byers Kilburn was asked to conduct a thorough investigation. Unfortunately for Mary, he had been Charles Cotton's doctor and had kept some samples taken from him. He had the boy's body exhumed and in the tests he carried out, he saw that the corpse contained arsenic. As a result, the again pregnant Mary Cotton was arrested and charged with murder. The trial was postponed until 10 January 1873, that is, until she had given birth to a girl, who was named Margaret Edith Quick-Manning Cotton.

As Mary stood in the dock she unsuccessfully tried to present an image of a concerned mother. Witness after witness painted unflattering portraits of her, some saying that she had treated her young stepson violently. In addition, Doctor Kilburn testified that he had found traces of arsenic in the body.

"Please tell the court, Doctor Kilburn," Mr Campbell Foster, Mary's defence barrister asked, "what colour was the wallpaper in the boy's room? Was it green? Paris green or Scheele's green?"

"No," replied Doctor Kilburn. "It was not green, and even if it had been it would not have caused the death of this young boy. It's true, I have read about arsenic in wallpaper causing death, but I doubt if this is what happened here."

Later on, Doctor Scattergood of Leeds College of Medicine was brought in as an expert witness for the prosecution. In his testimony he claimed that a tiny sliver of onion skin had been found in Charles Cotton's stomach and that this had contained arsenic. He also admitted that he had heard of wallpaper being 'injurious' to people's health, but that he had never heard of anyone actually dying because of it. He also suggested that arsenic may have been present in the house in the form of cleaning materials. In addition, in those days, arsenic was contained in the paint used for children's toys.

This question of arsenic being used in green wallpaper was a well-known concern. For instance, in this edition of the *South London Chronicle* (16 March 1878):

According to the present custom of the trade... [of using arsenic in green wallpaper] *as some recent analyses have resulted in the startling disclosure that many of the pale-coloured wallpapers contain from 15 to 25 grains of arsenic per square foot...*

Later, several of the other bodies of Mary's former children, as well as that of Joseph Nattrass, were exhumed, and they too were found to contain traces of arsenic. In addition, there was also discussion in the court and in the press that something should be done about paying out insurance claims when there was a question of foul play involved.

On 20 March 1873 the judge ordered the jury to retire to consider their verdict. It took them ninety minutes for their foreman to declare that Mary Cotton was guilty. That day, the correspondent for *The Times* wrote that after she had heard the verdict, she was sure that she would receive a royal pardon and not be hanged for murdering her several husbands and children.

Several petitions were presented to the Home Secretary, but they were to no avail. In a grim scene witnessed by fifty observers, Mary Ann Cotton, now nicknamed the 'West Auckland Borgia' (after Lucrezia Borgia, the late medieval much-married Italian [and rumoured] poisoner) walked to the gallows from her cell 'ghostly pale with a firm step, praying audibly and earnestly with her eyes uplifted. She never confessed to her crimes'.

She was hanged at Durham Gaol on 24 March 1873 in a botched execution. Instead of the noose breaking her neck, she died after being slowly strangled. Over one hundred years later when Durham Gaol was being refurbished, her grave was discovered and the shoes and some of her bones were removed and cremated.

Her death became a *cause célèbre* and children in County Durham and elsewhere happily chanted the following nursery rhyme as they played and skipped rope:

Mary Cotton, she's dead and she's rotten,
Lying in bed with her eyes wide open.
Sing, sing oh what can I sing?
Mary Cotton is tied up with string.

Where? Where? Up in the air.
Selling black puddings a penny a pair.

Mary Cotton, she's dead and forgotten,
Lying in bed with her bones all rotten.

Sing, sing, what can I sing?
Mary Cotton, tied up with string.

Over 140 years later, Mary Cotton would return to the British (and international) public through a two-part TV mini-series called *Dark Angel* (2016). This was part of a seven-episode series about notorious British serial killers which also featured the dramas *The Brides in the Bath,* about George Joseph Smith, (1872-1915) and *A is for Acid,* about the 'Acid Bath Murderer', John George Haigh, (1909-1949).

Mary Ann Cotton – Timeline

1832 – 31 Oct: Mary Ann Cotton (née Robinson) born in Low Moorsley, Co. Durham.

1834 – Margaret, (sister), born and died.

1835 – Robert, (brother), born.

1837 (or 1840) – Mary & family move to Murton, Co. Durham.

1842 – Feb: Father dies in coalmining accident. Family evicted from 'tied cottage'.

1848 – Mary moves to South Hetton, County Durham to become a nurse.

1852 – Mary marries William Mowbray, (first husband) and moves to Plymouth.

1852-56 – Five or six children born. All die young except one.

1856 – Margaret Jane, (daughter) born.

1858 – Isabella, (daughter) born.

1860 – Margaret Jane (daughter) dies aged two.

1861 – Margaret Jane #2 (daughter) born.

1863 – John Robert William (son) born.

1864 – John Robert William age one dies of gastric fever. Mary collects on his insurance.

1865 – Jan: William Mowbray (husband) dies of intestinal disorder. Mary collects on his insurance. Mary moves in with Joseph Nattrass (boyfriend). Mary Jane #2 dies aged 3½. Mary moves to Sunderland and works as a nurse at the infirmary. Sends Isabella (daughter) to live with Mary's mother. 28 August: Mary marries her second husband, George Ward.

1866 – 20 Oct: George Ward dies intestinal problems after 14-month marriage. Nov: Mary becomes housekeeper to James Robinson, shipwright. Dec: Robinson's baby son, John, dies of gastric fever.

1867 – Spring: Mary's mother dies of stomach problems. (It was suggested but never proved if Mary may have been involved with this). Mary's daughter Isabella Mowbray dies of stomach pains after moving to Robinson's house. Two of James Robinson's children, Richard and Elizabeth die of similar pains. 11 Aug: Mary marries her third husband, James Robinson. Nov: Margaret Isabella Robinson born.

1868 – Feb: Mary's daughter, Margaret Isabella Robinson, dies after three months.

1869 – June: George Robinson born. James Robinson throws Mary out for stealing his money.

1870 – 17 Sept: Mary bigamously marries her fourth husband, Frederick Cotton. Has son, Frederick Cotton Jr.

1871 – Spring: Robert Cotton (son) born. Mary meets Joseph Nattrass (past lover) in West Auckland, Co. Durham and Cotton family move to be near him. Dec: Husband Frederick Cotton dies of gastric fever.

1872 – Mary moves in with Joseph Nattrass. Becomes nurse to John Quick-Manning/Richard Quick-Mann. March: Frederick Cotton Jr. dies and son Robert dies soon after of gastric fever. Nattrass dies of gastric fever soon after changing his will in Mary's favour. Mary collects on the insurance. Mary pregnant with her thirteenth child.

1873 – Mary arrested after Thomas Riley, local assistant coroner, becomes suspicious of the number and similarity of deaths in Mary's family, including that of son, Charles Edward Cotton on 10 Jan. Mary's daughter, Mary Edith Quick-Manning Cotton born in Durham Gaol. 5 March: Mary's trial for murder opens. 20 March: Mary convicted of murder. 20-24 March: Unsuccessfully petitions the Home Secretary for a reprieve. 24 March: Mary hanged in botched execution in Durham Gaol.

Chapter Fifteen

Minnie Dean (1844-1895)
New Zealand's Baby Killer

Minnie Dean at the time of her marriage, 1873

What is your image of New Zealand? Is it a panoramic picture of green rolling hills dotted with woolly white sheep and dramatic mountains in the background? Is it a place where you find rocky coastlines and mountains reaching down to the sea? Perhaps for you, New Zealand is a place where people stand on high bridges before they throw themselves off into the river below in death-defying bungee jumps? Or instead do you think of people who roll down hills inside huge plastic balls while attempting to achieve a new zorbing record?

Perhaps you think of the Māori, that is, the native people, or of the black-uniformed rugby team, the All Blacks? Or does your mind's eye have a picture of European-looking towns such as Auckland or Wellington, complete with modern skyscrapers, harbours and green areas for sport and recreation?

Usually, apart from sports, that is, New Zealand as a country does not often appear in the world's headlines. If it does, it is because an event such as the massive earthquake that shook the city of Christchurch on the South Island in February 2011 was sufficiently dramatic, or else the terrible tragedy of the mass shooting that took place in a mosque in the same city in March 2019. This chapter covers an event not so internationally known as those recent cataclysms, but which was sensational enough to the press in 1895, when Minnie Dean, a fifty-year old woman from Invercargill, New Zealand, was charged with infanticide.

*

The early details of the life of Minnie Dean (born Williamina Irene McCulloch) vary according to which source you read. Some say she was born in 1844 in Greenock on the Clyde Estuary west of Glasgow in September 1844; others say she was born in Edinburgh in 1847. Similarly, some of the records state that her father, John, was a railway engineer or driver, and that her mother, Elizabeth, died from cancer when Minnie was a

226

teenager, while other sources draw a complete blank over her early years. However, what we do know is that by the time she was twenty, she may have been married to an unnamed husband and had two daughters. We do not know what happened to them, but it is recorded that by the 1860s Minnie had crossed the world and arrived in Invercargill, New Zealand's southernmost town. But whatever had happened to her, no evidence has been found recording her possible marriage, the births of her children and the death of her alleged first husband.

Why she decided to settle in this small, isolated town is another unanswered question, but according to Barbara Brookes, a New Zealand historian, Dean told people that she was the widow of an Australian doctor and the daughter of a Presbyterian minister back home in Scotland. The reason she lied was that when she arrived in Invercargill alone and pregnant, this would have definitely painted a suspicious picture in the mid-19th century. Another New Zealand historian, Lynley Hood, in her book *Minnie Dean: Her Life and Crimes* (1995), suggests that Minnie's lies were aimed to cover up the fact that both of her daughters, Ellen and Isabelle, were illegitimate and that perhaps she had been sent off to the colonies because she had brought shame to her Scottish family.

However, what we do know is that Minnie first lived there with an old woman she called Granny Kelly and who may have been a member of her family. When she was in her late twenties, Minnie became a governess and married Charles Dean, an innkeeper or farmer. They moved to his home at Etal Creek, an important railway stop in the area, particularly during the 1860s Otago Gold Rush. Unfortunately for the young couple, this gold rush lasted for only a few years. Sometime after the gold had run out they moved to the Larches, an abandoned house, as the pub which they had been running had failed. The Larches was a two-storeyed, seven or eight-roomed house sitting on a twenty-two-acre estate at East Winton. Here, some twenty miles from Invercargill, they started a pig or cattle farm. But now they had to face two problems.

The first was that the farm was unsuccessful and the second was that soon after they moved in, a fire burned their house down. In order to make sure that they had a roof over their heads, they built a two-roomed cottage with a lean-to and moved into that. In addition to losing their house, a man to who they owed money came and dug up all their fruit trees and took them away.

From their small hovel of a cottage Charles and Minnie Dean tried to sort out their future. But before they could do so, one of Minnie's infant daughters drowned in a well. Some people did not believe this story, as there was talk of the poverty-stricken Minnie killing the child in order to save on domestic expenses. But whatever was the reason, the 'accident' allowed the little girl to be given a Christian burial.

It was also at about this time that Minnie, desperate for a way of making some money, set up a 'baby-farming' business, inserting advertisements in the local press saying that she would care for babies and young infants. A typical ad read: 'Respectable married woman (comfortable home and more details) wants to adopt an infant'. Minnie Dean signed legal agreements for most of the babies that she took care of and collected sums of between five to eight shillings per week, or lump sums of between ten and thirty pounds paid in advance.

This meant that in most cases, poor women would hand over their unwanted babies or very young infants to 'baby-farmers' such as Minnie Dean, paying them to look after their unwanted offspring. Since most of these unfortunate children came from poor homes or were born to prostitutes, they were often not in good health and died soon after being taken over by the baby-farmer.

The term baby-farmer itself was deliberately insulting, as it implied that the woman in question was only undertaking the task for the money and not for the benefit of the mother, who would then be able to go to work. During the mid-19th century baby-farmers acquired a bad reputation, especially after some, for example Margaret Waters and Amelia Dyer in Britain, were found to have killed many of their infant charges in order to make a profit – as with the children dead they had few or no expenses. Waters was hanged in 1870 and it was believed that she had killed nineteen babies. In Dyer's case, although she was eventually hanged in 1896 for the murder of one child, it was thought that over a thirty-year period, she had killed about four hundred babies and infants. (A more detailed account of Amelia Dyer's murderous activities may be found in this book's companion volume, *Villains of Yore.)*

Minnie ran her business for over 20 years, looking after up to about nine children at a time, without arousing any suspicion. When one or two died, nobody asked any questions, as a high infant mortality was seen as natural in rural New Zealand at that time and several of Minnie's charges were known to have been sickly from the beginning. That Minnie was able to keep her activities under wraps for such a long time was probably due to the isolation of her house and also because the whole business of registering births and deaths was not strictly enforced by the local authorities. Another factor that kept the business flourishing was the shame felt by the mothers who had their babies farmed out who naturally did their best to keep their dubious arrangements secret. However, in either March or October 1889 Minnie and her business came to the attention of the authorities.

*

One evening while Minnie was preparing an evening meal for herself and her husband, there was a loud knocking on the front door.

"Charles," Minnie asked. "Can you be a dear and see who it is? I'm in the middle of making your supper you know, the way you like your lamb grilled, and I'm afraid it will burn or dry out if I leave it."

Charles grudgingly stopped reading about a murder in his local newspaper and went to open the front door. To his surprise he saw a young police constable standing there, holding an official looking document.

"Good evening, sir," the constable asked. "Is this the residence of Mrs Williamina Dean?"

"Yes, it is, although most people know her as Minnie.

Why, what do you want her for?"

"And does she take in babies and little'uns to look after?"

"Yes, she's been doing this for some time now, officer. Why, is there anything amiss?"

"Is your wife at home?"

"Yes, she's busy making supper. Can I help? Is anything wrong?"

"Let me please talk to your wife, sir, and we'll know soon enough."

Charles called Minnie to the door and the constable took out a small notebook.

"Mrs Dean," he began. "Have you been looking after a six-month old baby who died recently?"

"Yes," Minnie replied. "The poor little mite was not healthy when I started taking care of him and he died of convulsions. All blue and shaking he was. It was terrible to look at him and I was helpless to do anything about it." Minnie took out a large handkerchief out of her pocket and made a show of wiping her eyes.

"I see," the constable said. "Well, we'll have this recorded and I hope that the rest of the little ones who come into your care will have much better luck."

*

Minnie was lucky. The inquest concluded that the baby had died of inflammation of the heart's valves and congestion of the lungs. The coroner thought that Minnie had tried to care for the baby but that her premises at the

231

Larches were too cramped for her to continue in her line of work. However, if she wished to continue doing so, it would be advisable for her to accept fewer babies to care for. This did not stop her, although she did slightly reduce the number of the babies she took in. When she did take on new babies, she often used a false name with their parents. Two years later, in May or October 1891, she was questioned again after a six-week-old baby in her care died. An inquest was held and it was recorded that Minnie's small charge had died of natural causes, although some said that the real causes of death were cardiovascular and respiratory ailments.

By now the police were very suspicious of Minnie Dean and her activities and they decided to keep her under surveillance. However, they had to do so under very frustrating circumstances. They had no right to inspect the Deans' house without 'probable cause', and Minnie Dean and indeed all baby-farmers were not required by law to keep any records. In addition, the police were operating within a system that had very few child welfare laws. Those that did exist were inadequate.

In August 1893, the owner of a boarding-house in Christchurch contacted the police to say that a woman, later identified as Minnie Dean, had been given a three-week old baby while she was staying there. A detective was called in and he took the child away from the surprised Minnie. In his report he wrote, 'I believe this woman would have killed or abandoned this child before she got to Dunedin if it had not been taken from her'.

After this, Minnie began to run her business more

secretively and continued advertising using false names. It was during this period in 1894 that a very young boy in her care allegedly drowned, and instead of reporting this to the authorities, she buried the body in her garden. This, she must have hoped, would prevent her from having to attend yet another inquest. However, because the child was not seen again in the area local people become suspicious. This was especially so due to the grim reports of the large numbers of deaths at English and Australian baby-farms that had recently been sensationally reported. Another inquest was held but somehow, Minnie was not held responsible for the little boy's death. However, it did mean that this was yet another black mark against her name.

In the preceding decades, between 1872 and 1891, four baby-farming women had been tried for murdering their infant charges and were sentenced to death. All of these sentences were commuted to life imprisonment, but they set the general tone and background when Minnie Dean was eventually found out and brought to trial.

It all began in a very ordinary way. One day, a railway worker saw Minnie boarding a train near East Winton. She was carrying a young baby under one arm and a hatbox under the other. A day or so later, the same railway worker saw Minnie step down from the train carrying only the hatbox. This made the man suspicious. To be carrying a hatbox was a normal piece of luggage, but this particular box seemed to be very heavy and Minnie was having a hard time with it.

Knowing that the local police already had their suspicions about Mrs Dean, the railway worker reported what he had observed to the police. They began asking questions, and one thing led to another. At one point they went to speak to a Mrs Jane Hornsby.

*

"Good morning, Mrs Hornsby," the detective began once he had been shown into the lady's drawing room. "What can you tell us about any dealings you have had with a Mrs Minnie Dean of East Winton?"

"There isn't really that much to tell you, officer," Mrs Hornsby replied. "As my daughter is a working woman, she handed over her month-old daughter to Mrs Dean, who for a certain sum – I can't remember how much exactly it was – said that she would look after the wee one."

"Mrs Hornsby, did you or your daughter arrange to pay the money in instalments, or did Mrs Dean want it all in one go?"

"Oh, sir, she wanted it all in one lump sum. She was quite insistent on that."

"I see," the detective said, sucking on his pipe. "And if we took you to Mrs Dean's house, are you sure that you would be able to recognise her, that is, without a shadow of a doubt?"

"Oh, most certainly, sir. *That* would be no problem at all."

Soon after this, the police took Mrs Hornsby to Minnie Dean's house at Winton where she instantly recognised the baby-farmer standing in her front garden.

"Yes, sir," Mrs Hornsby whispered to the detective

behind her hand. "That is definitely Mrs Dean. I would swear to that on the Bible in court."

"Good," the detective smiled as he looked out of the carriage window. "Then this is what we'll do. We'll go into the house and I'll start asking some questions. While I am doing so, you will look around and see if you can see any evidence of your granddaughter having been there. Can you do that?"

Mrs Hornsby nodded, and they stepped out of the carriage and made their way over to the small house. They had hardly stepped inside when Mrs Hornsby clapped one hand over her mouth and started to wipe her eyes with her other.

"What's the matter?" the detective asked, thinking that the smell of urine which he had immediately smelt had affected her.

"Is it the smell of –?"

"No, no, sir," she said loosening her hand off her mouth. "Look at that little pink jacket, there in the corner. The knitted one with the little red and green flowers. I knitted that myself. Come, take me out of here. I cannot stay in here a moment longer."

*

The detective escorted her back to the carriage and then returned with his assistant to question Mrs Dean. An hour later, the detective left leaving his assistant behind to make sure that Mrs Dean and her husband, who had protested their innocence all along, would not leave.

Shortly afterwards the detective returned with the chief inspector and two other men in another carriage. The two other policemen had loaded several picks and shovels and empty boxes into their carriage before the party set off for the Deans' house. Once they had arrived, the chief inspector told the two policemen to start digging up the garden – the part of which could not be seen from the road and which was hidden by several tall kauri pine trees and bushes. As officers were doing so, Mr and Mrs Dean looked on without saying a word, apart from one moment when Mr Dean complained that they were harming his apple trees.

Within half an hour, one of the sweating policemen called out, "Sir, sir. I think I've found something!"

He was right. Under the gaze of Minnie and Charles Dean, the policeman then began to uncover the body of Mrs Hornsby's baby granddaughter. The half-rotten body of the infant was gently removed and lifted out of a leaf-covered shallow grave. After a quick inspection it was wrapped up in a long piece of cloth and placed in one of the boxes.

No sooner had the box been stowed aboard the carriage, than one of the other policemen, with his fingers to his nose, called out that he thought that he too had uncovered a body.

*

"Here, sir," he said to the Chief as he pointed down into the hole he had started digging. "There's a hand there. Can you see it? There by those brown stones."

Now surrounded by the other policemen, he continued digging, and soon he too was carefully uncovering the body of another baby.

"I think it's a girl, sir," the policeman said, wiping his brow. "Yes, I'm sure it is. Just look at its golden hair. She looks a bit like my Alice."

This little body was also carefully dug up, wrapped up and placed in another box which was taken to the carriage. Then the chief inspector turned to face the Deans.

"Are there any more? Or are we going to have to dig up the whole garden?"

Mr Dean looked blank.

"How should I know?" Minnie answered defiantly. "I never buried them there. Someone else must have done it and then blamed me. You know how the people around here hate me. Yes, one of them must have done it."

The chief inspector was not impressed. "Tie up their hands," he ordered, "and keep digging."

*

Another hour's digging produced yet another body, this time of a small boy. When it was clear after further digging that there were no more bodies to be found, at least in the garden, the two carriages returned to the police station. They contained the policemen, the Deans and the boxes with their tragic contents: three partly decomposed bodies of young children. It was later established that the second female body was that of Dorothy Edith Carter, a one-year-old who had died from an overdose of laudanum, a frequently used sedative. The identity of the third child, a young boy estimated to be about three years old, was never discovered.

The Deans were charged with infanticide and locked up to await trial. Soon after the police began their investigations, they discovered that Mr Charles Dean had had nothing to do with his wife's baby-farming, and at a hearing in a lower court, all the charges against him were dropped.

When the trial opened, on 18 June 1895, at the Invercargill Supreme Court, Mrs Minnie Dean was the solitary figure in the dock. Her defence lawyer was Alfred Hanlon, a barrister who was well-known for his successes in the courtroom.

The prosecuting lawyer claimed that Minnie Dean had taken the baby, Dorothy Carter, with her on a train from Winton and had changed trains to continue on to Lumsden. While she was on the second train, she had killed baby Carter and had then hidden the body in a hat box. She then spent that night at Lumsden, and boarded the train to Waimea Plains to continue travelling on to Gore the following day. There she took the Dunedin Express, getting off the train at Milburn, where she met Mrs Hornsby. While doing so, she left the dead baby in the hatbox in the storage office at the station.

Accompanied by Mrs Hornsby, Minnie Dean took the next train to Clarendon. She got off there and continued on another train to Dunedin as she carried baby Eva Hornsby in her arms. While she was on the train, she smothered the baby girl and then wrapped her body up in a parcel. Minnie Dean then took another train back to Clinton where she picked up the hatbox she had left behind in storage. Now with the two dead baby girls, the baby-farmer returned home to Winton.

After the judge and jury had heard the above, they also heard testimonies from several prosecution witnesses. Below are summaries of what they said:

A railway guard: 'I saw Mrs Dean board the train at Winton with a hatbox and a baby and then return carrying only a heavy hatbox and no baby'.

A friend of Mrs Dean: 'I have known Minnie Dean for quite some time and I can identify the signature, M. Grey, as Mrs Dean's handwriting on the Bluff poison register'.

A policeman: 'The clothing found at Mrs Dean's house was that of the dead child, Dorothy Edith Carter. In addition, we found several bottles of laudanum in the accused's bedroom, and the oilcloth we found in Mrs Dean's house was the same one that was used to wrap up the body of baby Dorothy Edith Carter'.

Grandmothers Hornsby and Carter: 'Mrs Dean was the woman that we entrusted our baby granddaughters to'.

Since Minnie Dean never stood up in court to give her own account of what had happened, the judge asked her lawyer, Mr A C Hanlon, to present her defence. He claimed that all the deaths were accidental and that his client had kept quiet about them because of all the bad publicity associated with baby-farming.

The judge was not impressed by the defence lawyer's impassioned speech, saying, "It seems to me that the real honest issue is whether the accused is guilty of intentionally killing the child or is innocent altogether." He also added that a verdict of manslaughter would be "a weak-kneed compromise."

On 21 June 1895, three days after her trial began for the murder of Dorothy Edith Carter, Minnie Dean was found guilty and sentenced to death. Between this date and the day of her hanging, 12 August 1895, she wrote a forty-nine-page account of her life. In this she claimed that she had looked after twenty-six (or twenty-eight) children in all, and that only six had died, naturally, under her care. One child had been reclaimed by its parents and five healthy children were present when the police raided her home. In addition, she and her husband had adopted two of the baby girls: Margaret Cameron and Esther Wallis. This detailed record still meant that around fourteen missing children had not been accounted for.

Dean was executed at Invercargill Gaol (the former site of which is now a carpark) and has the dubious honour of being the only woman who has ever been hanged in New Zealand. She was buried in Winton and now lies alongside her husband, Charles, who died later when his house caught fire in 1908.

One positive outcome of this gruesome story is that one year later, in 1896, the New Zealand government passed the Infant Protection Act. Unfortunately tens, if not hundreds of innocent babies and infants died in baby-farms run by Minnie Dean and other women before this act was passed.

Minnie Dean became part of New Zealand's folklore and it is claimed that flowers will never grow on her grave. In addition, Montbretia, an invasive wildflower nicknamed Minnie Dean, grows in Southland, New Zealand and local gardeners say that it should be uprooted if it starts growing in your garden.

Dean has also been the subject of at least two songs and one play, *A Cry Too Far from Heaven*, which was performed at the Edinburgh Fringe Festival in 2012. Songwriter Helen Henderson who was raised in the south of New Zealand wrote a ballad about Minnie Dean, its last verse being:

She dressed in black and carried a hat
In a hatbox when early to the courthouse she came.
"I'm innocent," she cried.
"They just disappeared."
But they hanged her from the gallows until she was
dead.

Chapter Sixteen

Belle Starr (1848-1889)
Wild West Outlaw

In the afternoon on 26 October 1881 in Tombstone, Arizona, cowboy Billy Claiborne together with two pairs of brothers, Ike and Billy Clanton and Tom and Frank McLaury, faced off against Marshal Virgil Earp, his two younger brothers, Wyatt and Morgan, and Doc Holliday. If you have not yet guessed, this was the famous 'Gunfight at the OK Corral'.

Within thirty seconds, the face-off and the shooting was over. Billy Clanton and the McLaury Brothers lay dead in the dust, Virgil and Morgan Earp and Doc Holliday had been wounded, while Claiborne and Ike Clanton were making a dash for the hills. This iconic Wild West gunfight has come to be one of the most well-known episodes in American frontier history. It has been immortalised in several films and also in a TV series about Wyatt Earp which ran for six years, (1955-1961).

The gunfight was typical of a showdown between the forces of law and order and the outlaws who tried to take over the part of the United States known as the Wild West – a vast area ranging from Montana and Idaho in the north to Arizona and New Mexico in the south. Most of these outlaws were rustlers, thieves and bank-robbers, who in this particular case were trying to impose their stamp on the growing town of Tombstone.

Today, much of our idea what life was like there during the last half of the 19th century has been influenced by Hollywood films. They have tended to depict either a romantic or an 'all guns blazing' version of everyday life. The truth is that it was something in between. While there definitely were rustlers and bank-robbers trying to make their fortunes, the agricultural economy of wheat, sheep and cattle was expanding, and the aforementioned lawlessness was not prevalent everywhere.

Life was certainly tough for the cowboys who lived an open life on the trails. In addition to rustlers, they had to contend with stampeding herds of cattle, tornadoes and the ever-present dust. The lack of medical care and constant exposure to the extremes of climate meant that the cowboys' average life, despite it being in the open air, was about forty years. In the end, this way of life came to

243

an abrupt end in 1886-87 when a particularly cold winter killed off thousands of cattle. As a result, many cowboys gave up their traditional wide-ranging way of life, or began to work on smaller and more controlled ranches instead.

Nevertheless, even before the advent of Hollywood films, several outlaws did achieve a certain infamy. This was so because at the time some of the stories about their exploits featured in cheap books and magazine articles. These included Billy the Kid (shot, aged 22 in 1881), Jesse James (shot by an accomplice in 1882, aged 34) and Butch Cassidy (shot aged 42 in 1908). However, not all of the 'baddies' were gun-slinging men. There were a few infamous women who had an equally bad reputation. The best known one was Belle Starr.

*

Belle Starr, christened Myra Maybelle Shirley, was born in Jasper County near Carthage, Missouri in February 1848. Everyone in the family circle called her May. Her father, John, made a good living raising hogs and horses and growing wheat and corn. Her mother, Elizabeth Pennington, was a member of the well-known Hatfield family. She was her husband's third wife. It was because John had divorced twice before marrying Elizabeth that he was thought of as the black sheep of the family.

When May was sixteen, her father sold his ranch and moved to Carthage, where he built a tavern, dealt in horses and became a blacksmith. His business thrived and, as an example of his respectability, he founded the Carthage Female Academy and sent his teenage daughter, an excellent student, to study the piano, foreign languages and gain a classical education.

It was during this period that the United States was torn apart by the Civil War (1861-65). Missouri was a border state and 110,000 men went to fight for the Union and 40,000 men for the Confederacy. The town of Carthage was the site of two battles. In the first, on 5 July 1861, the Confederate army won their first victory, in what was to be a small, insignificant skirmish. The second battle, on 22 October 1864, was much more important. Each side fielded armies of seven thousand men and by the end of the day, the Union forces had the Confederates on the run.

John Shirley was a Confederate sympathiser who strongly admired William the Confederate Clarke Quantrill and his guerrilla gang, 'Quantrill's Raiders'. Two well-known members of this gang, sometimes known as 'bushwhackers', were Frank and Jesse James. It was from this time in her life that May Shirley began to be associated with outlaws. May's older brother, John 'Bud' Addison, joined the gang and became a scout, but was killed in Sarcoxie, Missouri in 1864 by Union troops. Her father was devastated by his son's death, and consequently sold his business and moved his family to Scyene, Texas, three hundred and seventy miles to the south.

This was considered a step down socially as Texas was an open undeveloped territory and home to many outlaws and other rootless and destitute settlers. Here, near Dallas, May's family moved into a simple makeshift shack until they had built a better clapboard house. John Shirley obtained an eight-hundred-acre range through a land grant and started to establish himself again by growing crops as well as breeding and dealing in horses, hogs and milk cows.

It was during this period of chaos and confusion that followed the Civil War that many outlaws began making their presence known in the south. In 1866, the year after the war, the James-Younger Gang stole $6000 (well over $200,000 today) in cash and bonds from a bank in Liberty, Missouri and fled to Texas. There they sought refuge one night at the Shirley house, where they met May Shirley.

According to some stories, May became infatuated with Cole Younger and joined the gang. However, later, she, by then known as Belle, claimed this is when she became reacquainted with the man who would be her first husband, Jim Reed. They had met before in Missouri, where her family had been on good terms with his, and their connection now blossomed into marriage. The couple were married on 1 November 1866 then they moved back to Reed's homestead back in Missouri, where in September 1867 Belle gave birth to her first child, Rosie Lee, who later became known as Pearl.

It is from here that there are different versions about how deeply May/Belle became involved in outlaw activities. It was certainly about this time that the happy family story came to an end, as Jim Reed became more and more involved in crime. It seems that he murdered a man called Shannon, and when the law came knocking, Reed and Belle fled to California with Pearl. It was there that her second child, Edward 'Ed', was born in 1871. Then Reed was accused of passing counterfeit money, so they fled back to Texas where he became involved again in rustling and murder. After two years Reed and Belle fled yet again, leaving their children with her parents.

Soon after this, Reed and his gang stole $30,000 from the Grayson family (or possibly from a Creek Indian) and returned to Texas. Some reports say that Belle, disguised as a man, was involved in this robbery. But whatever the truth, their marriage was to end soon. By now, Belle had separated from Reed and was living with her parents, apparently having had enough of living on the run. Then she learnt that Reed, who had continued robbing stagecoaches and rustling, had been killed in Texas by John Morris, a former outlaw and friend who had become a deputy sheriff. She also heard that Reed had been seeing another woman.

After this, either Belle lived with Bruce Younger for a short while and/or had an affair with 'Blue Duck', an Indian outlaw. If this latter is true, it came to an end when she met a Cherokee named Sam Starr. He was the son of Reed's former partner in crime and in June 1880 May/Belle Reed married him to become the woman that she was known as hereafter, Belle Starr. Although various official records show different dates, Belle, aged thirty-two, was nine years older than her husband.

They settled on a sixty-two-acre property near Briartown on the north side of the Canadian River. This area was known as 'outlaw country' and even though Belle wanted a quiet life, they often hosted fugitives on the run, including Jesse James. This meant that willingly or not, Belle Starr became increasingly involved in the activities of various outlaws, and it was reported that often she was the brains behind the planning of various robberies and other crimes.

Unfortunately for the Starrs, the local magistrate was Judge Isaac Parker, also known as the 'Hanging Judge'. He was determined to put the couple behind bars and kept them under surveillance. One day in November 1882, one of his deputies, Bass Reeves, caught Belle red-handed attempting to steal a neighbour's horse. She was tried in Fort Smith, Arkansas and sentenced to two consecutive six-month prison terms. Both she and Sam, who was also found guilty, were sent to serve their sentences in the Detroit Federal House of Correction. Among other activities, she spent her time in prison reading and playing the piano. Sam on the other hand, was considered a troublemaker as a prisoner.

On their release, in 1886, Belle was tried again twice for robbery and stealing horses, but there was not enough evidence to prove the charges and she was acquitted. Sam, however, was less fortunate. At a Christmas party later that year he was killed by his cousin U.S. Deputy Indian Marshall Franklin West in a shootout in which each of the two men hit their marks, both of them dying at the same time.

It was during this period of her life that Belle became something of a celebrity. She was locally known as a western folk hero – a 'female Robin Hood and a Jesse James', even though the latter, who had been killed four years earlier, had never been known to have shared his ill-gotten gains with the deserving poor. She was called the 'Bandit Queen' and worked for a short while in a Wild West show playing the part of an outlaw. She was reportedly known to carry one or two guns, wear gold earrings, and in the iconic studio portrait of her – 'Queen of the Oklahoma Outlaws' – she posed while wearing a man's hat decorated with feathers.

Because Sam Starr had been a Cherokee, in order to keep her land, Belle had to marry another Cherokee. She solved this problem by marrying Sam's adopted Cherokee brother, another outlaw called Billy July. This time she was fourteen years older than her husband. It was at this point she was told by the Cherokee leaders that she must stop her criminal way of life, which included allowing fugitives to hide out on her property.

This marriage was not a success. The couple fought and stormed at each other all the time. After one particularly noisy argument, Billy July was reported to have offered $200 to a friend to kill his wife. The friend turned the offer down and Billy allegedly shouted, "Hell, I'll kill the old hag myself and spend the rest of the money on whiskey!"

A few days later, on 3 February 1889, Belle Starr was shot to death in an ambush as she was riding along a lonely country road. She was blown out of her saddle by a shotgun blast and when she tried to get up, the killer shot her again in the face and shoulder to make sure that she was dead.

It was never discovered who her murderer was. An unproven theory is that it was Edgar A. Watson, a sharecropper who had rented some of her land. The following incident may have been the cause of her death when she was only forty-one years old.

One evening in the winter of 1888, there was a knock on the door of Belle's house. Fortunately for her, she was on her own, as Billy July was out with some friends drinking down at the local saloon.

*

"Good evening, Mr Watson, how are you?" Belle began, pointing to a chair. "Please sit down. I've asked you to come over because I have something important to tell you about the land you rent from me."

"What is it? You want to put the rent up?"

"No, sir. I want to cancel the agreement between us."

"Why? I ain't done nothing wrong."

"I'm afraid you have. I heard this morning while I was in town doing my shopping that you are wanted back home in Florida for murder and –"

"But I –"

"And that I made a deal with the Cherokee owners of my land not to have anything to do with outlaws anymore. What do you say to that?"

"Well, I say it's a lot of nonsense and I ain't gonna cancel no agreement. And, Mrs High-and-mighty Belle Starr, or whatever you call yourself now, if you insist on it, I'll go and see your husband. He'll know what to do."

And saying that, the furious Edgar A Watson got up, marched out and left, slamming the door as he did so.

A few days later, Belle Starr was dead.

Another theory is that Watson murdered Belle, but not because she wanted to end the land rental agreement between them, but because she refused to dance with him when he was drunk at a local dance. Frank 'Pistol Pete' Eaton was a witness to this altercation, and later he claimed that after Bell turned Watson down, he followed her and shot her when she stopped to give her horse a drink.

Belle's granddaughter, Flossie, claimed that Belle was killed by her son, Ed, after she had punished him with a bullwhip for some unknown misdemeanour. Flossie said Ed was jealous of the way Pearl received the majority of his mother, Belle's, attention but she could never prove this. A fourth theory is that Belle's daughter, an angry Rosie Lee 'Pearl', shot her mother after Belle thwarted her wedding plans, which included having Pearl's daughter placed in an orphanage.

According to Kathy Weiser in *Legends of America*, Belle Starr was 'the undisputed leader of a band of cattle and horse thieves from 1875-1880'. She was buried in the front yard of the Younger's cabin at Bend. Carved on the gravestone was an image of her favourite mare, 'Venus' and the following inscription:

Shed not for her the bitter tear
Nor give the heart to vain regret,

'Tis but the casket that lies here,
The gem that fills it sparkles yet.

After all the speculation, the most accepted theory for Belle Starr's sudden demise is that Edgar A. Watson killed her – whatever the reason – and though he was known to possess a shotgun, after he was arrested and tried, he was acquitted. He eventually moved back to Florida and was killed there in 1910.

Belle Starr – Timeline

1848 – Born in Jaspar, County, Missouri.

1861-1865 – American Civil War and Bell starts meeting outlaws.

1864 – Family moves to Carthage, Missouri. Older brother, Jim 'Bud' Addison killed in war fighting the Union army.

1864-1865 – Family moves to Scyene, nr. Dallas, Texas.

1866 – Meets the James-Younger gang. Nov: Marries Jim Reed and moves to his homestead in Missouri.

1867 – Sept: Rosie Lee 'Pearl' (daughter) born.

1870 – Moves to California after husband Reed killed a man.

1871 – Edward (son) born. Moves back to Texas after Reed accused of passing counterfeit money.

1873 – New address in Texas. Leaves her children with her parents. Reed and his gang steal $30,000. Belle Starr and Reed separate and she moves back to her parents' home. Later she learns that Reed was killed in Texas.

1880 – Marries Sam Starr after an affair with Bruce Younger and/or another affair with Blue Buck, an Indian outlaw.

1882 – Nov: Caught red-handed trying to steal a neighbour's horse. Sent to prison for one year.

1886 – Tried again for robbery and stealing horses but acquitted. Dec: Sam Starr killed in a gunfight.

1886-1889 – Known as the 'Bandit Queen', she works for a while in a Wild West show.

1887 – Marries Billy July, outlaw, but marriage is not a success.

1889 – Feb 3: Killed in an ambush near her home at Eufaula, Indian Territory, now Oklahoma.

*

This was not the end of the Starr family featuring in the folklore of the lawless south at the turn of the century. Belle's daughter, Pearl, was twenty-one when her mother was shot. At first, she called herself Pearl Reed after her mother's second husband, but then after her 'famous' mother died, she changed her name to Pearl Starr. She was married for a short while to Will Harrison, and after their divorce in 1891, she became a prostitute in Van Buren, Arkansas, supposedly to make enough money to have her younger brother, Edwin, released from jail. Cashing in on a dime novel about her mother's life, she was able to buy his release two years later. She then moved to Fort Smith,

Arkansas and opened her own bordello. This claimed to have the 'most beautiful girls west of the Mississippi', sold good whiskey and featured a talented pianist. Her success here led her to open several more 'places of entertainment'.

It was during this period that she had an illegitimate daughter, Ruth, and married Arthur Erbach. She next had a son but within a year both he and her husband died of malaria. Three years later Pearl moved in with Dell Andrews and in November 1902 had another illegitimate daughter, Jennette.

Despite her being involved in the seamy side of life, Pearl Starr was only once implicated and sentenced for any crime. This was in 1911 when some stolen goods were found in her house. They had come from a general merchandise store that had been recently robbed, and Pearl was tried and found guilty of robbery. She was sentenced to a year in the Arkansas State Penitentiary, but after posting $2000 bail (nearly $60,000 today), her lawyers appealed to the Supreme Court and she was released.

The next brush she had with the law was in 1916, when Fort Smith made prostitution illegal. The local authorities turned a blind eye to her flourishing business for a few years, but eventually she was arrested. To stay out of prison she struck a deal. If she were to leave the town, she would not be indicted. She left Fort Smith for Douglas, Arizona in 1921, dying there in 1925 aged fifty-six.

Was Belle Starr really a wicked woman?

Today, if you look up any list of American outlaw women, you will find that Belle Starr is at the top of the list. Perhaps she was not really wicked, that is, not in comparison with some of the other women who appear in these pages. However, it does seem that despite the classical education she received, she did not make much of an effort to steer clear of the outlaws, infamous robbers and rustlers whose exploits achieved some form of dubious renown in the southern states of the USA over one hundred years ago.

Chapter Seventeen

Bertha Heyman (1851-1901)
Prussian-USA Con Artist

Bertha Heyman aged 30, 1881

This flattering description of Bertha Heyman appeared in the Buffalo Evening News, *1881:*

'*She had what is described by the French as a* 'belle figure'*... was a very attractive person and took your fancy the moment she fixed her big, brown, stag-like eyes upon you... Her wavy hair is soft and black, and her hands are white, taper-fingered and filbert-nailed. She sat quietly with her dress open at the neck, revealing a shapely throat* *of a complexion creamy as the inner petals of a lily, and her arms bare to the elbows, soft and dimpled.'*

In contrast, Police Inspector, Thomas Byrnes, in his book, Professional Criminals in America, *(1886) described her thus:*

'Thirty-five years old in 1886. Born in Germany. Married. Very stout woman. Height 5 feet 4½ inches. Weight, 245 pounds. Hair brown, eyes brown, fair complexion. German face. An excellent talker. Has four moles on her right cheek.'

These are two very different descriptions of one of the most successful con artists, Bertha Heyman, who made a fortune in the USA and Canada in the 19th century. The first description is from the Buffalo Evening News, *8 February 1881, the second appeared five years later in 1886. Both of these descriptions appeared while Bertha Heyman was at the height of her career as a con artist.*

*

Bertha Heyman (née Schlesinger) was born in 1851 in Kobly, near Posen in Prussia, and moved to the United States at the age of 27. We don't know why she emigrated then or what her childhood was like, except that it is on record that her father was jailed for five years for forging a cheque. All we know about her during the first part of her life is that she married twice. The first time was to Fritz

Karko, a mechanic, with whom she first lived in New York and then she moved with him to Milwaukee to open a milliner's shop. After that she (bigamously?) married John Heyman. For some reason this marriage came to an end soon after, either through divorce or because he left her.

The first record we have of her criminal career as a con artist dates from 1880, only two years after she crossed the Atlantic Ocean, and possibly this hints that she was already swindling people in Prussia before she left for the USA. Perhaps that was the reason for her transatlantic move. Whatever the reason was, one of her first cons in America took place in a train sleeping-car from Chicago to New York when Bertha found herself talking to a sleeping-car attendant.

*

"You don't look very happy day. Is anything wrong? By the way, what's your name?"

"It's Perrin, ma'am, E T Perrin. And yes, ma'am, nothing's really wrong. Just another long day, you know; aching feet, awkward customers and low pay. We've still got over twelve hours before we reach New York."

"Oh, you poor man," she said, smiling. "But tell me, how long have you been working on the railroad?"

"More years, ma'am, than I'd like to recall. More or less since I finished my schooling."

"How good are you with numbers, my man, with money?"

"Good, I'm fast, ma'am. You try me. After working on

258

the railroad for all this time, especially in this here railroad car, I must be the fastest man there is. Working out bills, giving change, calculating how much time we've got left for the journey. Yes, ma'am, I'm good. There's no doubt about it."

"So how about if I gave you a better job, one that was much better paid that would be good both for your pocket and your poor old feet?"

The tired attendant looked at the well-dressed passenger. "That'd be swell, ma'am. I was just saying to my wife yesterday that it was time I quit and found myself a better job. I'm telling you ma'am, my wife's always on at me about improving myself."

"So let me help you improve yourself."

"Why what would I have to do?"

"Well, it's like this. I have a large estate and it needs managing. I was doing all right while my husband, my dear Otto, was alive." At this point Bertha took out a handkerchief and dabbed her eyes.

"Well, that's me, ma'am. You'll find no-one better. And I'm honest, too. You ask my bosses at the office. I'm sure they'll vouch for me."

*

And so it was. Perrin quit his job after hearing that Bertha would employ him. She then informed him that she needed to borrow some money as she was in the middle of a legal battle with her agent, who owed her a tidy sum. Then after Perrin had swallowed this story, Bertha took her expectant new employee to see 814 Lexington Avenue, a large house which she claimed was hers.

"Is all that building, that mansion yours, ma'am?" Perrin asked, his eyes wide open in awe. "All those rooms and doors and windows? And this garden? It's huge."

Bertha smiled and nodded. "Yes, it sure is, and that's what you'll be running."

But the only running that happened after this was that Bertha ran away while Perrin ran after her trying to reclaim the money he had lent her to help her pay her alleged legal expenses.

The tale she told Perrin of her being a wealthy woman, was that she, together with her lawyer, Mr Edward Lauterbach, were in the middle of a legal battle to access her great fortune and she needed some more money to do so. This was her usual and practiced *modus operandi*.

Three years later, on 10 January 1883, *The Chicago Tribune* which by now was calling her the 'Confidence Queen', reported the above story in full, saying that she claimed that 'she was paying a New York lawyer $6,000' a year to look after her estate and that she had suggested to Perrin that he gave up his railroad job to manage this same estate.

The Chicago newspaper added some more details such as that Perrin, who was earning an annual salary of only $960, would supposedly have his wage more than doubled to $2000 per year. The report continued:

After Perrin had resigned his place [of work], the 'Queen' began borrowing money from him to pay small *debts. At least $1,038, had been obtained when Perrin insisted on entering upon the duties of his agency. The satisfaction that he obtained was her promise that when he came into possession of all her property through Mr Robert Bonner, who she said was her guardian and executor of the will under which she was the heir, the money he had loaned her would be refunded and his duties as agent would begin. Perrin finally came to the conclusion that the woman was not to be believed, and, despairing of ever obtaining from her his money without compulsion, brought suit against her.*

To prove how rich she was, like a spider, Bertha Heyman would lure her victims into the trap by meeting them at the best hotels – where she claimed she was staying – and then name drop affluent 'friends', such as the Vanderbilts, both William and Cornelius, as well as the Astors.

On 9 July 1881, Mark Twain, the budding writer and correspondent for the *Kansas City Times*, described Bertha Heyman and her nefarious schemes thus:

For years she lived in regal splendor in New York hotels, surrounded by luxuries and attended by liveried lackeys. She occupied different apartments at different times in the St. Denis hotel, the Grande hotel, the Gilsey house, the New York hotel and the Hotel Brunswick... Her plan was to pass herself off for a millionaire and then to borrow money on the strength of her prospects.

It was during this time that she swindled the firm of Bates, Reed & Cooley for $5000 (more than $115,000 today) and took a Mr Botty for a similar sum. However, he sued her and was able to recover his loss. She also tricked a Mr Brandt, a man she had known from the time she had been married to Fritz Karko, out of $1000, ($23,000 today), after persuading him to lend her money that she claimed she would repay soon. This repayment never happened, and the scam was repeated several times on all sorts of unsuspecting victims.

What is particularly interesting about Bertha Heyman is that she claimed that she did not con people in order to amass a fortune. She said that she gave most of her ill-gotten gains away and was quoted in the *New York Times* (3 July 1883) saying:

"The moment I discover the man's a fool, I let him drop, but I delight getting into the confidence and pockets of men who think they can't be 'skinned'. It ministers to my intellectual pride."

And this is how her 'intellectual pride' worked. She would dress up and make out that she was a rich woman who for various technical reasons, such as complicated banking or legal proceedings, was not able to access her money. She would have a paid phoney well-dressed maid and/or manservant at her beck and call while she stayed at the best hotels. Naturally, when she started reeling in her next 'mark', she would casually mention the names of her best friends, the financial elite of New York. Her way of operating was in general extremely devious and audacious. She believed that if you told a lie, it should be a big one. Her lies were as big as she was.

One year after taking the railway-car man for a ride, Bertha Heyman, together with a Dr J E Coombs, tried to trick a Montreal businessman out of several hundred dollars. This time she did not succeed and was arrested in London, Ontario. She stood trial four months later, in June 1881, and was also charged with stealing two gold watches and $250 from an old lady, a fellow tenant in New York. She was able to persuade the judge she was innocent and soon was happily walking out of the courtroom, where she was immediately re-arrested. This time she was charged with conning a Mr Charles Brandt and another businessman from New York out of $1460 ($33,600 today). This time she did not walk out of court smiling. She was sentenced to two years in prison and this was not to be her last prison sentence. While she was serving her sentence on Blackwell's Island, she did not waste any time. There she convinced a man to part with his life savings which netted her about $20,700 in today's money.

On another occasion she swindled a Mrs Schlarbaum from New York of $5000 and tricked the same amount from a Mr Theodore W Morris, one of the late Mr Schlarbaum's old friends. She had given the latter a fake bank draft for $13,000 drawn on a bank in Milwaukee and had also promised him a gift of some fine furniture, but then soon after she was arrested again by two men from the Pinkerton Detective Agency. When this incident was reported in the *Kentucky City Times*, Bertha Heyman described herself as the 'wronged' and 'injured woman'. As this newspaper continued in their report of 9 July 1881:

Since her arrest she has been a prisoner only by name. She occupies a suite of apartments in the courthouse; has been attended by a maid; and is treated to carriage rides every day. She has been at many excursions, and spends much of her time in attendance at scenes of festivity in the city. To such an extent is this carried that she is called the 'The Princess' by the residents of the village of Richmond. In conversation she is most plausible and graceful, and presents an air of injured innocence that induces many credulous persons to believe she is really a wronged and persecuted woman.

However, despite this luxurious lifestyle, at her trial in October 1881 for obtaining $500 from Mr Morris by false pretences, the jury took only five minutes to declare her guilty. The judge then handed down another two-year prison sentence. However, in typical Bertha Heyman style, this was not the end of this particular legal proceeding, as in the meantime she had run up a dental bill with the dentist employed by the judge. When the dentist demanded payment, she claimed that the bill was "so trifling a sum" and that she was very busy dealing with a $14 million deposit down-town that she had no time for him.

She was sent to Blackwell's Island Penitentiary, but that did not stop her from perpetrating yet another scam. There she contacted the gullible Charles Karpe. In the same way she had conned Mrs Schlarbaum and Mr Perrin, she spun a version of the familiar tale of not being able to access her considerable fortune. Karpe lent her $1000 after she told him that she owned a strongbox containing jewellery and bonds but that it was being stored in a bank.

*

"Mr Karpe", she told him, "I need the money to pay for liens for its storage. Please can you help me out and then I will repay you later, in fact, even ten times as much."

"Of course, and –"

"And yes, I also need some more money to cross the prison warden's palm with silver so he will shorten my sentence. Do you think you can help me with that as well?"

"Sure, how can he keep you, such a well-bred woman, locked up in this dismal hole?"

*

As with many others before him, Charles Karpe never saw any more money after he had 'lent' Bertha the requested sum, and so he joined the ever-growing list of her victims.

The Chicago Tribune reported Bertha Heyman's latest exploits, and after regaling its readers with an account of how the con artist operated, included the follow insight into how she fooled everyone, from the best educated to the most unsuspecting shop-owner:

The florist from whom she obtained the bouquets still

retains exceedingly lively recollections of her as an undesirable customer. She possesses a wonderful knowledge of human nature, and can deceive those who consider themselves particularly shrewd in business matters.

From Blackwell Prison, on Blackwell's Island in the Hudson River, Bertha's next stop was at the Hoffman House in New York. From there she continued conning those who were hoping to make a 'fast buck' out of her. However, on 22 August 1883, the 'Confidence Queen' was caught again, tried and sent to Sing Sing prison for five years. This was for conning several people, including a Wall Street banker, who she had told that her assets came to eight million dollars. What she did not tell him was that the share certificates that she showed him to prove her story were forged. She was to serve four years in that grim institution and was finally released in March 1887.

Surprisingly, her combined sentences of about ten years did not stop Bertha Heyman from continuing to do what she knew best. However, in 1888 she moved her base of operations from New York to San Francisco. She did not say why, but perhaps by now she was becoming too well known on the east coast. There in the west, nearly three thousand miles away, she could start afresh. And start she did. She changed her name to Bertha Stanley and took her son (or stepson) William 'Willie' Stanley, with her.

She became involved in the Jewish community, that is, not working in or for the local synagogue, but investigating those in the community she thought she could rip off. One of the first things she did was to approach Rabbi A J Messing, whom she had known more than thirty-five years earlier back in Prussia, and told him that she was now a very affluent woman who was looking for a husband, as her former husband had died. The rabbi's brother-in-law, Abraham Gruhn, quickly became attracted to this large rich woman, and soon after they met, he proposed.

This gave Bertha an entrance into the San Francisco Beth Israel Congregation, and there she continued her social round, financing her way with dud cheques and wearing expensive clothes bought on credit. However, before Bertha Stanley and Abraham Gruhn tied the knot, Willie Stanley asked his future father-in-law for a $500 loan. He also asked Gruhn for the jewels Abraham was going to give to Bertha so that he could have them reset for her in a more modern fashion. The unsuspecting bride was only too happy to oblige, until that week he learned that Bertha and Willie had disappeared. They had left San Francisco and gone south to Los Angeles.

The angry Gruhn went to the police and there he learned that his bride-to-be was already well known to the authorities. The wheels of justice started grinding, and several months later Bertha and Willie were found eighteen hundred miles away to the south-east in San Antonio, Texas. There they were arrested and were returned to San Francisco. Very aptly, on April Fools' Day 1888, the *Chattanooga Daily Times* described 'The Queen of Crooks' activities thus:

They ran up large bills in the various stores, through the clever fashion they had of shopping in the company of some wealthy Hebrew [Jew]. She had for a suitor a popular and wealthy young merchant whom she gave a check for $30,000 (nearly $700,000 today) on the LaSalle bank for safe keeping, and he in return gave her a $500 diamond ring and other gems aggregating several thousand dollars in value. After Bertha left, the duped suitor wired the LaSalle bank and discovered that the check was worthless...

As for their return journey to San Francisco, the Californian authorities, like their counterparts in New York, seem to have been captivated by Bertha Stanley's charm, as the *San Francisco Examiner* (14 June 1888) reported:

Bertha was treated with great consideration on the journey and no handcuffs being put on her. She and Willie... were in remarkably good spirits from the time San Antonio was left until San Francisco was reached and in jail they showed not the least trace of dejection...

The paper then went on to explain Bertha's charm and influence over her prison guards and escort:

A sight of Bertha is necessary to let one perceive how a woman with so much flesh and whose appearance has been often referred to as homely could attract the attention and win the confidence of men. Her power lies in her eyes. They are brown, but of such a dark colour they are bright enough to light up her entire countenance. She is not handsome, but she is not bad looking either... There is not a tailor's measure in the town that can encompass her ample form... Anyone with an eye for distances can readily perceive that the lady has passed her hugging days, but to one who has had such a contempt for men as she this can occasion little regret... the expressive contours of her person were studied by everyone in the jail. Yet she can carry herself without any unusual amount of effort.

Soon after this, Bertha and Willie were separated, she remaining in custody in San Francisco, while Willie was returned to face trial in San Antonio. There, so many people crowded the law-court, the *Daily Alta California* reported that the judge 'could hardly force his way through the crowd to reach the bench'.

*

At her trial in San Francisco Bertha Heyman consistently lied about her past:

Prosecution: 'Please tell the court briefly about your recent financial situation'.

Bertha: 'I have spent more money than I have ever received'.

Prosecution: 'Have you received any money from or checks from Mr Gruhn or anybody else?'

Bertha: 'No, never'.

Prosecution: 'Do you have a living husband?'

Bertha: 'No, Your Honour. I changed my name to Mrs Bertha Stanley after I divorced Mr John Heyman'.

Prosecutor: 'Were you first married to a Mr Fritz Karko?'

Bertha: 'No, Your Honour. Never.'

*

It was while Bertha was in court that her career took a surprising turn. Ned Foster, a local theatre impresario took one look at her and decided that by becoming her agent, he could make a lot of money. Therefore he bailed her out of jail and had large posters of her put up around town advertising a show featuring the 'Queen of Crooks'.

Bertha now appeared in a one-woman show, shamelessly recreating her past scandals while she posed on stage wearing flesh-coloured tights. It should be noted that this appearance was really sensational as it happened in a conservative America over one 140 years ago. However, that did not prevent Mr Foster from quickly recouping his outlay. Part of the act included some very un-Shakespearean scenes from *Romeo and Juliet* with an actor bearing the unlikely name of Oofty Goofty playing opposite her. This twenty-six-year-old ex-German sideshow performer made his living by having other people hit him on stage. This was called popular entertainment.

Ned Foster, seeing how successful his show was, then took Bertha Stanley on a tour of the West Coast. There, billed as 'Big Bertha', she would take part in wrestling matches or fight with boxers on the stage, very often knocking them out. Since she is said to have weighed four hundred pounds, it is perhaps not surprising she very often won.

The last we hear of her was of her taking part in professional wrestling contests in Spokane, Washington. She died in Chicago in 1901 aged fifty.

Her stage name lived on, although in a completely unexpected way. 'Big Bertha' – *Dicke Bertha* – became the name German soldiers gave to their huge howitzer guns during the First World War. However, they were so called, not after the ex-Prussian-American con artist, but rather in honour of Bertha Krupp von Bohlen und Halbach, the owner of the arms factory that produced these massive artillery weapons. The guns could fire a shell weighing 810 kgs over a distance of eight miles. Later in the war this range was extended so that the German army could bombard Paris from a safe distance of seventy-four miles.

Was Bertha Heyman really a wicked woman?

While it is true that she did not kill or physically hurt anyone, she deliberately fooled many people out of a lot of money and no doubt left much pain and sorrow in her wake.

Bertha Heyman – Timeline

1851 – Born as Bertha Schlessinger, Koby, Posen,

Prussia.

1878 – Moves to USA after two marriages. First lives in New York and then Milwaukee.

1880 – First record of her conning activities in USA. Sept: Arrested for conning sleeping-car attendant, E T Perrin, on Chicago train.

1881 – Feb: Charged with conning several hundred dollars from a Montreal businessman. June: Charged with stealing $250 and two gold watches from an old lady in New York but acquitted. Oct 29: Charged with theft but acquitted. Immediately re-arrested for conning Charles Brandt (New York) of $1,460 and sentenced to two years in prison. While there cons another man for $900.

1883 – Called 'The Confidence Queen' by *The Chicago Tribune*. Aug 22: Sent to Sing Sing Prison for five years for swindling a Wall Street broker using forged securities.

1887 – March: Released from Sing Sing Prison after two years.

1888 – March: Moves from New York to San Francisco and continues her conning activities there. Swindles members of the Jewish community and flees to Los Angeles, California. April 1: *Chatanooga Daily Times* calls her, 'The Queen of Crooks' and describes her activities. Starts new career as one-woman show and also takes part in wresting contests.

1901 – Dies in Chicago.

Chapter Eighteen

Thérèse Humbert (1856-1918)
French Con Artist Par Excellence

If your image of a female con artist is of a slim, fashionably well-dressed, smooth talking attractive woman, then think again. The 'star' of this chapter, Madame Thérèse Humbert, like Bertha Heyman, was a short, tubby woman whose career was based on many small lies and one extraordinary large lie. It was this fabrication of the truth that kept her living the high life in Paris for over twenty years at the end of the 19th century, before the whole mendacious edifice began to collapse, leaving her and many others penniless.

However, it was not just the wicked falsehood that kept Humbert in the manner to which she aspired, it was also the fact that the people who, knowingly or not, supported her, did so because they too wanted to exploit her for their own ends. In other words, for con artists to succeed, they have to be able to fool other people – their 'marks'. These are their gullible victims who want to believe in the con artists' stories, however outrageous they may seem, for their own benefit. However, when the con artist fails to deliver the goods, then their unfortunate victims often follow them down the financial drain. If you do not believe this, ask the thousands of people who lost billions of dollars thanks to the American con artist par excellence, Bernie Madoff, one hundred years after Thérèse Humbert began operating on the other side of the Atlantic.

*

"Oh, Thérèse, you and your imagination," Marie said to her sister, "you are always making up stories. Isn't that true?" she added, turning to her two brothers, Romain and Emile.

The three of them looked at their stocky, smiling sister and laughed as she told them how one day they would inherit a fortune. "One day," she said, "we will no longer live in our poor tumbledown old farmhouse. We will live in a grand château."

Thérèse d'Aurignac was born in 1856 in Aussonne, a small village in the south-west of France near Toulouse. Her peasant father was a dreamer and spent much of his time studying alchemy. He also filled his children's heads with stories of how their family had aristocratic roots and that the family had various hidden inheritances which were just waiting to be discovered. When his creditors showed up claiming their money, Monsieur d'Aurignac would show them a locked chest in which he said contained legal documents proving his wealth. This trick must have worked as it planted the seeds of ideas in his daughter Thérèse's head concerning how to convince people of her great (non-existent) wealth. When her father died and the locked chest was opened, it was found to contain nothing more than a brick.

However, little Thérèse was a quick learner. One day she persuaded some of the village girls to either loan or give her their jewellery so that she could fool some others into believing that she was rich. This little trick was just the first step in a long line of confidence tricks that would net her both a fortune and infamy.

Her next move towards acquiring her longed-for fortune came after she became a washerwoman. Since she needed the money she performed this menial task, probably most unwillingly, for her half-aunt, who was married to the Mayor of Toulouse, Gustave Humbert. There she met their son, Frédéric, and conned him into falling in love with her. She cemented her prospective rise in social status by telling him that when she turned twenty-one, she would inherit a château which had been bequeathed to her by the generous Madame de Marriott. Frédéric saw his own future suddenly becoming bright and proposed to Thérèse. His father objected to what he

275

believed was a scam, and so the young couple eloped from rural south-west France to the bright lights of Paris.

There they lived as if they had all the money in the world. They dined out in the most expensive and chic restaurants, bought the best tickets to the theatre and the most fashionable clothes as well as buying several properties. Naturally, they ran up huge debts, but Frédéric's father, now the Minister of Justice, paid off everything as he could not afford his family to be involved in any public scandal.

The next stage, the key stage of this saga of deception and avarice occurred in 1879, when Thérèse Humbert was twenty-three.

*

"Frédéric, *mon chéri*," Thérèse gasped breathlessly as she entered the *salon* of their sumptuous Parisian mansion. "You will never guess what happened to me on the train today. We are going to be rich, much richer than we are today."

"*Pourquoi? Que s'est-il passé?* What's happened?"

"I was sitting on the train reading my book when suddenly I heard some terrible noises coming from the next compartment. They were terrible, my dear – groans and cries like someone had been injured or who was dying. So, as you know me, I have a soft heart, I went to the carriage from where I heard these terrible noises, and guess what I saw there."

"*Quoi?*"

"There was this man lying on the floor of the carriage and it looked like he was having a heart attack or something like that!"

"*Alors, qu'as-tu fait?*"

"What did I do? The only thing that I could. I gave him some of my smelling salts and after a while he recovered."

"So, Thérèse, why does this mean that we are going to be rich? Did he give you any money or something?"

"No, no, he told me that he was an American millionaire and that his name was Robert Henry Crawford and that when he died, he would reward me for saving his life."

"But he didn't give you any money now, did he?"

"No, but he didn't look so healthy and so I wouldn't be surprised if he doesn't die soon."

*

Thérèse's prediction came true. Two years later she received a letter which stated that she was the sole beneficiary of Robert Henry Crawford's will. However, there was a small condition. The will stipulated that the family fortune which was locked in a safe would remain sealed until Thérèse's younger sister, Marie, was old enough to marry Henry Crawford, one of the millionaire's nephews.

Thérèse did not waste any time. Echoing her father's knowledge of financial scamming, she went to a bank and used the letter and its promise of a fortune to obtain a loan of six million francs. In expectation of making a good profit in the future, the bank did not ask too many questions. The result was that soon after, Thérèse and Frédéric moved into an even more opulent apartment on 65 avenue de la Grande Armée, one of the most prestigious boulevards in Paris leading off the Arc de Triomphe.

From here the lifestyle of the Humberts again improved, probably beyond Madame's wildest childhood dreams. They entertained royally, inviting French presidents, prime ministers and their wives and other notables to their numerous *soirées* and other parties. These well-dressed people were served the finest foods at banquets that *la cuisine française* could provide, while the proud hosts wore the most fashionable clothes that *les maisons de couture françaises* could produce. Thérèse became famous for her enormous hats, which were highly decorated with fake fruit and feathers. One of her most famous pieces of headwear became the talk of the town, as it resembled a leech feasting on Madame Humbert's expensively coiffed hair.

*

One day while Thérèse was resting at home, she heard some loud knocking on her door. She sent one of her servants to see who was there.

"It's a man, ma'am," the flustered servant said coming into the over-furnished salon, "and he says that he is a bailiff."

"Did he say what he wants?"

"No, ma'am, he just said he wishes to talk with you and

278

Monsieur Humbert."

"Then send him in and I'll deal with him. Monsieur Humbert has gone to the races."

The bailiff entered, no doubt his eyes wide open as he saw that the stories he had heard of the Humberts' wealth were true.

"*Oui, m'sieur*, what do you want? Can't you see that I am busy?"

"Madame Humbert," the bailiff began. "I have come here as the representative of my bank, they wish to know when you are going to start returning your loan. You see–"

"Tell your bank, *m'sieur* that I will contact them in a few days. And now go. Can't you see that I am in the middle of preparing a soirée for tonight? *Au revoir*."

That night when Frederic returned home, Thérèse told him about the bailiff's visit and how she had dealt with him.

"But it's true, Therese, we must start returning the loan or we will be in trouble."

"But you said that we don't have the money to do so."

"I know that, so…"

Thérèse clicked her fingers. "I know what we'll do. We'll borrow some money from another bank and pay the first bank back with that. I'm sure that knowing our name and standing in society, any bank will lend us the necessary money."

"But, *ma chérie*, don't you think that the bank will be suspicious – you know, the Humberts wanting to borrow some money?"

"Fear not, Frédéric. Don't you know that all what bank

managers think of are their rates of interest and their profits. I'm sure that they'll be delighted to lend us what we ask for."

*

Thérèse was right – the second bank lent their new, famous customers the necessary money. This allowed the Humberts to continue living their luxurious lifestyle unabated as they played one bank off against another. The banquets continued to be attended by the French capital's high society, the purchase of fine fashionable clothes and hats went on as before and the Humberts remained the talk of the Parisian *élite*.

One day in 1883, a flustered Frédéric rushed into the salon brandishing a copy of *Le Matin*.

"Look, Thérèse, look what they have published about us in their dirty rag of a paper! Look!"

Thérèse read the article, an investigative article asking how the Humberts had so much money and what they did with it.

"Frédéric," Thérèse said without wasting a minute. "Go and speak to your father. He was the Minister of Justice – see what he can do about this! Go now. Immediately. *Tout de suite*."

Frederic rushed off to see his father and told him about the scandalous report. Using his influence, Gustave Humbert pressurised the newspaper not to write any further stories investigating his son and daughter-in-law and in doing so, he bought his son's family a financial reprieve.

This potentially worrying incident did not put the brakes on Thérèse Humbert's attitude to money and life in any way at all. She continued to play her part as the inordinately wealthy society lady to the full. She put on weight and acted as if she were royalty itself. She wore high-piled hats decorated with peacock feathers, confections of fruit and birds' nests, and her dresses from the Parisian *couturiers*, Jacques Doucet and Maison Worth cost a fortune. In a biography about her, *La Grande Therese*, Hilary Spurling wrote that 'in a single year, she ran up bills worth 97,000 and 32,000 francs'.

However, despite the outward show of wealth and self-confidence, Thérèse Humbert felt at ease only when she was with her own extended family and her old friend and confidante, Catherine Parayre. It was as if that she knew that one day, her grand fraudulent bubble would explode with an almighty bang. And explode it did. Despite her brother Romain's bullying creditors and carrying out various murky financial deals, questions again were asked.

Then in the summer of 1901, rumours started swirling around suggesting that things were not as they should be with the Humberts. A meeting of her creditors took place, and even though they could not agree on what unified action they could take to regain the money they had lent, the fact that such a meeting happened at all was itself an important event leading to the eventual collapse of the *l'affair Humbert*.

It was now that one of the national papers, *Le Matin*, began to ask probing and pertinent questions, and many creditors started to panic. Then on 6 May 1902 an appellate judge, in response to public pressure, signed an order stating that Madame Humbert's famous strong box must be opened in three days' time. This was the strongbox that she had insisted all along was home to all the precious documents that enabled her to continue taking out enormous loans and 'borrowing from Peter to pay Paul'. The judge said that he wanted an inventory taken of its contents and to finally discover the secrets behind the whole saga. However, before this happened, Thérèse Humbert, her husband, Frédéric, her daughter, Eve, and her siblings Emile, Romain and Maria fled Paris to an unknown destination.

On 9 May 1902, ten thousand people crowded into the street in front of Thérèse Humbert's mansion on the avenue de la Grande Armée. Under the supervision of the state prosecutor, a locksmith smashed open the lock, as the Humberts had not left any keys behind. You can imagine the shock that ran through the crowds outside when it was declared that all that was in the strongbox was an old newspaper, an Italian coin and a trouser button! (Some accounts say that it contained only an English halfpenny and a brick.)

Everybody present now realised that an enormous con had taken place, and thousands of people who had placed their lifelong savings in the various banks that the Humberts had exploited now realised that they had lost their money. The newspapers printed lists of these creditors, which included such notable figures as the Empress Eugénie, the president's son and many famous lawyers, bankers, industrialists, Parisian jewellers and diamond merchants. All of these solid citizens knew that there was no way that they would ever see any of their loans, or even part of them, again. Aloyse Muller, one of these disillusioned investors, a man who had lent Thérèse Humbert nearly two million francs, shot himself two weeks later out of sheer desperation.

The Humberts' collection of paintings and their furniture and other goods were sold, but the proceeds did little to pay off their enormous debts. For months the newspapers asked pointed questions. Who had allowed this to happen? Why were there no checks on the banking system? And what should be done with this infamous family once they were apprehended? Perhaps the most pointed and immediate question was, where were they hiding?

The answer came seven months later, in mid-December 1902 when it was discovered that the Humberts were in Madrid. They were arrested on 20 December, and amid great publicity, brought back to Paris by train. The atmosphere at the station must have been similar to that of when Marie Antoinette and her family were returned to the French capital after trying to escape the country during the French Revolution, over one hundred years earlier.

According to Hilary Spurling's book, *La Grande Thérèse: The Greatest Scandal of the Century*, Paris went wild with excitement. People sang crude Christmas songs about the Humberts, toy Humbert dolls were sold, a board game based on their exploits was invented and the newspapers published caricatures of the family as a circus

or theatrical troupe staging melodramas such as *Humbugs'
Heritage* and *The Secrets of the Strongbox*. Thérèse herself
was portrayed as a whip-cracking ringmaster or wand-
waving magician.

The court case opened in August 1903 and Thérèse, her
two brothers, Romain and Emile, and her husband,
Frédéric, were charged with fraud. (Her sister, Marie and
daughter, Eve, had meanwhile been set free.) The French
and international press reported the case in full, and
despite the Humberts' protestations, Thérèse and her
husband were each sentenced to five years solitary
confinement with hard labour.

Thérèse served her sentence in the women's prison at
Rennes and Frédérick served his at Melun. When she
finished, she was fifty-two years old, Frederic, fifty-one.
Perhaps it is not surprising that they were never heard of
again.

As for Thérèse's two brothers, Emile and Romain, they
received two and three years respectively and the lawyers
who had protected this crooked family while they were
cheating the public, both the rich and the poor, never
practiced again.

Hilary Spurling comments that the lightness of their
sentences suggests that some sort of deal was struck
behind the scenes. It is quite probable that the 'movers and
shakers' in the French society also felt guilty by
association for not having done anything to prevent
Thérèse Humbert, the poverty-stricken little girl from
Aussonne near Toulouse, fulfilling her childhood dreams
of fame and fortune.

Was Thérèse Humbert really a wicked woman?

Like Bertha Heyman, Thérèse Humbert was not wicked in that she had killed or physically hurt anyone. However, she did exploit other people's desires to obtain a lot of money in a dubious way and by so doing, left a trail behind her of much misery and woe.

Chapter Nineteen

Kate Leigh (1881-1964) & Tilly Devine (1900-1970)
Rival Australian Organised Crime Bosses

Kate Leigh & Tilly Devine in 'People Magazine' March 1950

In Chapter Eight we read about two female pirates, Anne Bonny and Mary Read, who co-operated with each other and were known as two of the most fearsome pirates to threaten the mercantile shipping of the Caribbean. However, now is the time to read about another duo of female criminals, Kate Leigh and Tilly Devine, who hated each other's guts and fought over the same turf. This time however, the turf was in Sydney, Australia.

Perhaps it is no surprise to learn that these two latter-day crime bosses both came from poor working-class backgrounds: Tilly came from Camberwell, south London, and Kate from Dubbo, a small country town four hundred miles north-west of Sydney. They both married early, both became active in the 'Down Under' underworld at an early age, and both of them were involved in prostitution and brothels while becoming infamous members of the Sydney 'razor gangs'.

In the way their careers in crime developed, they would inevitably end up either as partners, like Anne Bonny and Mary Read, or as sworn rivals.

*

Kathleen Mary Josephine Beahan (as may be guessed from her name) was born into a Roman Catholic household in Dubbo, New South Wales in March 1881. Her father was a bootmaker and her mother a housewife. Kate grew up as the youngest child together with her seven brothers and sisters in this small, isolated town of three thousand souls, nearly four hundred miles away from Sydney.

She endured a tough childhood, was neglected, and when she was twelve, spent some time in a girls' home. She became pregnant and had a daughter, Eileen May, when she was only nineteen.

Two years later she married a petty criminal, James Leigh, who made his money as an illegal bookmaker. The marriage was not a success and they did not live together for long. After three years, Kate and James were separated

287

when he was imprisoned for assault and robbery. This marriage only ended officially sixteen years later in 1921. Meanwhile, however, Kate Leigh was convicted of perjury and aiding her husband in a case of assault. She was accused of lying under oath in an effort to protect her violent husband, but appealed this conviction and fortunately for her it was overturned.

Kate's second marriage did nothing to improve her life. One year after her divorce, in September 1922, she married Edward Joseph Barry, alias 'Teddy'. He was a petty criminal who 'specialised' in dealing with sly-grog – illegal alcohol – and who was eleven years younger than his wife. At first Kate adopted her second husband's name, but after this marriage broke up a few years later, she reverted to calling herself Kate Leigh.

Kate's lifestyle probably did not change much when, during the late twenties, she lived with Walter 'Wally' Tomlinson, another violent criminal who was also younger, by eight years, than Kate. They had come to know each other as she had originally employed him as one of her bodyguards. Like Kate, he too became involved in a life of crime at an early age. He was charged with murder or attempted murder when he was sixteen, and by the time he was twenty he was known as a hardened criminal. She never married Tomlinson, and when he walked out on her after several years, Kate became the *de facto* wife of Henry Baker. Like her previous men, 'Jack' Baker was younger than her, by six years this time, and he too was a criminal.

Kate married for a third time to a convicted criminal,

Ernest Alexander 'Shiner' Ryan, on 18 January 1950. Despite the fact that she had known him for years, this marriage like the others did not last, and they separated after six months.

Nineteen years after Kate Leigh had entered the world, Matilda Mary Twiss, later known as Tilly Devine, followed suit. Tilly was born on 8 September 1900 in a slum in Camberwell, south London. Her father, Edward Twiss, was a bricklayer and her mother a housewife. Tilly left school aged twelve and her connections with 'Down Under' began four years later when she married an Australian serviceman, James Edward Joseph Devine. He was a sapper serving in the Australian Imperial Force, one of the thousands of Australian soldiers who had served in the Allied armies during the First World War. They had one son, Frederick, who was born three years later.

However, long before this, Tilly, like her future rival, Kate Leigh, became part of the underworld. By the time she was sixteen she was involved in prostitution, a 'profession' she continued even after she was married. In her efforts to escape her childhood poverty, she became a streetwalker, applying her trade on the Strand near the bright lights of London's theatre-land. She continued to do this through the remaining war years, during which she was tried on several occasions and found guilty on various accounts of theft, verbal violence, assault and prostitution. On one occasion she was offered the choice of going to prison or paying a fine of forty shillings. She chose the latter. Her life of crime came to an end, at least in London, when at the end of 1919 she sailed to Australia with her husband on the *Waimana*. This ship was a 'bride ship', part of a centuries-long tradition of taking British brides and newlyweds to the colonies. Jim and Tilly Devine did not take their son with them, leaving him to be brought up by Tilly's parents in London.

Virtually as soon as the young couple landed in Sydney, they moved into the district of Paddington, which was well known for its low-quality housing and high level of crime. Naturally Tilly and Jim soon became involved in the city's world of crime, and they began dealing in narcotics, prostitution and running a brothel. In addition, and perhaps as a 'cover' for his illegal activities, Jim Devine became a car hire proprietor and chauffeur – and sometimes a 'getaway man' – while Tilly supplemented the family income by working as a prostitute, her pretty face allowing her to charge ten shillings a 'trick'.

She must have been a very busy woman as between June 1921 and May 1925 — she was convicted seventy-nine times on prostitution-related charges. These included offensive behaviour and using indecent language in public places. By May 1925, the Sydney authorities had evidently had enough of Tilly Devine, and imprisoned her for two years in Long Bay Women's Prison for maliciously wounding a man with a razor in a barber's shop. The police report at the time described her as a 'prostitute of the worst type and an associate of the worst types of prostitutes, vagrants and criminals'. However, despite this official description, within the prison she was called 'Pretty Tilly'.

The local press had a field day with the already notorious female criminal and described her as the 'Queen of the Night' and the 'Worst Woman in Sydney'. Her fame, such as it was, meant that large crowds would attend the courts whenever she appeared, charged with criminal activity.

In addition to all the above, Jim and Tilly Devine continued to deal in cocaine and sell illegal alcohol -'sly-grog'. In addition, they continued running their brothel which was registered in Tilly's name. This was due to a loophole in the law, as the 1905 New South Wales Vagrancy Act prohibited men from doing so, but it did not mention any woman's role in this business. Using the brothel as a base for their operations, they arranged for call girls of a better class to be available for businessmen, politicians and other well-paying customers. Lower class customers would have the use of 'tenement girls', while 'boat girls' were available for sailors or working-class 'johns'.

As Tilly Devine was busy raking in a fortune from her different illegal activities, so too was her future rival, Kate Leigh. She too made money from dealing in sly-grog, drugs, prostitution, and being a madam who ran several brothels.

The 1916 Liquor Act and the 1927 Liquor Licencing Act, which prohibited the sale of liquor after six o'clock, both encouraged the sale of bootleg alcohol. Something Tilly did at her more than twenty bootleg outlets throughout Sydney.

In the same way, Kate also exploited the 1927 Dangerous Drugs Act by organising a lucrative network for the distribution of cocaine. Her suppliers were corrupt doctors, dentists and chemists, who were well paid for their illegal co-operation. From here it is not surprising to read that with two feisty women running parallel criminal empires in the same city their rivalry would sooner or later spill over into violence, mayhem and murder. This happened in what became known as the razor gang wars of the 1920s and 1930s. But more about that later.

As Kate Leigh was netting a fortune from her enterprises, so too were Tilly and Jim Devine. Their businesses also made them a fortune, which they spent in a most ostentatious way. They invested their money in houses, gold and diamond jewellery, expensive cars and, when they went abroad, first class travel.

Whenever Tilly Devine appeared in court, you could be sure that she was flashing large, bejewelled rings, brooches and necklaces. The phrase, 'dripping with diamonds' was a very apt way to describe her. The Devines had by now moved from their Paddington slum to Maroubra, a suburb in Sydney, a move which meant that Tilly had left her childhood and past poverty behind and had joined the bourgeoisie. In contrast to this legitimate expense, the shadier side of their earnings went in paying the various fines that stemmed from their criminal activities, as well as towards bribing police officers to turn a 'blind eye' on occasion. Altogether, during her long criminal career – she continued to run her brothel in Palmer Street until 1968 – Tilly Devine was convicted over two hundred times and spent many years in prison. Not surprisingly, her reputation with the police was of the worst – she had a violent nature and was known to use guns when she thought it necessary.

This violent lifestyle was also reflected in the couple's marriage, and on 9 January 1931, after eleven years of marriage, Jim Devine was charged with the attempted murder of his wife.

*

"You stupid bitch," he shouted at her. "Why did you pay those girls so much? How d'you think we're gonna make any money if you carry on like that?"

"It's not my fault," Tilly shouted back. "You told me to pay them what I did. You said that if not, they'd rat us out to the police."

"Don't you be so stupid, woman! That would never have happened."

"Why not, wise guy?"

"'Cos I'd have paid off the police, then everyone would have been happy. But oh, no," he said, pulling out a pistol from the back of his belt. "You thought it best to give those stupid girls a fortune."

"Jim, you put that pistol away," Tilly shouted. "I'm warning you!"

"Oh yeah? I'm really scared. Your big mouth ain't gonna stop me."

*

And saying that, he swung the gun around in the air, finally pointing it at his wife. Tilly kicked a chair at him and tore out of the house. Swearing blue murder at the top of her voice, she slammed the front door and ran out into the street. As she did so, Jim fired a number of shots at her, but they all went wide. The neighbours, scared by the shooting and seeing Tilly tearing up the street, called the police. Jim Devine was arrested, charged but was acquitted as Tilly refused to testify against him.

But this was not a sign that Tilly had forgiven him. Their stormy relationship finally came to an end with a divorce in 1944. Like Kate Leigh, she linked her future as the lover of yet another well-known criminal, Donald Alexander 'Skinny' Kenney, who she married in Fremantle, Western Australia. The happy couple then returned to Sydney, but this marriage did not last long and after six months, they separated as a result of constant rows about where to live – Sydney or Fremantle.

It seems that Tilly did not like living on her own, as in May 1945 and she married Eric Parsons, an Australian ex-seaman. Despite the fact that this marriage did prove to be a happy one, it started off with Tilly shooting her husband in the leg soon after they were married. Tilly was arrested and charged but was finally acquitted. After this, they lived happily together in a comfortable bungalow in Maroubra, a middle-class suburb of Sydney. The marriage lasted for thirteen years, until Eric died of cancer in November 1958.

One of the most important changes in Tilly Devine's status came at the end of the 1920s, when she stopped prostituting herself and became a madam. By now she owned several brothels throughout Sydney, and apart from the girls of various classes who worked in them, Tilly also employed bouncers, bodyguards and 'standover' men – men who exhorted money through intimidation.

Larry Writer in *The Australian Book of True Crime* states that Tilly was known as a benevolent despot. She demanded honesty and loyalty, rewarded those who worked hard while providing food, housing and medical aid to her staff. In addition, through her bouncers and the like, she also provided her female staff with protection from dissatisfied 'johns' and other violent customers. However, if anyone crossed her, for example, if one of her girls hid some of her earnings, she would sack them immediately and even attack them physically, even with a knife or razor. In July 1943, Tilly was charged with maliciously wounding Ellen Grimson by cutting her face. At her trial, Tilly claimed that Ellen's injuries were caused in self-defence when she hit Ellen with her diamond-ringed fingers, not with a knife. She was acquitted.

As a result of her criminal empire, Tilly now lived in a respectable middle-class suburb in Sydney. However, this was to cause her problems of another sort. To their neighbours' disgust, the Devine bungalow was often used for wild and noisy parties. Her house was frequently raided by the police and more than one fatal shooting occurred there.

On one occasion, her first husband, Jim Devine, shot his rival, George 'Gunman' Gaffney, one of Kate Leigh's chief henchmen. Fortunately for Jim, the dying Gaffney refused to divulge who shot him. As a result, Jim Devine was acquitted by claiming that he had 'fired more to frighten' than kill, and that he was only defending himself and Tilly.

However, this was not just a case of a man defending himself, his wife and his property. Kate, as noted earlier, had her own sly-grog business going in Sydney, together with other criminal activities such as pushing cocaine as well as 'fencing' – dealing in stolen goods. Her illegal activities were parallel with Tilly's and on more than one occasion there were fights, shootings and stabbings between their respective groups of bouncers and henchmen in the streets of Sydney.

In 1936, Police Commissioner William Mackay had had enough of this gang warfare and he persuaded both sides to undertake a truce. Although Kate and Tilly and their men were naturally suspicious of the police, and of the opposing side, they did agree. The result was that the women were allowed to continue with their enterprises on condition that the violence stopped.

Kate's activities were controlled from her plush home in Lansdowne Street in the Surrey Hills suburb of Sydney, and like Tilly Devine, she too employed a small army of bouncers and standoff men for the purpose of protecting her 'girls'. They were also employed to keep an eye on her thirty-plus sly-grog hotels and brothels, as well as on her illegal betting, gambling and drug distribution centres. However, despite the 'peace-treaty', there were occasions when Tilly Devine and Kate Leigh also fought each other personally, as their respective gangs ambushed each other, often bringing razors to the fray. This was because the Sydney authorities, in their effort to fight the rising crimewave, had severely cracked down on the carrying and use of firearms. In addition, Kate was known to trash Tilly's brothels and attack her rival's sex-workers, while Tilly, not to be outdone, would smash Kate's groggeries and have her coke dealers beaten up.

Despite Kate's personal involvement in violent crimes she always managed to get acquitted. On 27 March 1930, she shot and killed John William 'Snowy' Prendergast, when he and other criminals broke into her house. In December 1931 she was indicted for killing Joseph McNamara, but again she was let off scot-free.

But her luck did not always last. In July 1930, Kate Leigh was sent to prison for dealing in drugs after her Riley Street house was raided by the drug squad. Because cocaine was found on the premises, Kate was sentenced to twelve months 'inside'.

However, this did nothing to deter her, and through her connections with corrupt police officers and other legal officials, she continued her various enterprises throughout the 1930s and 1940s. During this twenty-year period she was charged on over one hundred occasions and was sent to prison thirteen times.

Her extravagant lifestyle began to fall apart in the 1950s. World War II naval restrictions had already caused problems for her while the authorities in Sydney and the New South Wales state government began to crack down on one of the wealthiest women in Sydney. The restrictions meant that obtaining cocaine, which was very profitable, became more difficult, while the post-war

Taxation Office brought about Kate Leigh's final financial fall.

*

"Look at this," Kate declared one September day in 1954, and threw some sheets of paper onto the kitchen table. "I've just received this stupid letter from the tax people demanding I pay taxes on my income since 1942! That's twelve bloody years! Those idiots must have fallen on their heads."

"Don't you worry about that, dear. I'm sure it's all a big mistake, and if it isn't, one of your accountants will be able to sort it out," one of her friends said.

*

But Kate's accountants could not beat the system this time. When she appeared at the Sydney bankruptcy court – after claiming that her assets consisted of only '£1,960 [and] furniture and three properties in Devonshire Street' – the assessment was readjusted by the authorities to £7,130 (over £210,000 today). She was taxed on this figure, and also had to pay a considerable sum in fines also dating back to 1942.

Kate's finances received another blow in 1955, when the state government changed the law to allow legal hotels to sell alcohol until ten o'clock at night. Suddenly there was no need for thirsty Sydney-siders to purchase Kate's sly-grog, which meant that this major aspect of her business collapsed. Kate's reaction to the financial disaster was to say, "The bloom has gone off the grog."

By now, Kate Leigh was seventy-four years old. She was in poor health and living in a small room in one of her illegal hotels. She was virtually penniless and dependent on her nephew. Somehow she struggled on for another nine years, until she died following a severe stroke on 4 February 1964.

The major irony of her life was that despite her desire to escape her childhood poverty by turning to a life of crime, she died as poor as she had been when she had been born. Her funeral at St. Peter's Catholic Church was attended by seven hundred mourners and she was survived by her daughter Eileen May Ranson. Despite her terrible reputation, the press were more generous when she died and noted that she had helped the unemployed during the Great Depression of the early 1930s and they also noted her unofficial patriotic acts during World War II such as providing brothels and cheap beer for foreign servicemen.

At the same time that Kate Leigh making her illegal fortune, so too was Tilly Devine. Even when the razor gang warfare came to an end, Tilly continued with her brothels and drug trade. As a result, she too often appeared in court, her appearances becoming a show, she always being well-coiffed, dressed flamboyantly, wearing her diamond jewellery ostentatiously and wrapped up in an expensive fur coat. She was usually charged with a variety of crimes ranging from assault and indecent language to running brothels and various drug-related crimes.

In January 1930, Tilly Devine was charged with

assaulting a police officer and riotous behaviour. In order to escape from being sent back to Long Bay Prison, her lawyer promised that Tilly would leave Australia for two years. This she did and moved to London. She returned after two years to discover that Jim had been having an affair. This did not help her shaky marriage, which somehow continued despite her husband's philandering, domestic violence and drunkenness.

It was also during this period, in the early 1930s, that the world-wide Great Depression hit Australia. The lack of money and customers affected Tilly's businesses and she was only saved by the advent of the Second World War. Suddenly hundreds of Allied servicemen poured into Sydney, all looking for women and booze. Tilly supplied both and her business picked up. At the same time, she gained a certain amount of respectability by holding quiet and decorous garden parties for which she charged attendance or passed the hat around. She then donated the proceeds to the families of Australian servicemen, to the Veterans Welfare Association, and also some for the welfare of children in hospital.

Half-way through the war, in March 1943, she obtained a divorce from the brutal and unfaithful Jim Devine, concluding this twenty-seven-year chapter in her life. Like Kate Leigh, Tilly did not seem to like living on her own, and so in May 1945 she married the previously noted Eric Parsons. After forty-five years, Tilly Devine was at last happily married.

As already mentioned, the Second World War was good for Tilly. In fact it was so good that in 1953 she boasted that, "I am a lucky, lucky, girl. I have more diamonds than the Queen of England's stowaways – and better ones, too!" However, this financial situation did not last. As with Kate Leigh, the Australian Taxation Office played a major role in Tilly's downfall.

In October 1955, Tilly was ordered to pay the equivalent of twenty-thousand Australian dollars (nearly A$650,000 today) in unpaid income tax and fines. Naturally she protested and appealed but to no avail. This meant that she had to sell off many of her properties, and in the end she was left with one brothel in Palmer Street, Sydney.

Like her rival, Kate Leigh, Tilly Devine's final fall was one of pain and poverty. From 1950 she had suffered from chronic bronchitis, and in the end she died aged seventy on 24 November 1970 from cancer at Concord Repatriation Hospital, Sydney. Unlike Kate Leigh, hardly anyone attended her funeral and the eulogy, "She was a villain, but who am I to judge her?" was given by Norman Allan, the Police Commissioner.

Ron Saw in the *Daily Telegraph* was less kind. Although he had once described the ageing Kate Leigh as "a kindly and generous old trot with many friends," he said of Tilly Devine, previously known as the 'Queen of the Night':

A vicious, grasping high priestess of savagery, venery, obscenity and whoredom... She died friendless and alone, and for that she must be pitied. But if they hold a wake for

301

her the sorrow will be slobber and crocodile tears. She
was a wretched woman.

There was no wake and she was survived by her son,
Frederick Ralph, and two grandchildren.

Perhaps, the only bright spots in this tale of female
violence and avarice are that, apart from their donations to
charity towards the end of their criminal careers, the pair
of them did succeed in burying the hatchet in 1948. They
were now both well past their prime with very little close
family. Kate was sixty-seven and Tilly was forty-eight and
most of their friends and acquaintances were dead,
naturally or as a result of shooting and stabbing. In March
1950, *People* magazine published a report with a photo of
the pair of them close together and smiling, wearing their
jewellery and apparently at peace with the world.
However, it should be remembered that this happy picture
was taken several years before the tax authorities reduced
both of them to the poverty they had worked so hard to
overcome.

As with Australia's other iconic criminal, Ned Kelly
(1854-1880), Tilly Devine and Kate Leigh have both
become some sort of a legend – a pair of female Robin
Hoods. Bestselling books have been written about them
and the razor gang era of the Twenties and Thirties are
taught as a course, 'Sin City: A History of Sydney' at
Sydney University. Their criminal feud became the basis
of the Australian television drama, *Underbelly: Razor*,
while the central Sydney wine bar, 'Love Tilly Devine' is

still carrying on the tradition of selling alcohol, but legally this time.

Kate Leigh & Tilly Devine – Timeline

1881 – March 3: Kate Leigh born as Kathleen Mary Josephine Beahan, Dubbo, New South Wales, Australia.

1893 – Spends time in a Girls' Home.

1900 – Daughter, Eileen May born out of wedlock. Sept 8: Tilly Devine born as Matilda Mary Twiss, Camberwell, London.

1902 – May: Kate marries James Leigh, petty criminal.

1905 – Kate separates from James Leigh.

1912 – Tilly leaves school.

1916 – Tilly marries James Edward Joseph Devine, Australian soldier and is also involved in prostitution.

1919 – Tilly and James sail to Australia on 'bride-ship' and leave their newly-born son, Frederick, in London with her parents. Tilly and James become involved in Sydney crime scene. She runs a brothel.

1921 – Kate divorces James after unsuccessful sixteen-year marriage

1921-1925 – Tilly convicted on 79 charges of prostitution and other crimes.

1922 – Sept: Kate marries Edward Joseph Barry, petty criminal.

1925 – May: Tilly sent to Long bay Women's Prison for wounding man with razor.

1925-1930 – Kate lives with Walter 'Wally' Tomlinson, violent criminal.

1927 – Kate organises network for distributing coke in Sydney.

1930 – Jan: Tilly charged with assaulting a police officer and sent to England for two years. Tomlinson walks out on Kate and she becomes *de facto* wife of Henry Baker, criminal. March 27: Kate is charged with shooting John 'Snowy' Prendergast when he and others break into her house, but is acquitted. July: Kate sent to prison for one year for drug offences.

1930-1940 – Kate charged over one hundred times for criminal offences, sent to prison thirteen times.

1931 – June 9: James Devine charged with attempted murder of Tilly. Dec: Kate tried for killing Joseph Macnamara but acquitted.

1932 – Tilly returns to Sydney to find husband James, has been having a love-affair during her two-year stay in England.

1936 – Sydney Police Commissioner William Mackay persuades Tilly and Kate to 'bury the hatchet' between them.

1939-1945 – WW2 restrictions cause Kate's criminal business activities to fall financially. WW2 is good for Tilly's drink and brothel business. She donates money to veteran soldiers' charities.

1943 – July: Tilly charged with wounding Ellen Grison with a razor but acquitted.

1944 – Tilly and James divorce after 28-year stormy marriage. Tilly marries Donald 'Skinny' Kenny, criminal in Fremantle, Western Australia. Marriage lasts six months.

1945 – May: Tilly marries second husband, Eric John Parsons, ex-sailor.

1948 – Kate divorces Edward Joseph Barry after 26-year unsuccessful marriage. Tilly and Kate agree to make peace between themselves.

1950 – Jan 18: Kate marries third husband, Ernest Alexander 'Shiner' Ryan. Marriage lasts six months. Tilly starts suffering from chronic bronchitis.

1954 – Kate charged for failing to pay taxes since 1942.

1955 – Kate's grog business hit when government allow hotels to sell alcohol legally. Oct: Tilly ordered to pay A$20,000 in back taxes; has to sell off much of her property including brothels to do so.

1964 – Feb 4: Kate dies from a stroke, poverty-stricken. 700 people attend her funeral.

1970 – Nov 24: Tilly dies of cancer in Sydney hospital, poor and virtually forgotten. Only a few people attend her funeral.

Chapter Twenty

Marguerite Alibert (1890-1971)
Courtesan to Prince Edward (VIII)
& Other High-flyers

The word 'wicked' as used throughout most of this book usually describes women who have been considered as morally wrong, sinful, corrupt and evil. This is the Biblical use of the word and refers to such women as Eve (for tempting Adam), Jezebel (for denying God and encouraging the worship of false gods and murdering God's true prophets) and Delilah (for being an idol worshipper and also for seducing Samson, causing him to be blinded and to commit suicide).

However, language changes and, today, wicked when used as slang often means the opposite, that is, something 'wonderful', 'cool' or 'great'. This use of the word entered British English in the 1980s from Black American slang and is yet one more example of how a word which in the past described a morally bad concept is now used for something considered good. Similar modern examples include using 'evil' and 'brutal' for 'good'.

So keeping the above description of wicked in mind, how would you relate to women variously called prostitutes, whores and hookers? These are (and were) women who use their bodies and sexual assets to attract men and by doing so hope to improve their economic situation. The more 'classy' style of prostitute, the courtesan, also aims to climb up the social ladder while earning goodly sums of money at the same time. Are these women wicked because they do not wish to remain poor and downtrodden?

While society has always looked down on prostitutes and hookers who 'ply their trade' on the street or in dubious hotels, courtesans, their wealthier counterparts, often had a respectable role to play in high society. These women would use their natural charms on their royal or aristocratic patrons by providing sexual favours as well as being entertaining companions who could sing, dance and be witty conversationalists. Of course they had to be attractive and elegant, well-dressed and coifed, and much of their expensive jewellery and clothing would have been paid for by their adoring and wealthy benefactors.

Some well-known European courtesans include Nell

307

Gwynne (1650-1687), Charles II's 'pretty witty' favourite mistress; Madame de Pompadour, (1721-1764) who became the last maîtresse-en-titre *– chief mistress – to Louis XV, and Mata Hari (1876-1917) who in addition to being a courtesan, was a well-known singer and dancer before being executed for allegedly being a spy during the First World War.*

So was Marguerite Alibert, the subject of this chapter, a wicked woman or not?

*

Marguerite Marie Alibert was born in 1890 in Paris. Her father, Firmin, was a taxi driver (although he claimed that he was some sort of assistant in a lawyer's office) and her mother, Marie Aurand served as a maid. When Marguerite was a small girl, her four-year-old brother was killed when he was hit by a heavy vehicle. Her parents blamed her for this and sent her to the Sisters of Mary convent. She was badly treated and the only thing that she learned there was how to sing.

After she turned sixteen, the nuns made her become a house servant, and there she became pregnant. After giving birth to a daughter, Raymonde, the nuns threw her out onto the street. This was the toughest period of Marguerite's life. Without education or training, she was forced to do anything that would bring in money to support her and her baby girl. Eventually, as she had very little money, she sent her young daughter off to a farm in the country where she hoped she would be fed and well-looked after.

It was during this bleak period that she worked as a servant in a number of wealthy households. Here she saw how it was to live when you had plenty of money at your disposal, and so she decided to turn herself into *une dame à cinq heures* – a 'five o'clock girl' – that is, she aimed to become a high-class prostitute. Somehow, through sheer determination and the will to survive, she managed to acquire some impressive clothes and clean herself up. She was obviously attractive and soon she began to accompany wealthy businessmen on their trips or escort them to their clubs and restaurants. There she saw more of how high society lived and became even more determined to lead this life of luxury.

*

One evening, a well-dressed woman approached her in a restaurant.

"*Ma chérie*," the woman began, casually playing with a long pearl necklace. "I have been watching how you have been behaving these last two weeks with the gentlemen you have come here with, and I would like to make you a proposition."

"Why, who are you and what do you want of me?" the naturally suspicious Marguerite asked.

"My name is Madame Denant and I am the owner of a fine establishment which caters to the needs of gentlemen."

"Do you mean a brothel?" the unsophisticated

Marguerite asked.

Madame Denant coughed quietly. "I prefer not to use that word. Just let's say that I run a place, *une maison de rendezvous*, where men come in order to relax from the cares of the day."

"And what would I have to do?"

"You would continue doing what you are doing now, except that you would have a permanent roof over your head and food in your belly. You wouldn't have to wonder when your next client would turn up or how he will be because I will look after that side of the business."

"Can I have a day to think about this?" Marguerite asked.

"Certainly, my dear. Here is my card. Let me know if you are interested as soon as possible."

Marguerite nodded as Madame Denant gave her an embossed cream-coloured business card and added, "But please make up your mind quickly. Remember, you are not the only pretty girl in Paris."

*

The next day Marguerite went round to the address on Madame Denant's card and told her that she would like to work for her. The brothel owner had not lied. She did indeed run a very well-appointed establishment which catered for wealthy high society men. Marguerite quickly learned to become more attractive and sophisticated, two aspects which would help her for the rest of her life.

Soon after she began working for Madame Denant,

Marguerite was introduced to a Monsieur André Mellor. He was a successful married forty-year-old wine merchant, and as he told Marguerite at their first candle-lit meal, it was considered perfectly acceptable for men of his class to have a mistress. This was not news to Marguerite and she hoped that she would have a long-term relationship with this kind and wealthy businessman.

She was not to be disappointed. Soon after having been introduced to him, it became clear that he was very pleased with her and she became his latest mistress. He gave her a luxury apartment and bought her food, clothes and jewellery without laying down any irksome conditions. For Marguerite this was her aim. No longer did she have to worry about poverty or sleeping rough or selling her body for a few sous or francs in rundown hotels or back streets. Waking up late in the morning in a luxurious bed with fine sheets and having a servant to look after her, well, *that* was the life! But she must have asked herself, how long would it last? Would she ever go back to the stinking gutters?

Time passed and Marguerite remained with Monsieur André for six years. They lived together as a married couple and it was during this period that the now affluent Marguerite Alibert – who called herself Marguerite Mellor – brought her daughter, Raymonde, back from the farm and sent her to live in London (presumably with friends or family).

By now it was 1913 and Marguerite's relationship with her 'husband' was beginning to bore her. She began to have affairs with other wealthy men and André began to

311

grow increasingly jealous. In the end, they parted company, but not before he had paid her off with 200,000 francs. She then began to work for Madame Sonia de Théval, whose *maison d'affectation* was of an even higher class than Madame Denant's establishment. Marguerite was one of the most sought-after girls there and soon she began entertaining French noblemen and visiting members of the English aristocracy. One of her first well-known clients was the generous and fabulously rich landowner, Hugh Grosvenor, 2nd Duke of Westminster. From her connections with such men, it was more or less to be expected that the upward climbing Marguerite would come in contact with the next layer of society, royalty. And that is exactly what happened.

Sometime in 1917, Marguerite was introduced to the future King Edward VIII. At this time he was known as Edward, the Prince of Wales, and he was in France during the First World War serving as a captain in the Grenadier Guards. While he was on leave from the trenches of the Western Front, a friend introduced the somewhat sexually naïve prince to Marguerite, probably to expand this aspect of his education. It was not his first tryst with a courtesan, but it was certainly his first meaningful relationship with such an enticing woman. He used to see Marguerite when he came to Paris on leave and they would meet in quiet corners in exclusive hotel lobbies.

*

"Marguerite," the twenty-one-year-old prince said, taking

her hand and kissing her fingertips. "You are so beautiful that I adore you. You are all that I can think about when I am away at the Front."

"Non, non, mon chéri," she replied. "I'm sure you have to think about your men there and all that is happening. After all, you are an officer, *un capitaine, non?"*

"I know all that, but thinking about you takes my mind off the danger, the bullets and shells and the beastly filthy life in the trenches. But come, let me buy you another glass of champagne."

Later, after the champagne, she took him up to her room to continue with his sexual education.

"Oh, my Marguerite, you are so good at this," he panted later that afternoon. "You do to me what no other girl has done. I don't know how I lived before I met you."

"I'm sure you lived very well," Marguerite replied comparing her past and his. "You lived in a palace surrounded by servants and –"

"Yes, that is true, but *you* didn't have to cope with my family, did you? My parents," he continued, "are so boring and predictable. The only things that interest my father are the navy and his damned collection of stamps. And my mother, all she is interested in is *objets' d'art* and expensive knick-knacks."

"But surely it cannot be so bad back in London. After all, you have your four brothers and your sister, no?" she asked as she ran her hand lightly up his thigh.

"I know all that, but life in the palace is so formal," he sighed. "Here with you I can just be me. Even at the Front, they won't let me forget for a moment that one day I will be the king."

"Ah well, *mon chéri*, let us put all that behind us for an hour and see what else I can teach you before you have to leave."

The prince nodded eagerly and took her into his arms. "And when I'm not with you, I will keep writing to you. Is that all right?"

Now it was Marguerite's turn to nod. "*Oui, oui*, that is all right."

"And make sure you keep my letters," the infatuated heir to the throne added. "They are written proof of my love and how I am thinking about you all the time I'm away from you."

*

This intense relationship lasted for almost a year, but when the war came to an end in November 1918, so too did the love affair. Edward had to return to England to take up his princely duties, and in doing so he left a furious Marguerite behind in Paris. She felt that she had been abandoned and vowed to take revenge. She still had the twenty or so letters the prince had written to her, and she decided to use them to blackmail him. She knew that the British royal family would pay her a fortune not to publish this very private correspondence. But then she decided not to act right away, holding onto the letters as an 'insurance policy', to bring in more money in the future if necessary.

But in the meantime, she had to find her next meal-ticket. This proved to be Charles Laurent. He was a wealthy air force officer, and the two were married in 1919. This was the first time in her life that Marguerite lived with a man officially, and so she took his name and called herself, Marguerite Laurent. Despite the happy beginning, the marriage was a disaster and they were divorced after six months. Nevertheless, she now became even wealthier, as the divorce settlement included a luxury apartment, a ten-horse stable and two limousines. This of course was a distinct improvement for a woman who had spent her formative years being abused in a convent before being thrown out onto the streets.

As a result of this setback, Marguerite was soon looking for a new husband or partner, and her next man was to prove even richer and of a higher status than Monsieur André Mellor or Monsieur Charles Laurent. His name was Ali Kamel Fahmi Bey. He was a super-rich Egyptian businessman who had so much money that, although he was not really allowed to, he called himself *Bey* – prince – and no-one argued with him. Marguerite met Ali in Paris while escorting another businessman, who she rapidly dropped when her new lover took her around France on a gambling and touring trip.

After this, her new Egyptian conquest took her to Cairo. There she converted to Islam, and as part of a prenuptial agreement she was expected to agree to two conditions: that she would wear traditional Muslim clothes and not divorce her husband. The strong-minded, ambitious Marguerite refused to agree to the first condition, but did not make any complaint about the second. The couple were married in Cairo in 1922 and the service was followed by a formal Islamic wedding in January 1923. This marriage, like her previous marriage with Charles Laurent, began to fall apart very quickly. While Fahmi relented and allowed her to wear Western clothes, he insisted that, following Muslim tradition, he was allowed to take other wives as well.

They fought constantly and he made Marguerite perform sexual acts that she found disgusting. She became very unhappy and started to keep a strict record of her life with him. This, like the love-letters she still had under lock and key from Prince Edward, would prove to be very useful in the future.

One day in the summer of 1923, the wealthy couple went to London for a holiday. They stayed at the Savoy Hotel, and naturally were accompanied by several of their servants, a secretary, a maid and a valet. On 9 July, after returning from a production of the operetta, *The Merry Widow*, they had a blazing row in their hotel room. In the heat of the argument, early on the morning of 10 July, Marguerite grabbed her .32 Browning pistol, which she had hidden under her pillow, and shot Fahmi three times, in the head, back and neck. He was rushed to the nearby Charing Cross Hospital but died within an hour. Marguerite was arrested and taken into custody and the resulting 'trial of the decade' opened on 10 September 1923.

Huge crowds waited outside the court and the newspapers reported all the details they were allowed to; every revelation being accompanied by large dramatic headlines.

What the press was not allowed to publish were details of Marguerite's past courtesan life and her previous romance with the Prince of Wales, the future King Edward VIII. As Lord Curzon, the Foreign Secretary wrote at the time:

The French girl who shot her so-called Egyptian prince in London, and is going to be tried for murder, is the fancy woman who was the Prince's keep in Paris during the war, and they are terribly afraid that he might be dragged in. His name must be kept out.

Lord Curzon had no need to worry. All of this occurred before the changes in the sixties brought about a more open press and a less deferential media which was more than willing to hold the rich and privileges to account. Much of this was done of course by plastering their secrets all over the front pages of the popular tabloids. Therefore the post First World War I establishment was able to keep a lid on the prince's Parisian past and none of this became public knowledge.

Using all of his skill as a trial lawyer, the renowned Sir Edward Marshall Hull defended Marguerite by arguing that her husband had been 'a monster of eastern depravity and decadence, whose sexual tastes were indicative of an amoral sadism towards his helpless European wife'. By referring to the deceased Fahmi in racist terms and claiming that the shooting was a case of self-defence committed by a poor abused wife, the defence convinced the judge, Mr Justice Rigby-Swift, to drop all charges against Marguerite with the result that she was acquitted.

Following her success in the Old Bailey, Marguerite tried to claim her husband's fortune from his family in Egypt. The court there did not accept her claim, and so she had to return to her old gold-digging ways in order to continue living in the manner that she had become accustomed. She continued seducing rich men for the rest of her life, and she also took to acting small parts in films. She died a rich woman aged eighty on 2 January 1971.

Was Marguerite Alibert really a wicked woman?

In comparison with many of the women mentioned in these chapters, she was not a mass-murderer or poisoner, nor indeed had she duped tens of people out of their hard-earned savings. She had killed only one man who, according to her standards had regularly abused her. Her way of life, while frowned upon by the Church and the establishment, was the only way she saw available to her, without the benefits of a good background and education, to climb up out of the gutter and survive in comfort. As far as we know, the letters that Prince Edward wrote to her never surfaced and that whether they ever met again after the Second World War when they were both living in Paris is another unanswered question.

Chapter Twenty-One

Ilse Koch (1906-1967)
Nazi Concentration Camp Overseer at
Buchenwald & Majdanek

Ilse Koch in prison aged 41, 1947

Many of the women featured in this book were a bad lot, if not truly wicked in the full sense of the word, as defined by the Oxford English Dictionary, 'sinful, iniquitous, vicious, given to or involving immorality'. *But however bad these women may have been, none of them, including Elizabeth Bathory, who was alleged to have tortured and murdered hundreds of young aristocratic women and girl servants, or Guilia Tofana who indirectly poisoned hundreds of people four hundred years ago, can compare in any way with Ilse Koch, the commandant of the Nazi concentration camps, Buchenwald (1937-1941) and Majdanek (1941-1943). It was not that she, on a personal level, acted any worse than the aforementioned women in torturing and killing her victims; it is a question of scale. Whereas Elizabeth Bathory and Guilia Tofana had killed hundreds and Queen Ranavalona thousands, Ilse Koch, the 'Bitch of Buchenwald', served as a major contributor to the Holocaust's murderous total of at least twelve million victims. These included the 56,545 deaths at Buchenwald and the 79,000 victims of the Nazi death-machine who were killed at Majdanek.*

To put it simply, even though Ilse Koch was directly responsible for and personally murdered 'only' a few victims, she ensured that her concentration camps were run in such an organised way that the murder of tens of thousands in Buchenwald and Majdanek was carried out with extreme industrial efficiency. She made it her business to ensure that her well-oiled 'production line' of death, or as the US Holocaust Memorial Museum phrased it, 'the systematic bureaucratic state-sponsored persecution' machine ended the lives of hundreds of Jews, Poles, Russians, Gypsies and others **every day** *for six years from 1937–1943.*

*

Ilse Koch was born Margarete Ilse Köhler in Dresden, Germany in 1906. She must have been familiar with the

320

military way of life, as her father had been an army officer. She studied accountancy from the age of fifteen, and in 1932 joined the newly formed Nazi party. It was there that in 1934 that she met her future husband, Karl-Otto Koch. They were married three years later, when Karl was the commandant of the Sachsenhausen concentration camp, twenty miles north-west of Berlin. This camp held political and special prisoners such as Stalin's son, Yakov, the former French Prime Minister, Paul Reynaud, and Herschel Grynszpan, the Jewish assassin of a German diplomat in 1938. Here Ilse worked as a guard and as a secretary. Before this camp was liberated by the Russian army in April 1945, 100,000 prisoners had died there as a result of disease, being worked to death through slave-labour, and direct extermination. After their marriage, Ilse and Karl-Otto were transferred to Buchenwald, 180 miles south-west of Berlin.

This camp, which was originally intended to hold eight thousand prisoners, was the first concentration camp to be built within Germany itself and was surrounded by over 130 sub-camps. Buchenwald began to receive people from all over Europe, and almost 280,000 prisoners were incarcerated there between July 1937 and April 1945. The camp was the largest one to be set up in Germany itself and over 56,000 people died there as a result of torture, medical experiments and outright murder. More than eight thousand Russian soldiers were shot there in a specially erected building, and thousands of other people were forced to make equipment for the German army. When the Allies succeeded in overrunning the camp in April 1945,

General Eisenhower wrote, 'Nothing has ever shocked me as much as that sight'.

Between five hundred and a thousand female prisoners were kept at Buchenwald, and most of them were forced to work in the camp's brothel. This was run by the SS, and Ilse Koch worked as the head supervisor of twenty-two other female guards, overseeing the hundreds of female prisoners.

In addition, many medical experiments were carried out on the prisoners, including trials for vaccines against typhus and other diseases. Other tests, intended to find a balm for wounds from incendiary bombs, caused very severe burns to the victims' skin. In addition, Ilse Koch was known to take the tattooed skin of murdered inmates and use it for making lampshades, gloves and book-covers. According to testimony submitted at her trials after the war, the red-haired camp overseer would ride around the camp scantily dressed on a horse holding a whip and then savagely beat any prisoner who looked at her.

It was this 'factory of death' that Ilse Koch, nicknamed the 'Witch' and 'Bitch Queen', 'Beast' and 'Butcher Widow' of Buchenwald, built an indoor sports arena. This cost over 250,000 Reichsmarks, most of which came mainly from the camp's prisoners' stolen property.

Her four years at Buchenwald came to an end in 1941 when she and her husband were transferred to Lublin in eastern Poland in order to set up the Majdanek extermination camp. This camp, like Belzec, Sobibor, Majdanek, Chelmno, Treblinka, and Auschwitz, was built in Poland as the Nazis wanted to 'hide' them from the

Allies' prying eyes, the first three named here being the furthest away from Germany itself.

Majdanek ('Little Majdan') had seven gas-chambers, two gallows and over two hundred buildings for housing and torturing the mainly Polish and Jewish prisoners. Of the 150,000 people incarcerated there, nearly 80,000 were killed through forced labour, disease, inhuman living conditions and the gas-chambers.

On 24 August 1943, Ilse and Karl-Otto were arrested by the SS for financially exploiting their positions at Buchenwald. They were charged with embezzlement, private enrichment and murdering prisoners who knew too much about their illegal financial dealings.

Ilse was imprisoned until 1944 and then put on trial. She was acquitted through lack of evidence, but her husband was not so fortunate. He was sentenced to death and shot by a firing squad on 5 April 1945, one month before the war ended. The now demoted Ilse went to live with her family in Ludwigsburg near Stuttgart in the south of Germany.

On 30 June 1945 she was arrested by the US authorities, who were trying to catch and arrest as many top Nazis as they could. This was part of the denazification programme which planned to return Germany and the rest of formerly Nazi-occupied Europe to some sort of normality.

Ilse and thirty other Nazis were prosecuted in 1947 at the American Military Court at Dachau, near Munich, the site of the Nazi's longest running concentration camp (1933-1945). She was charged with 'participating in a criminal plan for aiding, abetting and participating in the murders at Buchenwald'. Although she was eight months pregnant at the time, she was still sentenced to life imprisonment.

However, in June 1948, the Military Governor of the American Zone in Germany, General Clay, reviewed her sentence and reduced it to four years imprisonment, saying that, 'there was no convincing evidence that she had selected inmates for extermination in order to secure tattooed skin, or that she possessed any articles made of human skin'.

This reversal of sentence caused a public furore and a Senate investigation back in the United States. The general tried to justify his decision by claiming that the skins found were goatskins, but this did not help Ilse Koch. She was put on trial again and this time she faced a West German civilian court. This new trial began on 27 November 1950 and lasted for seven weeks. Two hundred witnesses gave evidence for the prosecution and fifty for the defence. At least four witnesses testified as to how she had had prisoners killed for their tattooed skins.

Seven weeks later, on 15 January 1951, Ilse was charged with incitement to murder and attempted murder and incitement to committing grievous bodily harm. On 10 May 1951 she was found guilty and began her sentence on 15 June 1951. She appealed her sentence several times, but the West German Federal Court of Justice, the Bavarian Ministry of Justice and the International Human Rights Commission all took it in turn to reject her appeals.

Sixteen years later, on 1 September 1967 (28 years to

the day after the Nazis attacked Poland and started the Second World War), the sixty-year-old Ilse Koch hanged herself with a bedsheet in her cell in Aichach women's prison. Towards the end of her life she begun to be delusional and claim that survivors from Buchenwald and Majdanek were abusing her in her cell. Hers was not to be the only suicide in the Koch family. One of her sons killed himself, saying that 'he could not live with the shame of the crimes of his parents'.

Was Ilse Koch really a wicked woman?

Yes, there is absolutely no doubt that this Nazi extermination camp commander is the most wicked by far of all the women described in this book.

Chapter Twenty-Two

Bonnie Parker (1910-1934)

Bonnie Parker aged 23, 1933

If you watch sport, either live or on TV, read novels or study history, you will often see that people root for the underdog. In one of the most dramatic stories in one of the world's oldest books, the Bible, we hope that when young David faces the giant Goliath, (I Samuel, 17) David will win. After all, what chance does the young shepherd boy have? He is armed with his slingshot and 'five smooth stones', while the gigantic Goliath, the Philistine ('four cubits and a span' – nearly seven feet tall) is well-armed with a sword, spear and shield. As we know, David succeeds in killing his enemy with his first stone and our hopes for his success are fulfilled.

Similarly, Shakespeare in Henry V *was patriotically proud of the king's 'miserable little army' at Agincourt (1415) when they smashed the much larger armoured forces of the French King Charles VI. Not only does the Bard root for the simple English underdog archers in terms of weaponry, but he stresses that here is a case of 'We few, we happy few, we band of brothers' who will not bow down to what seems to be their terrible fate.*

Other well-known examples from military history of where the apparently weaker take on and defeat their stronger opponents occur when George Washington's small rag-tag army was determined not to be beaten by the British army in the American fight for independence; or when Davy Crockett and a handful of men took on the Mexican Army at the Alamo in 1836. On the eastern side of the Atlantic, Robin Hood has been cheered on for centuries for defying the nasty Sheriff of Nottingham, while several centuries later in 1879, one hundred and fifty British soldiers successfully beat off three to four thousand Zulu warriors at Rorke's Drift in South Africa.

We are also pleased to read 'rags to riches' stories, true or fiction, especially when poor children fight their way up the ladder to achieve fame and fortune. Cinderella is a good fictional example, while Abraham Lincoln, the boy who grew up in a simple log cabin to become one of America's greatest presidents, show that it is possible to beat the odds in real life.

For some reason, certain criminals and outlaws have

also been held in awe over the years. Is this because they fought the establishment and refused to be kept down? Or is it because they were hoping to make a fortune quickly, something that many other people would like to do? Examples of such folk heroes include Ned Kelly, the bushranger who took on the Australian police and was hanged aged twenty-six in 1880. In America, Billy the Kid and Jesse James were admired, perhaps more so in the past than today. However, their more modern counterparts include a pair of well-known criminals who have gone down in popular culture and are now known simply as Bonnie & Clyde.

*

Bonnie Elizabeth Parker was born in Rowena, Texas in 1910, the second of three children. Her father, Charles, was a bricklayer who died when she was four years old, and her mother, Emma, was a housewife.

Seeing that she could not cope on her own, Emma took her children back to her parents' home in West Dallas where she worked as a seamstress. Bonnie never completed her high school education as in September 1925 she dropped out to marry a fellow-student, Roy Thornton. This was just a few days before she turned sixteen and the marriage was a failure. Roy was often away from home, had problems with the law, and the couple separated soon after. He was later sent to Huntsville State Prison in 1933 for five years for robbery and was killed trying to escape in October 1937.

After her final separation, Bonnie moved back to her mother's house and worked as a waitress. From a diary she kept at this time, it is clear to see that she was bored with life and impatient to be doing something more exciting than serving customers in a cheap café. From this we know that one of her customers was Ted Hinton, a man who served in the posse who, eight years later, would kill her and Clyde.

According to several accounts, it was during this period, in 1929, that she met Clyde. This was at the house of Clarence Clay, one of Clyde's friends.

*

"Hello sugar," Clyde said, looking at Bonnie. "Who are you? What's your name?"

"Bonnie Parker, and who are you to ask?"

"Me? I'm Clyde Chestnut Barrow at your service, ma'am," he replied, making a sweeping bow. "Haven't I seen you working at the café near the bus station downtown?"

"Yeah, sure."

"So what happened to your arm," he continued, pointing to her plaster cast. "Did a customer get angry and hit you?"

"No, no, I slipped on the wet floor there and broke it. That's all. So now I'm back living with my mother. I suppose I'll find a place of my own when it gets better and I can go back to work."

"Yeah, yeah, rent costs money," Clyde nodded. "But

say, can I take you out to the movies? How about this Saturday night? There's this good picture, *The Bishop Murder Case,* showing. Its got Basil Rathbone and Leila Hyams in it."

"What, a murder film? I don't like seeing bodies all over the place."

"No, no. It's more like a mystery, y'know, a whodunit. Something like Sherlock Holmes. And only one guy is killed. My friend says he gets shot in the heart by an arrow."

"All right. Here is my mother's address. I'll see you then."

A few days later they were sitting in the dark in the movie theatre.

"I think I should tell you something about me," Clyde began as he put his arm around her trying to slip his hand down the inside of her blouse. "I may not be what you think," he said.

"What do you mean?" Bonnie replied, gently pushing his hand away.

"Well, if you think you're going out with a choirboy, you've got it wrong."

"How so?"

"I've served time –"

"Why? Where?"

"First time I was arrested was for not returning a rental car a few years back, then me and my brother, Buck, were arrested for stealing some turkeys."

"What! They'd arrest you for *that*?"

"Yeah, sure, and then I got caught for cracking safes,

stealing cars and robbing some stores and –"

"Weren't you scared?"

"No, it was fun, exciting, but then it wasn't funny anymore when they sent me to prison. Some guys there attacked me, so I hit one of them with this iron bar and killed him. After that the other guys left me alone."

"But that's terrible. So why didn't they send you to the chair or hang you?"

"'Cos another guy I was friendly with said that he'd done it. You see, he was in there for life, so what could he lose, eh?"

"Yeah, I guess you're right, but…"

"Yeah, but you ain't heard the rest. We had to work out in the fields and I hated that. So I got one of the guys there to chop off a couple of my toes with an axe so I couldn't work outside no more."

Bonnie clapped her hands to her mouth. "But didn't they –?"

"What I did was real dumb," Clyde continued, "because a few days later I was released anyway."

"Why? How?"

"I didn't know that my ma had petitioned for my release, and then it came through a few days after."

"So it was all for nothing."

"Right, but it didn't stop me robbing grocery stores and stuff when I got out."

"But why did you keep doing that? You could have got caught again and sent back to prison."

Clyde shrugged. "Revenge, Bonnie, Revenge. I wanted to get back at the system for what I suffered in prison, but ssh, the film's starting now. We can talk about what I done later."

*

Clyde, now accompanied by Bonnie and his friend, Ralph Fults, continued robbing filling stations and small shops. Bonnie and Clyde organised a loose-knit gang, meaning that the members joined and left and re-joined when it was convenient for them to do so. The aim of the gang was to make enough money so that Clyde could buy enough guns and ammunition to attack the Eastham Prison where he had been incarcerated.

During this period Bonnie and Clyde were very busy carrying out a series of robberies all over the south and central United States. They robbed small town banks, filling stations and grocery shops in Texas, Oklahoma, New Mexico, Louisiana and Missouri. To keep one step ahead of the law, they would often change their stolen cars, switch number plates and make sure that they stayed close to state borders, so that when the police gave chase, Bonnie and Clyde could cross the state lines and therefore evade capture. They even managed to return quite often to Dallas so that they could keep in touch with their families. The police heard about this and tried to ambush the couple, but until May 1934 they never succeeded.

In one of their raids on a hardware shop where they intended to steal some firearms, Bonnie and Fults were captured. Bonnie was sent to prison for a few months, but Fults had to serve a much longer sentence. Clyde was also caught robbing a store in Hillsboro. He could have escaped as he was the getaway driver, but the store-owner's wife identified him and he was sent to prison. He cannot have been 'inside' for long as four months later, on 5 August 1932, Clyde shot the first law officer of the nine that he and his gang eventually killed. Somehow they were not caught and by January 1933, they had murdered five people, law-officers and civilians.

Two months later, Clyde's brother, Buck, was released from prison and he and his wife, Blanche, together with Bonnie and Clyde moved into an old house in Joplin, Missouri. There they would drink, play cards and generally lead a noisy lifestyle. Naturally their neighbours objected and as a result the local police sent a five-man squad to check out the situation. A firefight took place and two of the policemen were killed. Clyde was slightly wounded but the gang all managed to escape. However, Buck was shot and later died of his wounds while Blanche was later captured. Their fellow gang member, Jones, was shot in the head, escaped and survived. When he was captured five months later, in November 1933, he told the police that Bonnie and Clyde used to take time off from their law-breaking to return home to Dallas to visit their families. This information became an important part of the story leading to the duo's demise.

One of the results of this raid was that the gang was forced to leave all their weapons and ammunition behind. When the police searched the house later, they found many photos of the gang pointing guns at each other for fun. The police printed these photos at *The Joplin Globe* press and very soon the picture of Bonnie, posing as a gun-moll, were seen throughout the United States. This became one of the most well-known photos taken of her. She can be seen proudly standing in front of a Ford, her foot on its bumper, a large cigar in her mouth, (even though she really smoked only cigarettes), while holding a gun.

In addition, the police found several poems that Bonnie had written about the lives of criminals and the women who suffered because of them. She grouped them together under the title of *Poetry from Life's Other Side*. One of them was entitled, 'The Story of Suicide Sal' and may be read as a reflection of Bonnie and Clyde's own story – the poem features characters she called Sal and Jack, two robbers living a life out of their control. The poem shows that Bonnie also had premonitions of her own early death.

I left my home for the city
To play in its mad glitzy whirl,
Not knowing how little of pity
It holds for a country girl.

...

There I fell for the line of a henchman,
A professional killer from Chi;
I couldn't help loving him madly;
For him even now I would die.

...

I was taught the ways of the underworld;
Jack was just like a god to me.

One day in January 1934 after Bonnie and Clyde had

successfully evaded an ambush on their way back to Dallas, Clyde decided that if he was to have any revenge on those who had hurt him, he had better do so very soon. Despite not being able to mount a full-scale attack on Eastham Prison, as no doubt he would have liked to, Clyde's Barrow gang managed to free Clyde's old friend, Raymond Hamilton. During the break-out several other prisoners escaped, but they also killed a guard at the same time.

After the break-out, the Barrow gang, which included Henry Methvin, one of the prisoners who they had helped escape, continued with their spree of robberies. Somehow, the police discovered that while Bonnie, Clyde and Methvin were on their way to Dallas, the last-named lawbreaker had become separated from the other two.

*

"Listen up, men," Texas Ranger Captain Frank Hamer said, looking at the five men seated around a table in his office. "I've been hauled out of retirement to catch this Bonnie and Clyde duo and that's what I'm, or we, are gonna do."

"How?" Officers Hinton and Alcorn asked together. "Every time we try and ambush them, they always get away."

"Right," Henderson Jordan agreed. "Those two must know every side road between here and New York."

"No, men, this time it's gonna diff'rent," Hamer tried to reassure his disillusioned team. "There's six of us and two of them. Not only that, but I think we've got the jump on them this time."

"What d'you mean, Captain?"

"Well, we've found out from that Methvin character how they behave, so we are ahead of them this time."

"So Captain, how's that going to change things?" Officer Oakley asked. "I mean, the last time we tried to catch those two bastards near Grapevines, Texas, they shot us up good and proper. Killed Officers Wheeler and Murphy."

"Yeah, so what are we gonna do this time, Captain? I don't fancy dyin' 'cos of those two."

"We're gonna use a decoy," Captain Hamer replied, chomping on his cigar. "We'll make 'em slow down by the side of the road and then we'll let 'em have it. We won't let them run us down or anything like that."

"What sort of decoy? A gorgeous blonde lady in distress?"

"No, Officer Gault, we'll use a truck – a broken-down truck."

"Excuse me, Captain, but that ain't gonna slow no-one down."

"Oh, yes it will. You see, we'll use Methvin's father's old truck and when those two hoodlums come along, you can bet your bottom dollar that Clyde Barrow will slow down to see what's up. I mean, he knows the truck and what guy don't want to show his gal that he don't know how to help another guy by fixing his truck?"

"And where are you planning to set up this ambush, Captain?" Officer Alcorn asked.

Hamer turned around and pointed with his pen to a large map of Louisiana on the wall. "Here," he said. "Here, on Highway 154 just south of Gibsland."

"What? Near Sailes?"

The captain nodded. "Yes, sir. Right there. That's where it's all gonna go down. We're pretty sure they're gonna come through this way on their way to Dallas to see their folks. We're gonna get those guys this time or my name's not Frank Hamer."

"Captain," Officer Hinton asked. "Do ya know what car they're drivin'? I mean it'd look bad if we shot up the wrong one."

Hamer nodded. "As far as we know they're driving a Ford of some sort. OK?"

Now it was Hinton's turn to nod as Henderson Jordan, the officer from Louisiana, asked, "It's a great plan, Captain, but are you sure it's gonna work?"

"It had better. I'm gonna be in deep trouble if not. Now let's get to work and see who's gonna be doin' what."

*

In the end Captain Frank Hamer organised a police posse of six armed officers to ambush Bonnie and Clyde in the way he described. He took Iverson Methvin's truck as a decoy and removed one of its wheels. Then he placed it on Highway 154 in such a spot in Bienville Parish that when Bonnie and Clyde's car came along, they would have to slow down even if they did not want to help the unfortunate driver repair his flat tyre.

The next day, 23 May 1934, the posse concealed themselves in the roadside bushes within sight and shooting range of the disabled truck. They heard Captain Frank Hamer give them their last instructions, "Keep yourselves well-hidden and don't fire till I tell you and remember, they're both probably armed and that the car we're looking for is mos' likely a beige coloured Ford V-8."

*

Half an hour after the men had settled down in their positions, Henderson whispered to Captain Hamer, "Here they are, Cap'n. I'd almost given up hope that they'd be coming this way."

"Me too, but be ready now."

The Ford Deluxe V-8 slowed down and pulled to a stop by Iverson's truck.

"Hey look, Bonnie," Clyde said. "That's Methvin's father's truck. I'd recognise that ol' heap anywhere. I wonder what's wrong with it?"

*

He got out of his car and strolled over to where the lopsided vehicle had caused them to stop. He leaned into the open passenger window and it was just then that when both he and Bonnie were off their guard that the whole police posse opened up with their guns. Within a minute the six policemen had blasted well over one hundred bullets into the bodies of Bonnie and Clyde. Clyde was killed as he was standing next to the disabled truck. On seeing this, Bonnie screamed just before she too was shot sitting in the passenger seat watching him. Her last sight was of her lover's dramatic bullet-filled death.

*

"Yeow, my ears are ringing, man," Oakley said, putting his hands to his ears as the sounds of the shooting died away.

"Me too," Henderson and Hamer said.

"Yeah, an' me," Alcorn and Gault both said as the posse walked over to the bullet-riddled Ford. All the men still kept their guns in their hands ready as if Bonnie, now hanging dead out of the front passenger door, would suddenly jump up and start shooting.

"Man, did you ever see a body like that?" one of them asked in awe looking at what they had done.

"Yeah, and just take a look at Clyde over there. He don't look much better."

*

Their bodies were taken to Dallas and publicly displayed, but not before souvenir hunters had tried to cut off pieces of their clothes and remove one of Clyde's ears and trigger finger. Such was the bad name that Bonnie and Clyde had gained, especially after killing the two policemen at Grapevine seven weeks earlier, that large crowds came to view the grisly display. Although Bonnie had asked that she be buried together with her beloved Clyde, her wishes were not taken into account and the pair were buried separately according to their families' requests.

Interestingly enough, when Bonnie's body was being prepared for her burial, they found that she was still wearing the wedding ring given to her by her husband, Roy Thornton, eight years earlier in September 1926.

At first, Bonnie was buried at Crown Hill Memorial Park, Dallas but later she was moved to the Western Heights Cemetery, Dallas, the same cemetery where Clyde lies buried next to his brother, 'Bud'. Carved on Clyde's gravestone it says, 'Gone but not forgotten'. The following is carved on Bonnie's stone:

As the flowers are made sweeter by the sunshine and the dew, so this old world is made brighter by the lives of folks like you.

The bullet-ridden Ford was later exhibited at fairs and carnivals, and in 1988 it was bought to be used as an attraction by the Primm Valley Resort and Casino, forty miles south of Las Vegas, for about $250,000.

Like Robin Hood, the legend of Bonnie and Clyde, the two criminals who took on the law, has never dimmed in the public memory. Several books have kept the story alive, while in 1967, Warren Beatty and Faye Dunaway starred in the film *Bonnie and Clyde*. This motion picture received mixed reviews on release, but was a massive hit at the box office, gained nine Oscar nominations (more than any other film for that year) and today is considered a classic. In the 2019 film, *The Highwaymen*, Kevin Costner played the part of Frank Hamer in an attempt to show the Bonnie and Clyde story from the lawman's point of view. It had mixed reviews. This may not be surprising as the film sought to show that Bonnie and Clyde's lifestyle was not as exciting nor as romantic as the public has been led to believe. In addition, at least two dramas based on this story were staged in 1958 and 1992 as well as a 2013 TV mini-series.

Part of the reason for Bonnie and Clyde's continuing legacy is that even while they were on their two-year law-breaking spree, they made sure that their names as a pair of runaway lovers remained in the public imagination. Somehow, the public, especially then, saw them as underdog young lovers and conveniently forgot their violence and their killing of at least nine policemen and four civilians in cold blood.

In fact, Bonnie and Clyde were a couple of selfish, thoughtless robbers. They robbed small town banks, small 'ma and pa' stores as well as filling stations. In addition, they shot and killed police officers and civilian bystanders who just happened to be in the wrong place at the wrong time. As robbers, they were not even very successful. Although they pretended to be like Robin Hood, in many of their robberies they only stole small amounts and they never ever scored the 'big time'.

Perhaps another reason that they were seen as heroes at the time is that all this happened during the Great Depression in the United States. Many people, especially

341

in Oklahoma and other states where they operated struggled to make a living. (See Steinbeck's novel *The Grapes of Wrath* which deals with this area in the 1930s.) Bonnie and Clyde were seen by some as rebels who had taken on the despised government through the police and the FBI. In addition, people saw their youth and audacity as appealing, a contrast to the miserable lives that many were enduring at the time.

Their carefree image was reinforced when newspapers published many of the photographs they themselves had taken, the pictures the police found after their raid at Joplin, Missouri. What enhanced their image is that they were seen as a pair of carefree lovers on the run and that Bonnie was an attractive looking woman. Bonnie being there, romantically tied up with Clyde, (with echoes of Robin Hood and Maid Marian?) more or less guaranteed that the couple would not be seen merely as a pair of murderous hoodlums. The fact that Bonnie also wrote poetry may have 'softened' the violent image that they may have acquired.

In one of her poems, the sixteen-verse *The Trail's End*, Bonnie foresees what will probably happen to them in the end. It begins:

You've read the story of Jesse James
Of how he lived and died.
If you're still in need;
Of something to read,
Here's the story of Bonnie and Clyde.

Now Bonnie and Clyde are the Barrow gang
I'm sure you all have read.
How they rob and steal;
And those who squeal,
Are usually found dying or dead.

and ends:

They don't think they're too smart or desperate
They know that the law always wins.
They've been shot at before;
But they do not ignore,
That death is the wages of sin.

Some day they'll go down together
They'll bury them side by side.
To few it'll be grief,
To the law a relief
But it's death for Bonnie and Clyde.
(Original spelling and punctuation)

Chapter Twenty-Three

Phoolan Devi (1963-2001)
Indian Bandit Leader turned MP & Lawmaker

It seems that all societies, whether European, North and South American, Asian or Australian, are home to organised gangs. Sometimes these exist in order to make money by robbing businesses and individuals. Other gangs and illegal organisations such as the German Red Army Faction (alias the Bader-Meinhoff Gang) and the Italian Red Brigades – Brigate Rosse – of the 1970s are political and aim to change society through their militant left-wing ideology. The right-wing also includes such groups as the Ku Klux Klan in the USA and Alternative for Germany and

the Austrian Freedom Party in Europe.

In contrast to these last two named gangs which were associated with terrorism, there are international Mafia-style gangs which have existed for many years and have no political agenda and whose activities cross national borders with impunity. Their activities include prostitution, loan-sharking, drugs, gambling and more on a vast scale. Other gangs are regional or local, such as the Red Brick Thugs in London, or the Moss Side Bloods based in Manchester.

Certain gangs are associated with specific countries or cultures. The original Mafia came from Sicily; the Triads are linked with organised crime in Hong Kong and China, while the Japanese have the Yazuka gangs. Australia is home to several motor-cycle gangs, including the 'Coffin Cheaters' and the 'Gladiators', while Mexico is home to the Sinaloa Cartel, which today specialises in money-laundering and drug trafficking.

However, in contrast to all these male gangs, there was an infamous long-running female gang of English shoplifters and thieves that ran from about 1870-1950. They were called the Forty Elephants Gang because they operated in the Elephant and Castle area in south London. (More about them in my book, Villains of Yore.*)*

Another of these early criminal organisations is the dacoits of India and Myanmar (called Burma before 1989). As an organisation, it had existed for at least two hundred years. This can be proved by the fact that the East India Company saw fit to establish a Thuggee and Dacoity Department in 1830 and several years later enacted the

Thuggee and Dacoity Suppression Acts. The areas in India where the dacoits – Hindi for bandit or armed robber – operated were the ravine-riven Chilapata and Chambal Forests near the Nepalese border.

During the time of the British Raj (1858-1947), the dacoits would attack local businesses and kidnap wealthy people to ransom. They would cut off their victims' noses, fingers and ears and send these body parts to the victims' families in order to persuade them to pay. In contrast, the dacoits would also play a 'Robin Hood' role, using their ill-gotten gains for the benefit of the poor. This included giving money to help them pay their medical expenses as well as donating funds to enable the poor to marry off their children.

Today, the dacoits as a large organisation no longer exists. This is due to the fact that they are no longer seen as popular or 'heroic'. If someone wants to turn to crime in India, it is easier to do so in the city and not in the remote forests in the north of that country. In addition, until the 1980s, the police in the north-centre of India carried out several serious and successful campaigns against the gangs to eradicate the dacoit presence.

An example of such a police raid occurred in 1983 when the local dacoit chief, a woman known as Phoolan Devi, surrendered to the authorities together with the remaining members of her gang. This woman was quite a phenomenon as the following story will show.

*

Phoolan Devi was born in a very poor home in the small village of Ghura Ka Purwa in the Indian state of Uttar Pradesh. Out of the four children her father, Devi Din Mullah, a fisherman and a sharecropper, and her mother, Moola, had, she and her older sister were the only two who survived to adulthood. What made their poverty-stricken situation even worse was that Phoolan's family were members of India's lowest caste, the Harijans or, as they prefer to refer to themselves, the Dalits.

The only asset of any worth that the family owned was about an acre of farmland with a very large, old neem tree on it. One day, soon after her paternal grandparents had died, Phoolan's cousin, Maya Din Mallah said that they should cut down the tree.

*

"Why?" Phoolan asked.

"Because then we'll have more land and so we can grow more crops."

"But I don't want you to cut it down," the eleven-year-old girl protested. "It gives us shade and its little white flowers are so pretty."

"Who cares about the flowers?"

"I do."

"Well, that doesn't matter anyway, because I've spoken to your father and he agrees with me. And anyway, it's no good as a tree. It's so old it's not giving us anything useful now, so say goodbye to your precious tree."

"Well, I'm not going to let you."

"So what are you going to do about it? You're only a stupid girl."

*

The next day Phoolan went into the village and came back with a group of her girlfriends. She told them what her cousin and her father wanted to do and they planned to stage a *dharna* – a sit-in – on the land near the tree. At first her father, cousin and a few other members of the family mocked them and said that when they were hungry, they would all go home, but that did not happen. The girls, led by Phoolan, stayed and refused to allow the men to come near in order to cut down the neem tree. But in the end, the inevitable happened. The male members of the family, together with the protesting girls' fathers and brothers, moved in to drag the girls away. The young girls put up a fight, and it was only when Phoolan had been beaten up and knocked unconscious that the battle for the neem tree was over.

Soon after this, Phoolan's father decided to get rid of his rebellious daughter, and he arranged to marry her off to a villager, Puttilal Mallah, who lived several miles away. In exchange for his daughter, Phoolan's family would receive a cow.

The marriage was a disaster. The husband, a middle-aged widower, abused Phoolan sexually and physically. This situation became so humiliating for the twelve-year-old girl that she broke all social taboos and, after several unsuccessful attempts, ran away and returned to her family home. Her husband decided to take revenge by telling the police that she had stolen various goods from him. The police locked her up for three days, beat her up and then returned her to her father's family.

Her family were not happy to receive her as now she was no longer a virgin in addition to being a social outcaste. But not only that, she was an outcaste from the lowest caste of all. In order to rid themselves of this shame her father suggested that she commit suicide by jumping into the village well. When she refused to do so, her parents, by offering various presents to her in-laws, persuaded them to take Phoolan back. This second time did not work any better and Phoolan, together with the presents she had brought with her, returned to her family home once again.

She was married off again, this time to one of her cousins, who already had one wife. This marriage did not last and once again she returned home. Despite the fact that her social status was of the lowest of the low, this determined young woman took on the local authorities and, as well as defending herself, she fought for her father's land rights in the court. Naturally this did not endear her to the authorities, and a year later they arrested her on a trumped-up charge. She was accused of robbery and held in custody for over a month. As a social outcast and a 'fallen woman' she was seen as 'easy meat' and during her stay in prison she was beaten and raped.

In the summer of 1979, aged sixteen Phoolan either escaped or was rescued by a band of dacoits. Their leader, Babu Gujar, beat her up, but then he was killed by Vikram

Mallah, a dacoit member of her own caste. He initiated her into the dacoit lifestyle and soon she was ready to have revenge on all those who had abused and humiliated her. When she told Vikram that she wanted to kill a specific person, he replied, "Kill twenty, not just one. If you kill twenty, your fame will spread; if you kill just one, you will be hanged as a murderess."

After this, despite the fact that she was officially married and that Vikram already had a wife, they moved in to live together. Soon after this, Vikram's gang attacked her former husband's village and in front of everyone present, Phoolan stabbed her ex-husband Puttilal Mallah and left him for dead. They also left a message on his body warning the village's older men not to marry young girls. In fact, Puttilal Mallah did not die, but he did spend the rest of his life living as a recluse. The fear of the dacoits was so strong that the other villagers did not want to have anything to do with him.

It was during this period that Phoolan learned how to be an active member of the gang. They stayed hidden away from the local authorities by living in the forests and ravines of the Chambal River. Vikram taught her how to shoot and, according to dacoit tradition, she took part in raids on villages and attacks on wealthy people.

However, the dacoits were not a united organisation. Two upper-caste brothers, Shri and Lalla Ram, joined the gang and held Phoolan responsible for killing their former leader, Babu Gujjar. They also resented her because although she was regarded as a dacoit leader, she was lower caste than they were. As time passed, the Ram brothers recruited more upper-caste members to join the dacoits until Vikram suggested that their band should form two gangs: one upper caste and the other lower caste. The brothers refused and said that the dacoits traditionally had consisted of mixed castes. In addition, the other Mallahs resented Vikram or were jealous of him because of his relationship with Phoolan.

All of this came to a head and there was a major argument and shootout between Shri Ram and Vikram, after which Phoolan and Vikram fled in the night. They were tracked down and Vikram was killed. Phoolan was captured and taken as a prisoner to Behmai, the Ram brothers' upper-caste village. There she was locked up by the Thakurs, beaten and gang-raped for three weeks before she was paraded naked in the village. Then to publicly shame her even further, they forced her to act as their slave and draw their drinking water from the village well. Finally, at the lowest point of her humiliation, in the late summer of 1980, several low-caste members of Vikram's gang, including a Man Singh Mallah, helped a vengeful Phoolan escape.

She moved in with Man Singh and they became lovers and the joint leaders of a new Mallah-only dacoit gang. Like true dacoits, they carried out more raids on upper-caste and wealthy people. According to some stories, although these were denied by the Indian authorities, they distributed their spoils, Robin Hood style, among the poor lower-caste locals.

Phoolan never forgave or forgot how the men of Behmai had treated her when she was incarcerated there.

On the evening of 14 February 1981, while a wedding was taking place, Phoolan and her dacoit gang invaded the village. Disguised as police officers, they demanded that Shri and Lalla Ram be produced. They could not be found and so, according to some accounts, twenty-two young men of the village were rounded up, marched to the river and shot. Some say that Phoolan, using her .315 Mauser rifle, shot many of these men herself.

This massacre produced two sharply contrasting reactions across India. The Mallah caste and other low castes as well as some higher castes admired Phoolan for her audacity and defiance, whereas the authorities launched a massive manhunt to track her down. It took them a year to do so, partly because she was held as a folk hero by so many people. She was called the 'Bandit Queen' and seen as the poor underdog struggling in the world while trying to achieve some form of justice.

After two years on the run, the government decided to negotiate a surrender. Phoolan agreed to the terms, as in addition to her not being well, many of her gang had by now died in skirmishes with the police or with members of rival gangs. When she finally surrendered, she laid down four conditions:

- *The prison term for the other gang members would not exceed eight years*
- *No gang member would receive the death penalty*
- *She would receive a plot of land*
- *Her whole family would witness the surrender under police escort*

In a controlled ceremony, witnessed by about ten thousand people, including three hundred policemen, Phoolan Devi and other members of her gang surrendered while standing in front of the portraits of Mahatma Gandhi and the Goddess Durga, the goddess of motherhood, strength and protection. After this she was charged with forty-eight crimes (thirty of them were concerning dacoity or banditry) and imprisoned for eleven years before she even went to trial. While she was imprisoned she underwent a hysterectomy and an operation for ovarian cysts. She was finally released in 1994, after the government withdrew all charges against her. This last action caused much extreme public discussion among those who said she should be tried for her crimes, and those who claimed she had been unjustly imprisoned as her case had not gone to trial.

After this, now aged thirty-two, having spent one third of her life in prison, Phoolan's life took on a completely new turn. Soon after her release, Dr Ramadoss, a politician who later became the Minister of Health and Family Welfare, invited her to take part in a conference about alcohol prohibition and women in pornography. This caused her to become involved in politics and she became an MP, sitting from 1996-1998. She lost her seat in the 1998 elections but regained it the following year.

However, she was not fated to hold public office for long. On 25 July 2001, while she was outside her bungalow in New Delhi, three masked gunmen assassinated her. She was hit nine times and was pronounced dead on arrival at hospital.

The chief suspect, Sher Singh Rana, eventually gave himself up, and in his defence said that he had assassinated Phoolan in revenge for the Behmai massacre. Thirteen years later, on 8 August 2014, Phoolan's assassin was tried in a Delhi court, found guilty and sentenced to life in prison. Another ten men were accused of involvement but were acquitted. Phoolan's sister, Rukman Devi, told reporters that she would seek a retrial for Rana's accomplices and also seek the death penalty for Rana. In the meantime the Delhi High Court released Rana, after granting him bail in October 2016. In February 2018 he married and the following year formed a political party.

Was Phoolan Devi really a wicked woman?

Does she deserve to be included in this book? For much of her life as a member of a dacoit gang, she was engaged in illegal activities. In addition, in an act of premeditated murder, she helped kill twenty-two young men in Behmai. It is true that they had seriously humiliated and gang-raped her several times during her imprisonment in the village, but does this mean that they deserved to be punished by being shot down in cold blood? Although the New Testament (Romans 12:9) says, 'Vengeance is mine; I will repay, saith the Lord', this can be counterbalanced with, 'Life for life, eye for eye, tooth for tooth...' (Exodus 21:23).

Perhaps the answer lies in Phoolan's legacy. Although she was seen as a murderous dacoit leader by some, she did change completely to become a model for young women trying to break out of the stranglehold of the caste system. She also demonstrated that despite her own violent past, people could change. In the end, before she was gunned down, she had made the extreme transformation from being a dacoit leader to a peaceful citizen, as well as a member of a political party and parliamentarian whose aim was to improve the society in which she lived.

A message from the Author

First of all, I would like to say thank you for buying my latest book published by Cranthorpe Millner, *Wicked Women of Yore*. It was great fun to write and do the necessary research. I hope that you get as much out of it as I put into it. My other books that have been published by Cranthorpe Millner are also a good read:

Villains of Yore
Colonel Blood: Soldier, Robber and Trickster
Kill the King: And Other Conspiracies

If you enjoyed reading *Wicked Women of Yore*, I would be very pleased if you would write a positive review and post it on one of the many online book sites, or write to me personally via:

Email: dlybooks15@gmail.com
Website: www.dlybooks.weebly.com
Facebook: David Young (facebook.com/dlyfcb)
Twitter: @ly70473845

Thank you,
David Lawrence-Young

About the Author

D. Lawrence-Young was an English and history teacher and lecturer in schools and universities for over forty years until he retired in 2013. He is happiest when researching Shakespeare, English and military history or quirky aspects of British history. In addition to editing *Communicating in English*, a best-selling textbook, he has written twenty-five mainly historical novels which have been published in the UK, USA and Israel.

He has been a frequent contributor to *Forum*, a magazine for English language teachers and also to *Skirmish*, a military history journal. He is a board member of the Jewish History Society of England, and from 2008-2014 was the Chairman of the Jerusalem Shakespeare Club. He is also a published (USA) and exhibited photographer (UK & Jerusalem). He loves travelling, plays the clarinet (badly) and is married and has two children. This is the fourth book he has had published by Cranthorpe Millner.

Bibliography

Achtemeier, Paul J., (Gen. ed.), *Harper's Bible Dictionary,* Harper & Row, San Francisco, USA, 1985

Ashley, Mike, *British Monarchs*, Robinson publishing Ltd., London, 1998

Becker, Helaine, *Pirate Queen: A Story of Zheng Yi Sao*, Groundwood Books, Toronto, Canada, 2020

Brennan Stephen, (ed.) *Murderers, Robbers & Highwaymen,* Skyhorse Publishing, New York, 2013

Brooke Alan & Brandon, David, *Tyburn: London's Fatal Tree*, Sutton publishing Ltd., Stroud, Gloucs., UK, 2005

Byrnes, Thomas F., 247 *Professional Criminals of America*, Castle Publishing, Auckland, New Zealand, 1989

Codd, Daniel J., *Crimes & Criminals of 17th Century Britain*, Pen & Sword History, Barnsley, S. Yorks., UK, 2018

Connolly, Martin, *Mary Ann Cotton: Dark Angel*, Pen & Sword History, Barnsley, S. Yorks., UK, 2016

Cook, Petronelle, *Queen Consorts of England*, Facts on File, New York, 1993

Cordingly, David & Falconer, John, *Pirates: Fact and*

Fiction, National Maritime Museum, London, 2021

Dame Enid, Rivlin Lily & Wenkart Henny, *Which Lilith? Feminist Writers Recreate the World's First Woman*, Northvale, New Jersey, USA, 1998

Deary, Terry, *The Peasants' Revolting...* Crimes, Pen & Sword History, Barnsley, S. Yorks., UK, 2019

Eastman, J. Tamara, & Bond, Constance, *The Pirate Trial of Anne Bonny & Mary Read*, Cambria Pines, Fern Canyon Press, California, USA, 2000

Gilbert, Martin, *The Holocaust: Maps & Photographs*, The Jerusalem Post, Jerusalem, Israel, 1978

Gilchrist, Catie, *The Worst Woman in Sydney: The Life and Crimes of Kate Leigh*, New South Books, Sydney, Australia, 2016

Glenn, Shirley, *Belle Starr and Her Times: the Literature, the Facts and the Legends*, Norman, University of Oklahoma Press, 1990

Graham, Ian, *The Ultimate Book of Imposters*, Sourcebooks, Naperville, Illinois, USA, 2013

Hallam, Elizabeth, (Gen. ed.), *The Plantagenet Encyclopaedia: An Alphabetic Guide to 400 Years of English History*, Tiger Books International, London, 1996

Hillam, David, Kings, *Queens, Bones & Bastards: Who's Who in the English Monarchy from Egbert to Elizabeth II*, Sutton Publishing, Stroud, Glosc., UK, 2006

Hood, Lynley, *Minnie Dean: Her Life and Crimes*, Penguin Random House, Hawthorn, Australia, 1995.

Knight, James R. & Davis, Jonathan, *Bonnie & Clyde: A Twenty-First Century Update*, Eakin Press, Austin, Texas, USA, 2003

Laidler, Keith, *Female Caligula: Ranavalona, the Mad Queen of Madagascar*, John Wiley & Sons, London, 2005

Lawrence-Young, D., *Villains of Yore*, Cranthorpe Millner Publishers, London, 2020

Lewis, Brenda Ralph, *Kings & Queens of England: A Dark History – 1066 to the Present Day*, Barnes & Noble, New York, 2005

Philips, Charles, *The Complete Illustrated Encyclopaedia of Royal Britain*, Anness Publishing, Leicester, UK, 2014

Rapaport, Helen, *Beautiful For Ever: Madame Rachel of Bond Street – Cosmetician, Con-Artist and Blackmailer*, Long Barn Books, Ebrington, Gloucs., UK, 2012

Rose, Andrew, *Scandal at the Savoy: The Infamous 1920s Murder Case*, Bloomsbury Publishing PLC., London 1991

Segrave, Kerry, *Women Swindlers in America 1860-1920*, Mcfarland, Jefferson, NC.USA, 2014

Spangler, Anne, *Wicked Women of the Bible*, Zondervan, Nashville, Tennessee, USA, 2015.

Spurling, Hilary, *La Grande Thérèse: The Greatest Scandal of the Century*, HarperCollins Publishers, New York, 2000

Stow, John, *A Survey of London: Written in the Year 1598*, (Revised 1603), Sutton Publishing, Stroud, Gloucs.,

UK, 2005

Treherne, John, *The Strange History of Bonnie and Clyde*, Stern & Day, New York, USA, 1984

Williamson, David, *Brewer's British Royalty*, Cassell, London, 1996

Wilson, David, *Mary Ann Cotton: Britain's First Female Serial Killer*, Waterside Press, Hook, Hants., UK, 2013

Wilson, Derek, *The Tower of London: A Thousand Years,* Allison & Busby Ltd., London, 1998

Writer, Larry, *The Australian Book of True Crime*, Pier 9, Murdoch Books, Sydney, Australia, 2008

Zsuffer, Joseph, *Countess of the Moon*, Griffin Press, S. Australia, 2015

Additional note: unless otherwise stated, all references to the Bible (Old & New Testaments) are from *The Holy Scriptures: Hebrew and English*: Authorised Version, published by the Society for Distributing Hebrew Scriptures, Hitchin, Herts, UK, 2014.

If you enjoyed this book, try these other history books by D. Lawrence-Young, published by Cranthorpe Millner:

Colonel Blood – Soldier, Robber, Trickster

Colonel Blood – Soldier, Robber and Trickster has it all: royalty, aristocrats, love-affairs, lusty wenches in taverns, war and fighting. But most of all, an incredible robbery. This is the life of self-styled 'Colonel' Thomas Blood, the 17th century swashbuckling Anglo-Irish adventurer who achieved fame by (almost) succeeding in stealing the Crown Jewels from the Tower of London in 1671.

But Blood did much more. He changed sides from being a Royalist cavalier to a Roundhead during the Civil

War before becoming involved in several treasonous plots. In addition, he also dramatically saved a friend from being hanged and twice attempted to kidnap his longtime enemy, the Duke of Osborne. But despite being caught after his failed jewel robbery, he was saved by King Charles II. Why was the king so magnanimous? What hold did Blood have over the 'Merry Monarch'?

Villains of Yore

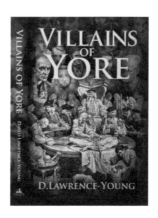

Take some twenty British villains. Then add their dastardly crimes and their miserable backgrounds. Mix in some nefarious conversations and combine all this to produce this exciting collection of stories.

This book describes in an entertaining way through facts and conversations how criminals such as, Richard Pudlicott in 1303 up to the 20th century Elephant Gang operated on the wrong side of the law to make their fortunes. Reading your way through these 700 years, you will meet other well-known characters including Dick Turpin, Burke and Hare and Moll Cutpurse, as well as some lesser known but equally nasty villains such as Colonel Blood, Mary Carleton and Jonathan Wild, the 'Thief-taker General'.

Kill the King & Other Conspiracies

Being the ruler of England has always been fraught with danger. In *Kill the King!* you will see that many people wanted to assassinate you! At least two plots were aimed at Henry VII and George III, four against Elizabeth I, and more than three against James I. Queen Victoria survived eight plots while the present Queen Elizabeth II has survived three. William II was accidentally (?) killed hunting while two Anglo-Saxon kings were also murdered – one of them while he was in the loo!

Several of these stories such as the Gunpowder Plot are well-known, but how many people know about the

Ridolphi or Babington plots? Would history have changed if Guy Fawkes had succeeded?

Kill the King! describes over thirty murderous plots in a serious but light-hearted way, and this book should shed much light on your understanding of England's murderous and regal history.

BV - #0001 - 291122 - C3 - 197/132/22 - PB - 9781803780962 - Gloss Lamination